One Boy, Two Bills and a Fry Up

One Boy, Two Bills and a Fry Up

A Memoir of Growing Up and Getting On

WES STREETING

HODDER &
STOUGHTON

First published in Great Britain in 2023 by Hodder & Stoughton
An Hachette UK company

1

Copyright © Wes Streeting 2023

The right of Wes Streeting to be identified as the Author of the Work has been
asserted by him in accordance with the Copyright, Designs and Patents Act 1988.

All images are from the author's personal collection.

A CIP catalogue record for this title is available from the British Library

Hardback ISBN 9781399710107
eBook ISBN 9781399710114

Typeset in Celeste by Hewer Text UK Ltd, Edinburgh
Printed and bound in Great Britain by Clays Ltd, Elcograf S.p.A.

Hodder & Stoughton policy is to use papers that are natural, renewable
and recyclable products and made from wood grown in sustainable
forests. The logging and manufacturing processes are expected to
conform to the environmental regulations of the country of origin.

Hodder & Stoughton Ltd
Carmelite House
50 Victoria Embankment
London EC4Y 0DZ

www.hodder.co.uk

With love to my parents, step-parents,
grandparents, and Joe

In loving memory of
Bill Streeting
Libby Crowley
Bill Crowley
and Annie Knott

And with thanks to all my teachers, especially
Ann Howarth
Dorothy Eden
Colin Nash
Elena Soto
and Derek James

Contents

The Big C and the Rest of My Life

IT WAS A cold and overcast day in Greater Manchester in early April – perhaps the heavy, grey clouds were an omen as they filled the darkening sky. I was in Bury to campaign for the Labour Party in the upcoming 2021 local elections, having just finished the long drive up from Ilford – my home on the London–Essex border and the place I've been proud to represent as a Labour MP since 2015. Just as I turned off my car engine, the phone call from the hospital took me by surprise. I hadn't been expecting them to call for another few hours, but there I was, sitting by myself in an almost-empty car park, listening to the news that would change my life.

'If I've understood you correctly, this is obviously terrible news because I've got cancer, and I'm only thirty-eight.' I needed to say the words out loud to process the news. 'But you've caught it early, so I'm not going to die and although you're going to whip one of my kidneys out, it's OK because I've got two of those and I only need one, so all in all, I'm pretty lucky,' I continued, blurting out the jumbled thoughts that were swirling around in my head to the doctor on the other end of the phone.

He laughed cautiously. 'Erm, yes, that's a positive way of looking at it, Wes.'

'Well,' I replied, 'if you'll excuse my language, Doctor, you've delivered this shit sandwich rather well.'

The journey leading up to that dreaded phone call had started a month earlier, on Budget Day. I had woken up at about four in the morning with what I'd thought was a stomach ache. I tried to sleep it off, but I was getting increasingly uncomfortable and anxious about the pain. Worried I would wake my partner, Joe, I took myself downstairs to lie on the sofa, until a sharp, excruciating pain gripped my back and sides and an agony which left me breathless set in. I began to panic and phoned the NHS 111 service, who took my symptoms and advised me to get to a hospital straight away. I managed to stagger upstairs to wake Joe, who immediately leapt into action and drove me to our nearest accident and emergency department at King George Hospital – ironically, this was the very A&E that I had fought successfully to save from closure as the local MP. But that irony was lost on me in all the pain – the overwhelming, debilitating pain.

Joe walked me to the door of the emergency department and had to leave me there, alone. Covid rules – no plus-ones. After what felt like an eternity of agony – but was probably more like five or ten minutes – I was seen by a nurse, who gave me something for the pain before a bed was found for me.

I was given every type of pain relief possible – in my mouth, in my arm, even a suppository (if you don't know what that is, you'll have to look it up because there's only so much detail I'm willing to share with you). I was in too much pain to care about being embarrassed as the doctor explained what it was, where it went, and where the toilet was where I could insert it. I was just grateful for the relief it gave me.

Because the searing pain was focused around the middle of my back and on my side, the doctors called for a scan of my kidneys. After the scan, the real waiting began. Minutes turned to hours and the hours became even longer once my phone battery started to die. This was Budget Day, one of the biggest moments in the Westminster political calendar, when the announcements made by the Chancellor of the Exchequer can shape the political weather for years to come, for better or worse. And I was missing it all.

Lunchtime came and went. By the time I'd finished my standard hospital-issue cheese sandwich and a cup of stewed tea and been given a fresh saline drip, the doctor came through to give me the news. 'You've got a kidney stone,' he said in a matter-of-fact tone. 'It's on the big side, about 6 mm, we reckon. It should pass naturally, but if not, you'll need a small procedure to get it removed.'

If there's one thing I know about kidney stones, from having had one years before, it's that they're bloody painful, but there are worse things in life, so the diagnosis came as a small relief. As I didn't have any questions, the doctor wrinkled his eyes in the way we did when wearing a mask to show that we were smiling underneath it and whizzed out of the room.

I was getting ready to be discharged, and the cannula was being removed from my arm when the doctor returned. I didn't need a facial cue to tell he wasn't smiling this time. 'The urology team just called again,' he said, quite calmly.

'They've seen something on the same kidney that we want to investigate. Given your age and your health it's very unlikely to be something to worry about, probably some fatty tissue or blood vessels, but we just want to reassure ourselves and you with another scan.'

At that moment, I wasn't worried – if anything, I was impressed by their due diligence. The scan was scheduled at the nearby Queen's Hospital in Romford, but by the time I got there, after an age waiting for Covid-safe patient transport, I'd missed my slot and was sent home with the promise of a scan in the coming weeks. When I went back a week and a half later, there was another cock-up – a second ultrasound instead of the CT scan I needed. My stomach turned to knots as the radiographer slid the scanner across my jelly-covered abdomen. 'It's definitely a solid lump ... not fatty tissue or blood vessels ...' he murmured quietly, as though he was talking to himself. Then came the words that really pricked my attention: 'It's most likely benign.' Benign. My mind went straight to tumour. Although I knew that benign tumours were the harmless sort, it was the first time I'd felt a pang of worry since my visit to A&E.

Then came the warning: 'You need to keep on top of this, Wesley. You need a CT scan as soon as possible. Timing is really important. Keep chasing. Don't feel guilty about chasing. The NHS is under a lot of pressure right now, but you just have to be persistent,' he urged as I sat up from the bed.

I left the treatment room in a daze and plonked myself down on an empty chair in the waiting room while I tried to gather my thoughts. I took my phone out from my jacket pocket, my thumbs hovering over the internet icon on the screen. I sucked a deep breath in through my teeth and googled kidney cancer for the first time. As I scrolled, I searched for any information that would ease the panic that had begun to grip my chest. It's one of the most common types in the UK, but it usually affects people in their sixties and seventies. Surely I was too young? I looked down the long list of symptoms, but realising I was veering into the realms of hypochondria, I dumped my phone back into my pocket and pulled myself together. Putting a brave face on, I went outside to meet Joe, who had been waiting in the car. I decided not to panic him, and so I simply told him they'd sent me to the wrong scan, and sat quietly worrying to myself on the short drive home.

Four weeks and another scan later, I was in Bury when I answered the phone to a withheld number. I initially thought it was good news from the hospital. 'I hope you don't mind me calling early, Wesley, but I have some difficult cases today and wanted to speak to you early on,' said the urologist at my local hospital. I instantly relaxed. This must be a good sign, I thought, getting me out of the way early. Nice and straightforward.

So I wasn't prepared for the bombshell that followed. It was a tumour. About five centimetres – so not a small one. And then he dropped the C-word. What were the chances? I was thirty-eight years old with kidney cancer. The doctors had told me again and again that this was so unlikely. Statistically, they were right, but in my case they were wrong.

Reality seemed to be suspended around me. I could hear my pulse racing in my ears. Alone in my car, I took some deep breaths and tried to take it in, but I was in shock. The surreal moment of receiving this diagnosis over the phone in a random car park in Bury was compounded by my friends James and Kevin tapping on my car window to tell me a whole team of Labour Party volunteers were waiting for me to join them.

I allowed myself a moment for one quick, deep breath, got out of the car, and forced myself to smile before heading off to knock on doors and talk to complete strangers. Meanwhile, the looming clouds burst, and rain, snow and hailstones each took a turn to pelt down on us. It was tough, but it was also a useful displacement activity and one that I would come to rely on during the weeks leading up to my surgery. Talking to residents about the issues they were worried about worked well to take my mind off my own problems.

'You've got cancer, but you're going to be OK,' were the words I repeated over and over in my head in between conversations on the doorsteps and with the local Labour team.

I checked into the Bury Best Western that afternoon and went upstairs to my room to receive the follow-up call I'd been promised from the nurse. She had been listening to my call with the urologist and was phoning to see how the news had sunk in and to take any questions – I had a host of them. When would I need to go into hospital, for how long, and would I need chemotherapy or radiotherapy? Most importantly, would I need to stop working and start isolating?

The news was reassuring. Because the cancer was low-grade, I wouldn't need radiotherapy or chemotherapy – just an operation – so I didn't need to isolate until closer to the surgery. Even better: unless I felt ill I could carry on working to my heart's content.

This was such a relief. It felt so important to me to be able to carry on with life as normal while I waited for my operation. So, after the hardest of calls to Joe and my parents, who took the news as well as could be expected, I threw myself into campaigning across every corner of England and Wales for the local elections, as if nothing was wrong.

Sometimes we help others without even realising it and this was true for every person I spent time with: they had no idea about my diagnosis and no idea how much being with them helped me through those weeks leading up to my operation.

My boss, the leader of the Labour Party, Keir Starmer, could not have been more supportive. On a visit to my Ilford North constituency he pulled me to one side to ask how I was and, touchingly, how Joe was doing. He told me to take off whatever time I needed and said that the Labour Party would be waiting for me when I returned. I felt lucky. There are so many people for whom a cancer diagnosis isn't just a health worry, but a work worry and a money worry as well. Far from holding me back, after the local elections were out of the way, he conducted a small reshuffle of his shadow cabinet and promoted me from my previous job as Shadow Schools Minister to a new brief covering child poverty – attending shadow cabinet. As well as being delighted with the promotion to a post that covered an issue close to my heart, I wondered how many other bosses would promote a member of their team, knowing they'd be out of action for a few months?

There was an air of unreality about it. On the surface, life was great: there was the joy of being surrounded by people, doing the job I love, and enjoying the spell of warmer weather as spring began to turn towards summer. But all of this was punctured by the truth that lay beneath it all.

When the time came to visit the centre for kidney cancer at the Royal Free Hospital in Hampstead, I was told that, once more, due to Covid, family weren't permitted at appointments. So, there I was, alone again, desperately wishing Joe could be beside me as I waited to meet my surgeon.

Ravi Barod was the Consultant Urological Surgeon and Clinical Lead at the Specialist Centre for Kidney Cancer at the Royal Free Hospital. He was also a master at putting his patients at ease. I called Joe and put him on speakerphone so that he could hear what Ravi had planned for me. I listened intently as he repeated much of what I had already been told about my tumour, before turning to the proposed treatment. He would be performing robotic surgery on me, and he was proposing to save my kidney with what's known as a partial nephrectomy, where they cut out the tumour and save the remaining kidney. Alternatively, I could opt for a full nephrectomy and have the whole kidney removed with the tumour.

'It's your choice,' said Ravi gently.

'But you're the one who's been to medical school,' I quipped. 'If you think you can save my kidney, I trust you. Let's try that.'

As we wrapped up the conversation and Joe was given an opportunity to ask some questions, I was taken next door to meet my clinical nurse specialist, David Cullen. Between the two of them, Ravi and David would make the following weeks so much more bearable.

I was back in the Royal Free on 5 May 2021. A Wednesday – memorable because it was the day before the local elections – or 'eve of poll', for political anoraks. Normally, I would have been out pounding the streets trying to find those final Labour votes; instead, I was in hospital for my biopsy. I arrived early in the morning with Joe by my side, but I felt a pang of loneliness and anxiety as I said goodbye and made my way inside.

The biopsy was a horribly intrusive procedure – deeply unpleasant and painful. Despite the local anaesthetic, I felt movement inside my body. 'You're doing really well,' said the nurse, as I dutifully followed instructions on breathing.

Then it was over. I was returned to the ward for observation for a few hours before I was allowed to go home. I was in more pain than I had expected, so the next day, as predicted, I sat in bed, making some phone calls until I conceded defeat to my body, and dozed in and out of sleep.

When the biopsy results returned, they confirmed the diagnosis, and preparations were well underway for surgery.

I needed to decide whether to say something more publicly about my diagnosis and, if so, how. I didn't feel I could have the luxury of privacy. I worried I might be criticised for missing votes in the House of Commons or not doing my job if I didn't explain why I was absent, so my team and I put together a plan. I would record a short video on my mobile phone, publish it on Twitter and Facebook, and a note would be sent around political journalists – known as the 'Lobby'. All very straightforward.

I didn't anticipate the reaction. Just after the video was published, I watched as the BBC News Channel flashed

'Breaking News' across the screen with a photograph of me and the news that I had been diagnosed with kidney cancer. I'd expected friends and colleagues to be in touch and some online news articles, but – perhaps naively – I didn't think this would be big enough for rolling TV news coverage. The video was on a number of news sites and viewed more than a million times via my own social media channels. My phone began to melt with a deluge of well-wishers. It was completely surreal.

One of my favourite reactions came from a regular Twitter troll who had once wished me dead. Now he was quick to take to Twitter to say that, whatever disagreements he had had with me, he wouldn't wish this on anyone! Needing a skin like a rhinoceros is a prerequisite for the life of an MP, but it was consoling to know that half the time trolls don't really mean what they say.

The kindness from my harshest critics came with an abundance of love from family, friends, colleagues and people I had never even met. Again, I was feeling lucky.

Then came the day. Friday, 21 May 2021 – the surgery. As with the rest of my appointments, Joe wouldn't be able to see me until I was discharged, so we found ourselves sharing another teary-eyed goodbye at the hospital door before I made my way inside. That agonisingly long walk from the entrance to the ward was the loneliest I had ever felt in my entire life.

I came around in the recovery room, dazed and confused, to find Ravi Barod at my bedside. While I blinked a few times to shake off the sedation, he told me that the procedure had been a success, but that he hadn't been able to save the kidney.

The tumour had been growing into the organ, so he was unable to get a clean cut. If I'm honest, I was relieved. I didn't care about the missing kidney; I was just glad to see the back of the tumour. Ravi had also thoughtfully phoned Joe to tell him the news, which was another weight off my mind, as I was feeling less than coherent.

In the days and weeks that followed, I focused entirely on my recovery. I realised that it was the first time I had truly stopped to rest since I graduated from university almost twenty years before. It gave me time to contemplate the rest of my life and just how far I'd already come.

When I gave an interview to Rachel Sylvester at *The Times* after my return to work that September, I began to realise, from the huge response to the interview, just how unusual my story is: that there aren't many MPs who were born to teenage parents, grew up on a council estate, experienced poverty, received free school meals and had grandparents in prison, yet had also excelled at school, made it to Cambridge University and been elected to Parliament. I wanted to say more about why that is and how it was that I had bucked the trend.

When a note arrived in the post from Tom Perrin, who had read the interview, asking me if I'd like to write a memoir, I was initially reluctant. Memoirs feel like something that politicians write at the end of their careers, and I hope I've still got some years left in me. I worried too about telling stories from my childhood that I've never told beyond close family and friends. As politicians, we aren't supposed to show vulnerability.

But if cancer has taught me one thing, it's that you never know what life holds for you around the corner. I came back from cancer with a new lease of life, so why not tell the story now of how a boy from the East End ended up in Westminster? But this story doesn't just belong to me; it belongs to every single person who helped me out of the poverty trap that so many people never escape – my family, my friends, and some wonderful teachers. This is for them.

CHAPTER ONE

The Fry Up

Nanny Libby and Mum. Early 1980s.

A FRY UP saved my life. Literally.

It was Monday. A spring morning in May 1982. My mother, Corrina Crowley, was up early and in the kitchen doing something she never normally did: cooking herself breakfast. She knew she wasn't supposed to. The instructions from the hospital were clear – do not eat before coming in for the procedure – but she had already decided that she wasn't going through with it.

Mum had made the decision some days before, but nobody knew as yet. She had been at work at Ribbons, a clothes factory not far from where she lived in London's East End, near Whitechapel on Hanbury Street, a place made famous for being the gruesome site where the body of Jack the Ripper's second victim, Annie Chapman, was found.

Mum had been chatting to one of her friends about the latest workplace gossip, but her mind was elsewhere. All she could think about were her three all-consuming secrets – her very unexpected pregnancy, the termination she had booked to deal with it, and how desperately she wanted to keep the baby. Those closest to her knew the first two, but nobody knew the last, because she had only just made up her mind. One thing you should know is that when Corrina's mind is made up, there is nothing anyone can do to change it. She would keep the baby, whatever the cost.

She knew there would be consequences, of course. No one had judged her for falling pregnant, at least not to her face. Teenage pregnancies were not unheard of on Mum's side of the family. Her own mother had her first child at the age of nineteen. These things happen, was the general response. But there had been a unanimous consensus that an abortion was the right response to my eighteen-year-old mother's predicament.

Mum still lived at home with her mother, Libby, her younger brother, My Uncle Billy, and her younger sister, my Auntie Eve. The three-bedroom council flat they shared on the fifth floor of Bengal House, on the Ocean Estate in Stepney Green, was no place to raise a baby – Billy was sixteen and wouldn't be leaving home any time soon; Mum didn't even have her own room, forced to share with her ten-year-old sister due to the limitations of space. And as a factory hand, she wasn't exactly in a position to move out and set up home on her own.

The decision to have an abortion had been straightforward; the decision to keep the baby much less so. So as she stood in the kitchen on that Monday morning in May, Mum was preparing to face the biggest challenge of all: her mother, Libby Crowley.

At five foot two inches and three-quarters – the three-quarters being important to her – with dark hair, brown eyes and olive skin, my Nanny Libby was a strong woman. Born in Newport, South Wales, she had moved to Liverpool and then to East London, where she married a man with a less-than-decent reputation who had been in and out of prison for most of his life – more on that later. In her day job, she campaigned against the regeneration of London's Docklands with the Joint Docklands Action Group. At home, she was bringing up her children alone and working hard to keep the roof over their heads and food on the table. She was a tough cookie, to say the least, and at forty-one years old, she wasn't ready to be a grandmother. She certainly did not believe her daughter was ready to be a mother, either.

Mum knew she was about to face the music – cooking breakfast was an act of defiance against the planned abortion, but it was also a guarantee to herself that, whatever pressure she came under from Nanny Libby, she wasn't going to the hospital that day. By the time Nan arrived in the kitchen, the deed was done. There wasn't so much as a rasher of bacon or a crispy sausage left in sight.

'We need to get you to the hospital,' Nanny Libby ordered, taking a long draw of an ever-present cigarette.

'I'm not going through with it,' was Mum's matter-of-fact response.

'What do you mean you're not going through with it?' Nan said, her voice going up an octave.

'I've eaten breakfast. I can't go now. And I'm keeping it, anyway,' Mum replied nonchalantly, putting the breakfast dishes away.

All hell broke loose. Until that moment, Nan had greeted the news of her daughter's pregnancy much like everyone else in the family: with shock and disbelief but also a level-headed focus on solving the problem. Now that Mum was unsolving the problem, Libby blew a gasket.

'Right, that's it!' Nanny Libby yelled at the top of her voice, ciggie in hand. 'You ruin your bloody life!'

To a passer-by, the drama that was unfolding might have struck terror, but the harsh tones and strong language, unprintable here, were just a reflection of a mother's fear for her daughter and the future she was giving up. Having been just a year older than Mum when she'd given birth to her first son, my Uncle Paul, Libby knew all too well what her daughter Corrina's choice would mean for the rest of her life.

Mum was all too used to such screaming and shouting, having borne the brunt of Nan's misdirected fury far too often as a child. Mum's parents had a toxic relationship, and she witnessed many of their arguments. When the fighting broke out, she would scream at the top of her voice for them to stop. (She is convinced that this is what gave her repeated bouts of tonsillitis until she had her tonsils removed.)

As the oldest daughter in the home, Mum took on a huge burden of the emotional trauma that affected the family, not only witnessing the domestic and emotional violence between her parents but also often being on the receiving end of it. It was during one of these rows that Mum made the discovery that she had spent the first six weeks of her life in prison. It was a revelation that she would find both startling and distressing.

My grandad mistreated my nan and, too often, she mistreated my mother in return. When not dishing out beatings with everything from her hands to the buckle end of her belt, she would tell Mum, 'I hate, loathe, detest and despise you.' On one occasion, the beating she was dishing out to Mum was so severe that my great-grandmother, Nanny Knott, hearing the commotion from the flat next door, where she lived, barged in, lifted Nan up off the floor with one hand and shouted, 'Don't you ever touch that child like that again or you'll have me to deal with!'

By now, Mum was used to her mother's temper and was determined to protect her unborn child, so she remained defiant.

'Don't think I'm looking after it either!' Nanny Libby threatened. 'You made your bed, you lie in it!'

'I will,' said Mum, with the defiance I owe my life to. Unlike her mother, who wouldn't carry through with her threats, Mum remained resolute.

*

A month earlier, on 7 April, Corrina Anne Crowley had turned eighteen. The whole family had gathered at the residents' association club on the Ranwell Estate in Bow, East London, to throw a huge party for her and her grandmother, Nanny Annie Knott, who had celebrated her seventieth birthday on the same day.

They had sectioned off a corner of the social club, with balloons, sandwiches, cocktail sausages, sausage rolls and an assortment of sweet and savoury nibbles on display. Two big cakes had been ordered from Anderson's bakery on the Roman Road. They were almost identical, except Mum's read 'Happy 18th Birthday' and Annie's read 'Penblwydd Hapus' – happy birthday in Welsh – as a nod to her Welsh heritage. For a family that never had a lot of money, it was quite the spread.

Pictures from that night show Mum looking stunning in a black all-in-one suit and a bright red belt; her blond curls were cut short and her huge smile lit up the room. For some reason, Annie – fifty years her senior – had decided to pull off the same look, much to everyone's affectionate amusement.

There was always laughter when the Knott family got together and a double celebration made them the life and soul of the party in the Ranwell club that night. Cheap drinks were flowing from the bar and a DJ kept the party going until the small hours.

Also there that night was a boy named Mark – a boy who would soon become Dad. He was six foot tall, with dark brown hair swept to one side, bright blue eyes, and rosy-red cheeks that betrayed his youth. He had only turned seventeen two months earlier in February and was there to celebrate his girlfriend's birthday.

He had met Mum through her older sister, Amanda, and his best friend, Kevin, about a year earlier. They had both agreed to go to 'the pictures' with Amanda and Kevin. Dad was then sixteen and neither he nor Mum had realised it would be a double date, but Mark and Corrina hit it off instantly. Over the course of their blossoming romance, they did what teenagers of their age in London's East End did at that time: hung around their estate, went to the pictures, went to parties, were in and out of each other's houses and in and out of each other's good and bad books.

Dad lived barely a ten-minute walk away from Mum in a two-bedroom council flat in Walter Besant House on Bancroft Road, with his father Bill Streeting – my soon-to-be grandad. Dad had just left Bow School for Boys, and after completing his O levels, he did exactly what was expected of him by his father: he went out and got a job. As a shipping clerk, his first wage was just over £2,000 a year, the bare minimum wage even in those days.

To say that Dad was shocked by the news of his girlfriend's pregnancy would be an understatement. They'd had what he thought were mature conversations about contraception – it shouldn't have been possible. When Mum told him the news, they immediately talked about abortion. He wasn't ready to be a father – emotionally, financially or otherwise. This wasn't how he intended his life to pan out.

Despite being a devoutly religious, ex-Navy Conservative voter, Grandad Streeting's reaction was supportive and non-judgemental. When Mum told him that she planned to have a termination, he said he understood and would be there to support them both however they needed him.

So it was a bombshell of earth-shattering proportions when Mum changed her mind. When she finally confessed to Dad that she wasn't going to go through with the abortion, he gave her an ultimatum. If she didn't get rid of the baby, it would be the end of their relationship.

Mum chose to keep me, leaving Dad bewildered at how she could make such a big decision without regard for his wishes or any real consideration of how a baby would change his life, as well as hers. But ultimately, it was her decision to make – he was powerless.

Dad remained adamant that he would have no part in the baby's future. He even convinced himself he had nothing to do with the pregnancy and said I could have been anyone's. A harsh and unfair judgement on Mum, but easier for him to live with than the truth. So, for the rest of the pregnancy, my parents had no contact, bar one meeting when Dad visited Mum at Nanny Libby's to try and clear the air about six months in. It didn't go well.

*

For weeks, only Nanny Libby, Dad and Grandad Streeting knew about Mum's secret pregnancy, until one afternoon, my auntie Amanda called Mum with news of her own.

'How would you like to be a bridesmaid?' asked Amanda excitedly. Kevin had proposed to her just the day before. Amanda was probably expecting a simple, 'Yes, of course!' from Mum. Instead, Mum responded by asking, 'How would you like to be an auntie?' There was silence on the other end of the line. Amanda, like the rest of the family, was in shock.

The news of my impending arrival spread like wildfire around the family and around Stepney Green. Teenage pregnancies still came with a great deal of stigma in the 1980s. It was only when I turned seventeen myself that I had any comprehension of just how terrifying an experience this must have been for Dad, or how much courage Mum must have had to defy the wishes of everyone around her and go through with the pregnancy. Thankfully, the reaction within the wider family was mostly supportive. Even my grandmother, Libby, had mellowed.

Later that year, Tower Hamlets Council relocated Nanny Libby, Mum and her two siblings. They left their flat on the Ocean Estate for more space in a three-storey terraced house on Crofts Street in Wapping. From the front bedroom on the top floor, you could just about see St Katherine Docks, right next to the Tower of London, separated only by the bustling traffic of the Highway beyond brown brick walls and the narrow steps of the estate. It was still a council property, but it was a house nonetheless, with a front and back garden, a decent-sized kitchen and living room, and three bedrooms. Still not big enough to cater for a daughter with a newborn baby, but a vast improvement on the flat in Bengal House.

As Mum grew more heavily pregnant, Nan did everything she could to support her daughter. When my Uncle Billy helped himself to her last Mars bar, Nanny Libby offered to go out and buy her another one. This was unprecedented. Mum couldn't remember a time in her life when her mother had ever bought her a Mars bar, or any other chocolate, as a sweet gesture. But the pregnancy marked a new chapter in their lives. Cuddles, care, attention. This was a novel experience for Mum, who began to understand what a real mother–daughter relationship was like for the first time.

Meanwhile, over in the visitors' room of Maidstone Prison in Kent, her father, Bill Crowley, could only sit in stunned silence as his daughter told him the news that he was to be a grandfather. She had gone to visit him by herself, as he and

Nanny Libby had long since divorced and she was sick of dealing with him, to put it mildly. But Mum still wanted a relationship with her father despite his flaws, of which there were many. By the time he found his voice, all he could say was, 'Oh. I can't believe it. Oh. I can't believe it.' Bill – Grandad Pops, as he was later known to me – was doing time for armed robbery and had just been moved from Albany, the higher-security category-B prison on the Isle of Wight where he'd been for years. It wasn't his first time serving at Her Majesty's pleasure, and it wouldn't be his last. On top of everything else he'd been missing on the outside, he was now going to miss the birth of his first grandson.

It was the early hours of 21 January 1983 when the telephone rang at 18, Walter Besant House, waking Grandad Streeting, who leapt out of bed to take the call. Despite the fact that he had been fast asleep only minutes before, he answered as he always did, firmly polite and well-spoken, albeit perhaps a little groggier than usual: 'Hello, nine eight oh, two double three nine?' The call was from Amanda. Despite Dad's protestation that he wanted nothing to do with the baby, she thought he should know that Mum had gone into labour at the Mile End Hospital – not 200 yards from where he was sleeping soundly in his childhood bedroom – and that he was wanted at the hospital.

Grandad promised to wake Dad and pass on the message, before calmly replacing the receiver in the hall. Whatever his son's misgivings about the baby, he was about to become a grandfather for the first time – and he was over the moon. Trying to keep a lid on his own excitement, Grandad made his way up the stairs of their maisonette to let his sleeping son know he was about to become a father. Loud enough to stir, but quiet enough not to startle, he gave his son the news. 'Mark . . . Mark . . . Corrina is in labour. She's just up the road. Do you want to go to the hospital now?'

Dad stirred. 'No. It's nothing to do with me. I'm going back to sleep,' he said defiantly, before rolling over, lifting the duvet over his head and doing just that.

Sensing he wasn't going to get any more movement or response out of his son, Grandad closed the door and went back to bed, worried that his first grandchild was arriving at the end of the road without their father there to see the moment.

The morning arrived, but I still hadn't – it seems my struggle with punctuality started in the womb. Around 7 am, Dad's best friend, now Mum's brother-in-law, Kevin, arrived at the door. 'Corrina's still in labour. Mandy's down there with Libby. You can still be there when the baby's born if you want to go to the hospital,' he said, hoping to urge his friend into action.

But still Dad wouldn't budge – whatever was happening in the hospital at the bottom of his road had nothing to do with him, as far as he was concerned. So he just got himself washed, dressed and ready and left for work.

The labour was long and difficult. For Mum, it was traumatic. She had been awake all night, enduring the agony of childbirth without my father, willing me to arrive.

Nanny Libby and Amanda were by Mum's bedside the whole time. Well, most of the time, anyway. Whether it was the appearance of the forceps or something else, no one can recall exactly, but everyone can remember that at some point during the birth, it all became too much for Nan, who passed out on the floor.

Just before lunchtime, the nurses came in en masse like an SAS squad mounting a rescue, with the same bedside manner. Eventually, the rescue mission was a success. A long, stringy body emerged with a purple head, arms and legs and a little pink body. A baby boy. The ordeal was over. Mum was finally looking down on the son she had fought so hard to keep and even harder to deliver.

Dad was now a father, but it wasn't until he arrived home from work late that afternoon that he was even aware that Mum had had a baby boy. He was still refusing to accept any responsibility or involvement. My grandad, however, couldn't wait any longer. Throughout the previous nine months he had supported his son through the emotional roller coaster he had been on: learning his girlfriend was pregnant, agreeing to the abortion, learning that the abortion hadn't happened, feeling helpless, deciding to have nothing to do with the baby, convincing himself that I was nothing to do with him. But just as Nanny Libby had understood why Dad wanted nothing to do with her daughter once she had made her decision, Grandad had understood why Mum had been determined to see the pregnancy through. He never sought to judge her, only to support the pair of teenagers as best he could.

But now that he was officially a grandfather, there was no way that he wasn't going to walk to the end of the road to see his grandson that day. So he did. From the moment he held me in his arms that Friday afternoon, it was clear to all those present that we would become the best of friends.

By the time Grandad returned home, Dad had already received a string of deputations from family and friends at the front door and on the telephone, urging him to go to the hospital, but he continued to refuse.

'You have a son. You are a father now, and you need to be there,' Grandad urged. 'Go and see him. He's yours. There is absolutely no doubt about it. He has his mum's blond hair, but your blue eyes.'

My grandad hadn't raised his son to shirk his responsibility in life. There was no way he was going to allow him to sit there at home, under his roof, pretending his own son didn't exist. He'd supported Dad in everything else and had indulged him when the phone had rung in the middle of the night, but this was where he drew the line. Dad had to face up to the reality waiting for him at the end of the road.

He knew his father well enough to know that he wasn't going to let this go – Grandad could talk the hind legs off a donkey – so Dad relented.

Dad told me that he walked down the street and through the doors of the Mile End Hospital that evening, and when he saw me for the first time, any doubts that he'd sowed in his own mind were vanquished by an overwhelming paternal instinct of love and pride. I was his son, and he loved me. He might have missed my arrival, but he was there then and has been there ever since.

CHAPTER TWO

Stepney Way

A rare photo of the three of us. Eastbourne, 1983.

WHEN I WAS born, my mother decided that I should take my father's surname – after a bit of grovelling about how he had behaved during her pregnancy. The choice of my first name was also my mother's, and it was one she had made years before she even became pregnant. Wesley wasn't a family name. I was named after Wesley Jordache from *Rich Man, Poor Man*, an American TV miniseries that Mum watched when she was growing up. It wasn't that she loved the character that much – an orphaned child sent to live with his uncle – she simply liked the name. As for my middle names, Paul represented her oldest brother, and William represented my two grandfathers, Bill Streeting and Bill Crowley. So Wesley Paul William Streeting it was and remains.

Due to the traumatic birth and subsequent long recovery, it was ten days before Mum was able to leave the hospital. When departure day finally arrived, the relationship between Mum and Dad was still uncertain, but the three of us left the Mile End Hospital together – Mum was exhausted, Dad was terrified, and I was fast asleep in Mum's arms. They didn't have a pram or even a baby carrier. Instead, Mum carried me, wrapped up in a blanket, up the road to Grandad's maisonette in Walter Besant House to give him a bit more time with his new grandson, before they called a cab to take us on the fifteen-minute drive from Stepney Green back to Nanny Libby's house on Crofts Street in Wapping, the place Mum and I would call home for the coming weeks.

The family couldn't afford a cot initially, so my bed for the first couple of weeks was a drawer that had been taken from Nan's dresser in her bedroom, placed on the floor of the living room – which was now doubling up as our bedroom – and padded with light bedding. At seven pounds and four ounces, I fitted like a glove. When my Auntie Amanda came to visit and take photos of her newborn nephew, she couldn't contain her laughter at the sight. 'What are you laughing at, Mand?' Mum asked, a little defensively. 'He looks like he's in a coffin!' my aunt squealed through fits of giggles in response.

But Amanda's coffin joke might have been too close to the bone. My makeshift bed would be a source of anxiety for Mum during those early days of motherhood – she'd seen stories about infant cot death in the news and worried that the risk of this might be even higher in a drawer. So for a while, her sleeping schedule was even worse than to be expected for the mother of a newborn baby. Mum would wake through the night almost hourly, anxiously lean over the drawer where I was sound asleep, put her ear close to my tiny lips, hear my soft breath and then, relieved, collapse back onto the chair beside me.

While Mum's new nightly routine might have worked to put her mind at ease, her lack of sleep, ironically, presented other risks. In the small hours one morning, after I had woken Mum crying for a feed, she went downstairs to warm a bottle in a saucepan on the hob, before swiftly returning to placate me so I didn't wake the whole house. In the process of soothing me, she fell back to sleep herself. Soon, she was woken up by the commotion that had broken out downstairs. The bottle had boiled dry in the pan and was now burning. My Uncle Billy, sleeping next door to the kitchen, had woken up to the smell and, shuffling into the kitchen, half asleep, to trace it, was horrified to see flames erupting from the stovetop. Fortunately, his fast action in extinguishing the blaze with wet tea towels prevented the fire from spreading. The only damage inflicted was to Mum's pride as she learnt a cautionary lesson in needing to take care of herself, as well as me. Oh, and a bottle warmer was purchased to avoid a repeat of the fiasco.

One of the challenges Mum faced as a parent was of her own making – she refused to accept help from anyone who would offer it. She knew what some people had been saying during her pregnancy: that she was too young, that she wouldn't be able to cope, that she was too volatile to provide the patience good parenting required. So she was determined to prove herself, to show people she could cope – and be a great mum.

Mum's natural defiance was emboldened by the hollow threats her own mother had made all those months before in their kitchen in Bengal House. Nanny Libby might have moved on, but Mum hadn't forgotten. She replayed Nan's words in her mind: 'If you think I'm looking after it, you've got another thing coming. You made your bed, you lie in it.'

Even though Libby had turned into a proud and loving grandmother, she was now having to do battle with her daughter to even get a look in with her grandson. 'I'll look after him, love. You have a break,' she would say. 'No, I'm OK, thanks, Mum,' would come the curt reply.

It would become a regular cause of contention between the two. 'Why don't you have a night off to enjoy yourself? I can look after him,' Nan would suggest eagerly.

'No thanks, Mum,' her daughter would respond.

'It's a lovely day out. Why don't I take him for a walk and give you a rest?' Nan would offer.

'That's all right, Mum. I'm taking him out today,' would be the defiant answer.

It took three or four months of this futile back and forth before Nan eventually had to beg her daughter to let her be a doting grandmother. Mum finally relented. She'd made her point, and besides, she wanted Nanny Libby to have some quality time with her grandson. As stubborn as she was, family was the most important thing to her, and she wasn't going to deny me the attention of a loving nanny.

Throughout those early months at Crofts Street, Dad really wanted to make things work as a family, and they still had feelings for each other, so my parents decided to give their relationship another go. Dad had learned to drive a couple of weeks after I was born and went out and got an old Morris Marina that needed some work – to say the least. One of Grandad's friends gave him his old Marina to raid for parts, but the car that had been donated turned out to be in better shape than the one he'd bought! It was good timing: Dad would be back and forth between work, home in Stepney Green and his young family in Wapping. Being able to drive meant he could travel between all three within the hour.

The car also allowed my parents the chance to escape the confines of East London and drive to the East Sussex coast together for the first time to see my other grandparents, Dad's mum Heather and her husband Robin, and their children. It was a bright but chilly spring day and one of the very few occasions during that first year where photographs were taken of us together – Mum, Dad and me – as a family. One of my favourite pictures is of Mum beaming at me as my little face scrunches into a cheeky, toothless grin, while Dad clutches me in the slightly awkward grasp of a first-time parent. We look every bit the happy family.

My parents' first priority in those early weeks as a couple again was to set up home together. Crofts Street was a vast improvement on the pokey flat in Bengal House, but there simply wasn't room there for the three of us. Their best bet was applying to the council – there was no way they could afford to rent a flat by themselves. But they knew they would face a long wait. Contrary to the popular myth that teenage mothers pop babies out for council housing, it has never been that simple. Even in the 1980s, social housing was in short supply, and as far as the council was concerned, my mother had a stable roof over her head, which should have been enough. They wouldn't care if it was somewhat overcrowded with Libby, Billy and Eve already occupying the three bedrooms in the house.

So, my parents did what so many others did at the time: they played the system to make sure that they had a place of their own in which to bring me up. Mum phoned Tower Hamlets Council feigning distress and told them that her mother had thrown her out and she had been made home-less. It's never been in Mum's nature to lie, but she felt she had little choice if she wanted to be housed any time soon. Since the council would be wise to this manoeuvre, Mum knew they would send a team to Crofts Street to inspect the premises for signs that mother and baby were still living there, so we moved in with Dad and Grandad Streeting in Stepney Green, just to be safe.

Grandad's house was a small two-bedroom maisonette that occupied the top two floors of the four-storey block of 1960s flats on Bancroft Road. When it was just Dad and Grandad living there, it had suited them perfectly well – Dad was lucky enough to get the big bedroom at the back of the flat to himself. Even the constant hum of the InterCity trains running along the elevated railway tracks at the end of the street wasn't too bad – they got used to it, after a while.

But when Mum and I moved in, it was a different story. If Crofts Street had felt overcrowded, Walter Besant House was far worse. Even with the men out at work for most of the day during the week, the flat felt cramped with just me and Mum – never mind when three adults and a baby were there at the same time. Mum thought Nanny Libby had been bad for fussing over us, but she paled in comparison to Grandad. There was nothing he wouldn't do for his grandson and his newly adopted daughter. For Mum, still fiercely independent and determined to prove herself as a capable young mother, Grandad was helpful to the point of being overbearing. She knew he meant well, but he was driving her up the wall. So when the offer of a two-bedroom flat came in the autumn of that year, my parents practically sprinted to their new home. Another top-floor maisonette in a four-storey 1960s block, just off Stepney Way, only a mile from the house they were leaving behind.

But when my parents first moved into 22 Clichy House, it was as far removed from love's young dream as it was possible to be. It was drab, cold and completely empty. There wasn't a stick of furniture in the place, and my parents couldn't exactly afford to redecorate. But it was theirs – their own little taste of freedom. The kitchen could barely fit the two of them at one time, but it did the job; the living room was a decent size – there would have been enough room for a handful of visitors if there had been a sofa for them to sit on. There was a little balcony that looked down on the street below and a standard white bathroom upstairs. Most importantly, though, there were two bedrooms – one for my parents, and one for me. It was certainly an upgrade from sleeping in a drawer in Nanny's living room.

*

Mum wasn't able to work when I was so small, and Dad's salary as a shipping clerk in Stratford didn't get us very far.

The best he could do to get us started was to bring the portable TV that he'd had in his bedroom at Grandad's and prop it up in the corner of the otherwise empty living room on his repurposed hi-fi stand, flanked by two cheap-and-cheerful steel-framed chairs from MFI. All I had in my bedroom was a cot, a brown teddy bear, a few other small toys and some books that Mum had been collecting during her pregnancy. There wasn't even any carpet, just old, worn, creaky floorboards. I'm sure Mum wasn't in a rush for me to start learning to crawl on them.

The cupboards were as sparse as our empty rooms, so Grandad would come over most Sundays with two big bags of shopping full of fruit, vegetables and meat, to help my parents for the week ahead. Mum felt guilty for feeling suffocated by his insistence on helping when she was under his roof – they wouldn't have been able to survive without his help now. Nanny Libby would do what she could to help too, but she was on a single wage with three mouths to feed; Mum knew she couldn't spare as much as she would have liked.

For Dad, the pressure must have been enormous. Still only eighteen years old, he was trying to play the role that was expected of him: going out to work, providing for the family, being a good partner and a caring father. But on a salary of £2,500 a year, this was a burden of responsibility beyond his means. He would get home from a long day at work on a Wednesday and find there was nothing for them to eat and no money left to do any shopping. The extra support from their parents helped, but inevitably when there were more days left in the month than there was money, Dad started to incur debts.

As the pressure mounted, so did the stress on their relationship. This had been both Mum and Dad's first serious
relationship, so it would not have been expected to last even
in normal circumstances – and these circumstances were
anything but normal.

Even without the financial pressures, their relationship was
volatile. Love had been absent when Mum was growing up, so
she struggled to cope with being loved now. She found it hard
to be close to someone else. She didn't exactly have an example of a healthy, romantic relationship to follow from her
parents – on top of a plethora of negative traits, Grandad Pops
was a womaniser and would have affairs behind Nan's back,
even introducing women he described as girlfriends to Mum.

Dad would come home from work dreading the inevitable
arguments that started the moment he stepped through the
door. They tried their best, for my sake, but they were living
beyond their means and becoming deeply depressed in the
process. But despite the poverty and the fights, my parents
did have some happy times together during that first year as
a family. They were quite a sight at a fancy-dress party held
in the Scout hall on the Clichy Estate, with Dad sporting some
fetching black eye make-up, a trend at the time that would
later enjoy a revival as 'guyliner' in the early 2000s. And if all
else had failed, Mum could have had an alternative career as
a Boy George impersonator. Her handmade costume – braids
made of brown cotton and ribbons, and red lipstick – made
her the spitting image of the Culture Club frontman in the
video for 'Karma Chameleon'.

If only the happy moments had been enough to outweigh
the bad, but after a year or so of trying to make things work,

Dad decided it was time to move out. He confided in Grandad and asked if he could move back in with him. 'If you're sure that's what you want, of course, you can come home,' he said. Dad was sure. He knew it wasn't going to work, and calling time on the relationship sooner rather than later would also spare me the pain of the break-up. I would be too young to remember anything different than my two parents being apart.

So their relationship ended, and this time it was final. Mum had half expected it, and her determination to prove she could stand on her own two feet kicked back in. Thankfully, they remained on amicable terms and establish a new routine. From the week that Dad left, he would come to collect me from Mum's on a Saturday morning and return me home on Sunday night. Occasionally, Mum would make plans to go out on a Friday night, and Grandad willingly collected me an evening earlier than planned, leaving my parents to start enjoying the freedom of a night out in the way that people in their late teens and early twenties should. At some point, the Friday night routine became formalised. Grandad was happy to give up his evening down at the Three Crowns pub to spend more time doing the thing he loved most: being a doting grandfather.

I have scant recollection of the only other serious relationship Mum had during those early years, which is just as well. Mum started seeing Lenny when I was around two years old. He seemed like a nice guy at first, but appearances can be deceptive. Underneath the charming exterior was a violent, controlling brute, and my mother was on the receiving end of his terrible abuse. Mum made sure Lenny never hurt me, but it was the threat of harm that led her to hand me over to the care of Dad and Grandad temporarily while she tried to extract herself from the relationship. She had grown up in a household where domestic violence occurred, and she was determined to protect me from experiencing what she had. Lenny was prepared to threaten people she loved as part of his coercive control. On one occasion, he dangled Mum's thirteen-year-old sister, Eve, over the balcony and threatened to drop her three storeys to the ground below as Mum looked on in horror, pleading with him to stop as my aunt screamed at the top of her lungs.

This was the straw that broke the camel's back – for Mum, who knew this relationship had to end, and for Nanny Libby, who went to give him a piece of her mind – and succeeded.

My nan tracked Lenny down to the building site where he worked. She stormed into the yard, one hand scrunched in a tight fist, the other gripping a bicycle chain that trailed on the ground alongside her. Surrounded by his workmates, she proceeded to beat Lenny black and blue with the heavy, oily chain and with each lashing, she told him exactly what this hiding was for.

Whether they were frozen in shock or Nan had told the other men on the site what Lenny had done before she dealt out his punishment, I cannot say. But they stood and watched as this five-foot-two-and-three-quarter-inch woman described the abuse he had inflicted on her daughter and chose not to intervene, some even laughing, as she dished out a taste of his own medicine. Then, when Nan told the foreman later what Lenny had done to my mother and her family, he was fired. I can't quite imagine the Nanny Libby I knew dishing out this rough justice and, though she shouldn't have taken matters into her own hands, it is hard, all these years later, not to feel that Lenny got exactly what he deserved. Unfortunately, it wasn't the last we heard of him.

The worst incident of all, perhaps the most painful for Mum to recount, and the hardest for a son to write about, was when she was abducted by Lenny. When she told him that the relationship was over, he took the news badly. Mum had hoped that the hiding he had received from Nanny Libby would put an end to any threat of further violence, but she was wrong. On her twenty-first birthday, Mum was dragged from the street in Stepney Way and taken to his dingy flat, where she was held hostage for twenty-four hours. She has never told me exactly what she went through during that day from hell, and I have never asked. Only when she promised Lenny to stay in the relationship did he release her, and as soon as he did, she made straight for the nearest police station.

Had it been fifteen years earlier, the police would most likely have ignored her – the term 'domestic violence' had only come into use as a term to describe abuse within the home in 1973 through the campaigning Labour MP for Stoke-on-Trent South, Jack Ashley. Even by today's standards, far too many abusive men fail to see the inside of a courtroom, let alone a prison cell. But thanks to several dutiful police officers, the courage of my mother and her younger sister Eve, who bravely testified in court, Lenny was ultimately brought to justice. He received a custodial sentence, and thankfully, a dark chapter in Mum's life was closed. I cannot imagine what she went through, but I do know that, like so

many other women trapped in abusive and violent relationships, it took a hell of a lot of courage to escape and to put
him behind bars.

*

My memories of Clichy House are few, but happy. Mum
continued to work hard to prove herself and make the flat
feel more like a home: the rest of the rooms were carpeted,
eventually; over Christmases, birthdays and runs of good
luck in between, the small collection of toys I had arrived
with grew into a bigger collection in my bedroom and in the
'toy corner' that I was allowed to keep in the living room.

One thing in our house that was never sparsely populated
was the bookcase. For as long as I can remember, I had a little
bookcase full of books – all the Ladybird classics like *The
Three Little Pigs*, *Goldilocks and the Three Bears* and *Chicken
Licken*, Mum had been keen to add to the collection she had
started when she was pregnant. She was determined to make
sure that, as I grew up, I was never made to feel stupid as she
had been when she was at school. Mum's difficult childhood
meant that she was in and out of school and left education at
sixteen without any qualifications, despite being sharp-witted
and clever in many respects. She would read to me during the
week and Dad and Grandad would read to me at the weekends. Between them, they turned my literal appetite for books
– I used to chew on the thick, cardboard corners of my favourite stories when I was small – into a love of reading.

Making the flat feel like a home fit for a small child wasn't
all plain sailing. One particular night – rather, in the early
hours of the morning – Mum had been up late talking to

friends on her CB radio (a radio with an attached walkie-talkie device, similar to what you would see in a police car in a TV detective programme), which was the 1980s equivalent of social media, when she heard what was at first a muffled disturbance outside, but which then escalated into deafening thumping on our front door. She crept out onto the landing and stood at the top of the stairs, leaning down to catch a glimpse of the door to check that it was still in place. All of a sudden, that same door burst open and in stormed police officers who stood at the bottom of our stairs with their guns trained on her. 'Armed police! Put your hands in the air – slowly,' one of them shouted. Mum was shaking from head to toe and couldn't even muster enough control of her arms to raise them. 'Put your hands in the air!' they repeated, their guns still fixed on her. She made a feeble effort to follow their orders. Hands raised as best she could and shaking, elbows glued to her waist, she slowly crept down the narrow staircase as instructed, stammering, 'My son . . . my son . . . he . . . he's . . . upstairs in his bedroom sleeping . . . Please, please don't hurt him . . .'. Mum had an instinctive suspicion of the police owing to her father's – Grandad Pops' – encounters with the law. Her first thought was that they must have been looking for him until she remembered he was still serving time.

As she trembled down the stairs, all she could think about was the risk that I would wander, half asleep, out of my bedroom into the line of sight of any one of the guns that were trained on the upstairs landing. Thankfully, there was little chance of that. I was out for the count and none the wiser. If there is one trait I've kept with me throughout my life, it's the ability to sleep through anything.

As Mum stood beside the tattered front door, the police did a sweep of the premises before finally providing a vague, perhaps embarrassed, but completely unapologetic explanation of what on earth had led to an armed raid on our flat. It turned out they weren't expecting to find us there at all. They were on the lookout for a dangerous criminal on the run and 22 Clichy House had been the last address they'd had for him. Mum didn't receive so much as an offer to repair the door as they disappeared into the night in pursuit of their man. Typical of the police, she thought. Break down the door, ask questions later, and leave others to clean up the mess.

The neighbours had heard the commotion and one of them must have tipped off the *East London Advertiser*, the local paper, because the following morning a reporter turned up to ask Mum what had happened as a photographer snapped some photos of her clutching onto me in our doorway. She had recovered from the shock of the ordeal, but remained baffled by it and told the paper the full story. Most kids make their first appearance in the local newspaper in the births, deaths and marriages column or in a bonnie baby contest – I made my debut in a front-page spread reporting an armed police raid!

After the event, Mum didn't have to worry about forgetting to take her keys out with her. She could just give the front door a shove and it would pop right open.

I might have missed that moment of high drama at Clichy House, but I will never forget the next traumatic experience there: our infestation of fleas. I must have been about three years old when my Aunt Amanda offered to give us her old settee. It was an improvement on what we had before, so

Mum gladly accepted the offer. There was just one problem: Amanda had always had cats, and unbeknownst to her and us, it arrived at our place in Stepney, absolutely covered in fleas. What started with us getting a few flea bites soon turned into a mammoth infestation, and we were forced to stay over at Nan's in Wapping until the flat could be fumigated. Unfortunately, though, we had to pay the flat another visit before the fleas had been dealt with.

I was standing just inside the doorway, where I had been ordered by Mum to stay, when my legs started to tickle. I giggled, until I felt the biting. Looking down, my ankles were smothered in so many fleas that they looked like black socks. I let out a blood-curdling scream and Mum appeared quick as a flash, scooped me up, fleas and all, and slammed the door behind us.

Fleeing from the fleas, the ones that had found me already kept on biting, so I was stripped down to my pants on the rapid half-hour walk back to Wapping. Once back, I was whisked into the shower while my horrified grandmother doused my remaining clothes in boiling-hot water.

We would remain in the safe harbour of Crofts Street until it was okay to return to our flat. It was no hardship. I would always enjoy staying with Nan and our extended family across the East End. This became more frequent when Mum landed a job that was about as far removed from our lives and her upbringing as was possible to be – she became a silver-service waitress.

The job, which mainly involved evening shifts but also the occasional daytime event, took her to the Guildhall and the Livery Halls of the City of London, the Henley Regatta, and golfing tournaments like the Bob Hope Classic at Twickenham. She would even find herself serving banquets attended by the Queen and other senior members of the Royal Family, and once, Michael Caine put on a dinner where a boar's head was paraded. She had never seen anything like it. In the kitchen, she was experiencing exotic new tastes like kiwi fruit, to her delight, but even the taste of fresh salmon was new to her, having only previously eaten salmon from a tin.

Years later, as a member of the House of Commons Treasury Committee, I would be regularly invited to events in the City of London, including the famous Mansion House Dinner. I enjoyed telling the Lord Mayor of London that decades earlier, Mum had worked at events like the one I was attending. I was as proud of her as she is of where my career has taken me.

While Mum was serving the Establishment, my grandmother was busy fighting it. Nanny Libby was always a fighter, not just for her family, but for social justice. During those early years of the 1980s, the East End of London formed one of the battlefronts in the fight against Thatcherism, and she was on the front line.

The East End was undergoing profound change. In 1981, the government had established the London Docklands Development Corporation to regenerate the docklands in Tower Hamlets and Newham to the north of the River Thames, and Greenwich, Lewisham and Southwark to the south. The scheme proved hugely controversial. The centralisation of decision-making powers and relaxation of planning restrictions in the hands of the Corporation heightened the fears of campaigners that the scheme would serve the interests of big corporations and wealthy executives and ride roughshod over the views of local residents, some of whom would have to be rehoused to make way for new commercial developments.

One of those campaigners was my grandmother, who worked to mobilise community opposition to the regeneration scheme. When the Docklands Light Railway was first opened in 1987 she would sit in the modern, driverless carriages with me and Mum, pointing out of the window towards the new buildings springing up along its route, saying, 'See those buildings? Every one of them has cost us five pounds a brick.'

She was similarly appalled when Rupert Murdoch's News International group relocated its operations to a big site in Wapping, just off the Highway and a short walk from her front door. When the print workers went on strike in 1986 over News International's decision to relocate printing to its Wapping base, costing huge numbers of jobs, Nanny Libby joined the picket lines with her loudhailer. I always laugh when I think about Nan with a loudhailer because, given that she was never low on decibels herself, she didn't exactly need one. But it did make her a rabble-rouser and, during one of the worst clashes between police and the 5,000 protesters who had gathered in Wapping, she found herself rammed up against a wall with her loudhailer plunged into her chest.

It wasn't just the job losses that Nan opposed. She detested Murdoch's newspapers and their cheerleading for Mrs Thatcher. Visitors weren't even allowed to mention the *Sun* newspaper under her roof, let alone bring a copy in, and this was years before its appalling coverage of the Hillsborough disaster which led to its boycott on Merseyside.

When Maggie Thatcher announced that she was abolishing the Greater London Council (GLC) in 1986 after regular political confrontations with the GLC and its leader, 'Red Ken' Livingstone, Nan hatched a plot. She and a group of friends would smuggle themselves into the GLC's County Hall headquarters on the Southbank, almost directly opposite Parliament across the Thames, posing as international students. They would then mount an occupation in protest at Mrs Thatcher's assault on London government. Libby left that morning with a bag full of tins and supplies to sustain the occupiers. There was just one problem – having successfully completed the earlier parts of the mission, they then found themselves ensconced in County Hall with lots of tinned supplies, but no tin opener! The occupation was as successful as the efforts to save the GLC. It was disbanded.

Given how much Nanny Libby's Labour politics and campaigning spirit inspired my own involvement in politics, I can't help but feel saddened that my nan never entered elected politics herself. She was a Labour Party stalwart, and she was encouraged to stand for the local council on a number of occasions, but she always refused. I'm not sure whether she ever gave them the real reason why, but the family knew it was because she had a criminal record, of which she was incredibly ashamed.

The reason for that criminal record was still serving out his sentence in Maidstone Prison during the early years of my life. The crimes of Libby's estranged husband, Bill Crowley, had consequences for Nan, our family and, of course, his victims.

For me, the only hint of Grandad Pops in my life at that time was a bright yellow duck, with big round beads for eyes, a bright orange beak and feet, and two small wings with blue-and-white-striped linings on their undersides. He made this soft toy for me in prison. I loved it and took 'Duckie' everywhere, clinging onto its neck so tightly that the stuffing migrated into his head and body, leaving him with a floppy neck. It was a beautiful toy that looked so professionally made. Grandad Pops was a man of many talents, which makes the story of his life, his criminal activity and his impact on the rest of his family all the more tragic. But that's not to say the rest of Mum's side were completely normal. In fact, chaos and the Crowleys seemed to go hand in hand. Let's meet them, shall we?

CHAPTER THREE

Bill Crowley

Bill Crowley, 1960s.

TO SAY THAT Grandad Pops, Bill Crowley, had a hard childhood would be an understatement. He was born on 31 January 1940 in Wandsworth, South London, in the same month that rationing was introduced by Neville Chamberlain's government. Britain was at war with Germany, but it wasn't the falling bombs of the Nazi blitzkrieg or the hardships of the home front that young William was most afraid of: it was the suffering he experienced at the hands of his own father.

Although he would speak fondly of his late mother and his five sisters, it would not be until he was in the departure lounge of life in his sixties that he would finally share the dark secret he had been keeping throughout his life. His father had abused him – physically and sexually – from the age of four. Whether he kept his silence through fear or shame or a combination of the two, he didn't need to tell us. Nor did we expect him to relive the ordeal by recounting the trauma he had experienced. That he finally felt able to open up was all that mattered to us. The torture of silence must have been unbearable. The horror of his suffering, unspeakable. But it explained a lot about his childhood and the life that he led.

Zennor Road, where Grandad Pops lived with his father, also called William Crowley, mother Daisy and five sisters, had a reputation for being rough. As it wasn't a thoroughfare to anywhere else, it was somewhere you went only if you really needed to. The terraced houses were three storeys tall, but often housed two or three families. William Crowley senior was a labourer and the sole breadwinner for his wife and six children. While Grandad Pops suffered at the hands of his father, he loved his mother, Daisy, and his sisters enormously.

From an early age, Grandad Pops was rebellious. He would spend hours out around the streets of Balham getting up to mischief, and it didn't take long for mischief to evolve into serious trouble. In fact, his first conviction was at the age of eight.

The Woolworths on Balham High Street had stood on the same site since 1928. By the late 1940s, hundreds of 'Woolies' had opened up across the country, providing a range of general goods at low prices that would make it a family favourite for decades to come. It had survived a near miss in 1940 when a German bomb landed in the middle of the street, right in front of the store, crashing down to the Northern line platform of Balham station below. The shop front was shattered, and a number 88 double-decker bus had crashed into the huge crater created by the blast, in what became known as the Balham Tube disaster. But Woolies remained, and by 1948 the flat roof of the store, jutting out from the brown-brick housing that stood behind it, made it a tempting target for the eight-year-old aspiring thief, my grandfather. One night, he climbed up onto the roof and attempted to gain entry to the store below to make off with some spoils.

It would have been rich pickings if he had succeeded, but he was caught red-handed. Thus began his lifelong association with the criminal justice system. He spent time as a child in a borstal and approved schools – residential detention centres for children who'd committed crimes or were deemed to be beyond the control of their parents. The conditions were harsh. (He'd later describe receiving just bread and water, three days on, three days off.) Discipline was enforced by corporal punishment – unruly boys would receive the cane according to the severity of their behaviour. Boys who tried to abscond would receive up to eight lashes, which would leave them marked and sore for a week.

You might think that such conditions would deter a young child from reoffending, but knowing what we know now about the abuse he was subjected to by his father, we can hazard a guess as to why a borstal might feel safer than being at home. Later in his life he would recall with a wry smile what one of his instructors would say to him: 'Bill Crowley, you're a born leader, but the trouble is that you lead people astray.'

Mum has a photograph of Grandad around the time of his attempted Woolworths heist, wearing a beige jacket with big lapels, matching trousers and a checked woolly jumper with his mousy-blond hair swept to one side in a parting. Although his tongue was cheekily planted into his cheek, he didn't look like a happy child. Even from the aged, sepia-toned photo, it's clear that his eyes were slightly puffy with faint dark rings around them. He would be a casting director's dream for the role of the Artful Dodger in a West End production of *Oliver!* But the grim reality of his childhood was far from a rosy musical with a happy ending.

However hard the conditions of his punishment were, they didn't deter my grandfather from going on the job again throughout his youth, which earned him greater notoriety and brought him into contact with more serious operators. He taught himself to drive as a teenager and helped himself to other people's cars, and by the time he was eighteen, my grandad was serving time in a real prison. We only know this because he would later recall that it was in prison that he learned of the passing of his mother, Daisy, in 1958. Although she had suffered with a weak heart for years, her death hit him hard. He loved her dearly and was distraught when the prison authorities refused to allow him out on day release to attend her funeral. That was probably the worst punishment he would ever receive.

By the time he'd reached his twenties, he had established a reputation within the criminal underworld of South London as a fast getaway driver, a valuable skill for his line of work. When he first met Nanny Libby in 1962, she had recently made a getaway of her own – from Liverpool to London. Nan had left her hometown of Newport, South Wales, for Liverpool, where she had gone to work and start a new life, living with a family who owned a Cantonese restaurant in Liverpool's Chinatown. It was while she was in Liverpool that she fell in love with a local man and had her first son, Paul. Pregnant with her second child, my Aunt Amanda, Elisabeth Knott – as Nanny Libby was then – had discovered that the man she had been in a relationship with, the man she loved, the man with whom she had a two-year-old son, was already married with children. She wouldn't divulge the man's name until Amanda was an adult, only that she had followed him home to where he lived with his family, and that when she confronted him, he pointed at her pregnant tummy and snarled, 'That's probably not mine, anyway.' She decided to leave Liverpool and return to her mother, Nanny Knott, who had since moved to West London with the rest of the family from South Wales.

It was a remarkable stroke of bad luck to leave behind a cheat and land herself a crook, but when Nan was introduced to Grandad Pops by her oldest sister, Esme, they got on like a house on fire. It was Grandad who first called her Libby and the name stuck with the rest of the family and pretty much everyone else who knew her since.

It said a lot about their relationship and their love for each other that when Nan went into labour in January 1963, Grandad Pops was there by her hospital bedside, holding her hand throughout the birth of Amanda. Although they weren't his children by blood, he loved and accepted Paul and Amanda as his own. He even insisted that they took his surname.

Grandad Pops had been told he had a talent for leading people astray, and sadly this was true for Nanny Libby. His criminal enterprise became something of a family business. He would involve Nan in 'drumming houses' – driving out to big homes in the country and knocking on doors posing as a couple, looking for a local dog breeder from whom to buy a puppy. Anyone answering the door would be greeted by the sight of an apparently respectable couple, who would then claim to have the wrong address before saying their good-byes and moving on. If nobody was home, Grandad would break in and make off with whatever valuables he could find. When Mum told me this story, it came as a shock. It seemed so out of character for the woman that I grew up with: the caring grandmother, the social justice warrior. But she was blinded by love and foolishly would do anything for him.

Their lifestyle soon caught up with them. By 1964, both of my grandparents were in prison. I'm not sure what Grandad had been banged up for – he had so many spells in and out of prison that family accounts of what he did and where he was are confused, and it will be some years before his criminal record is publicly available. Nan was so ashamed of her own conviction that she never discussed it and it remained a source of deep embarrassment for her throughout her life. But my understanding is that because Nan refused to cooper-ate with the police and their enquiries about Grandad, they had pinned a stolen radio on her and it landed her a convic-tion and a custodial sentence.

This version of events is supported by the account of the woman with whom Nan shared her cell in Holloway Prison, Christine Keeler. For a time, Christine had been one of the most famous women in the world, having found herself at the centre of the Profumo Affair, a scandal that rocked the

British Establishment and led to the resignation of John Profumo as the Secretary of State for War in Harold Macmillan's government. Profumo had lied to Parliament about his relationship with Christine, a model who had also been romantically involved with the Soviet naval attaché Yevgeny 'Eugene' Ivanov.

Christine had received a nine-month prison sentence in December 1963, having been advised by her lawyer to plead guilty to perjury in her case against Aloysius 'Lucky' Gordon, the jazz singer who had stalked and brutally attacked her. It had been a terrible injustice that saw Christine put behind bars while her attacker went free. Lucky Gordon indeed.

Her memoir refers to her time in prison with Nan, whom she described as 'a good friend in prison . . . in for helping her burglar husband.' Nan was utterly convinced of Christine's innocence and they both felt a sense of injustice, not only for themselves but for the women around them in Holloway Prison, many of whom seemed to be there because of the actions of the no-good men in their lives.

Nan was not only doing time on account of Grandad, but she was also pregnant and would give birth to her third child, their first child as a couple, 'inside'. That daughter was my mother. Corrina Anne Crowley was born in 1964 at the Whittington Hospital in Islington. What her birth certificate doesn't record is that, on top of the pain of childbirth, Nan had to endure the humiliation of being under prison guard and handcuffed as she gave birth. She would later tell Mum that the nurses were so horrible to her that when one of them asked her what she was imprisoned for, she replied, 'Murder – and the next one will be you!' She was returned to Holloway after the birth (probably to the relief of the nurses) where Mum would spend the first few weeks of her life.

Holloway Prison was a cold and hostile environment. The cells were cold, the food was cold, most of the people were cold. It had been no place for a pregnant woman and was certainly no place for a newborn baby.

After six weeks, Nan had to undergo the additional trauma of having her newborn daughter ripped away from her and handed to Nanny Knott, who would care for the baby with Paul and Amanda until Libby was released.

Christine Keeler's memoir also describes helping Nan to 'get back on her feet' when they were both out of prison later that year. Nanny Libby visited her at her pad on Linhope Street, in Marylebone, a very exclusive part of North West London near Baker Street and Regent's Park. Nan later told us that Christine would give her some of her glamorous clothes and that she would use them to act as a decoy for her infamous friend from time to time, taking advantage of their similarly dark hair, good cheekbones and thin frames to fool the following paparazzi.

This was about the only glamorous period in poor Nan's life. After she was released, it wouldn't be long before the far-reaching consequences of her conviction would start to become clear. While Mum and Paul, now four years old, would return home to live with Nan, now living in Brockley in South London, Amanda no longer recognised her mother and refused to return. She would scream and cry at the thought of being left with a woman she didn't know. I can't even begin to imagine how Nan must have felt looking into the tear-filled eyes of her daughter who looked back as though she were a complete stranger. So to avoid causing Amanda any further pain, but to Nan's heartache, it was agreed that she would continue to live with Nanny Knott where she had settled.

Whatever regrets Nanny Libby had at the time, they apparently didn't include her relationship with Grandad Pops. On 15 September 1964, they married at St Nicholas Church in Gloucester. Grandad wore a navy-blue jacket and tie with a crisp white shirt and dark trousers. Nan wore a dark-purple two-piece dress with three cream roses on the jacket lapel, black shoes and a matching hat. Aside from the absence of a white dress, the photograph of the newlyweds looks like any other wedding day. But what it doesn't show are the prison guards just out of shot. Grandad was still serving out his own prison sentence and was on day release under guard. It would be a running joke in the family for years to come that if you looked closely enough at the bushes behind my grandparents, you could see the police keeping watch. The wedding certificate was itself a source of comedy. Grandad gave his occupation on the wedding certificate as 'painter' and his address as 'Barrack Square'. I suppose these are more respectable than the more truthful and direct answers of 'convict' and 'HMP Gloucester'.

The newlyweds and their children moved to Stepney Green in East London in the late 1960s, but there was one child missing – Paul. One afternoon in late March 1966, when the family were still living in Brockley, my Uncle Paul took himself off to the shops. It wasn't that unusual for a six-year-old boy to do so in those days in that part of London. It was while crossing the road near Brockley railway station that Paul was hit by a car. He was rushed to hospital, and during the coming days, doctors fought hard to keep him alive, but Paul died early in April as a result of his injuries. Grandad Pops had been released from prison at this point, so both Paul's parents were by his bedside. To them, he looked as if he was asleep, with just a bruise on his cheek. They were completely devastated. Grandad later described his distress at driving past the scene of the accident just a couple of days later and seeing Paul's little shoe still there by the side of the road. Just days After the accident, Nanny Libby put all her time and effort into a successful campaign to get a crossing installed where the collision took place.

I grew up seeing the same faded photograph of Paul on mantelpieces and shelves at homes across the family, including ours – the happy, smiling face of a blond-haired, blue-eyed boy beaming out beyond the frame. Although he was in every house we went to, Nan never spoke of Paul, and even at an early age, I had enough tact not to ask. But those who knew him spoke of a bright, happy, well-spoken little boy who wanted to grow up to be a doctor. It was never to be.

Nanny Libby had joined the Salvation Army during her time in Liverpool, but after Paul died, she lost her faith. The pain of separation from Amanda had been bad enough for my grandmother. The grief from Paul's death must have been unbearable, and the birth of my Uncle Billy a month later, though joyful, was no consolation for the loss of her first son.

*

When the Crowleys moved to Stepney, it marked the start of a new chapter. They were moving up in the world, it seemed, but only insofar as they were moving north of the River Thames.

The Ocean Estate was a sink estate long before the term came into common use, ravaged by poverty, crime and drugs. Stretching from the Mile End Road all the way back to Ben Jonson Road, it contained dozens of tower blocks as high as ten storeys. Each block of flats was given a name with a nautical connection: Atlantic House, Adriatic House, Magellan House and so on, presumably as a nod to the East End's place as a gateway to the world through London's Docklands.

The Crowleys had arrived in Bengal House following my grandmother's side of the family, the Knotts. Nan's sister Esme had a flat on the sixth floor with her daughters, Dawn and Sara. My grandparents had their three-bedroom flat on the fifth floor, where they lived with Mum and uncle Billy. And next door, via a connecting balcony between the two flats, lived Nanny Knott.

Nanny Knott was the towering figure on Mum's side of the family, despite her small stature. For my generation in the family, having a great-grandmother so full of life was a rare blessing. I can still picture her big smile and the mischievous little twinkle in her eyes. As a kid, I loved visiting her flat, which was in Bow at the time I was born. There were always loads of kids from the family there and a hot pie in the oven, some chips frying in the pan, or corned beef rissoles on the go. How this little Welsh matriarch came to be an East Ender was a riches-to-rags tale worthy of the BBC soap opera's storyline. I wish I knew more of it, but it was never altogether clear when we were growing up. I do know that she was born Annie Pope and came from a well-to-do family of medics and professionals in Newport who led a very comfortable life. Her upbringing meant that Annie's marriage to Frank Knott, a mere butcher, was not approved of by the family. Even at her funeral in 2006, a snooty relative told my Aunt Amanda, 'The trouble with your grandmother was she married beneath her.'

I don't know what happened to Frank Knott, but after giving birth to ten children and surviving the family defying him in the first place, Annie then upped sticks and left him in Wales, moving the whole family up to London in the late 1950s, where her eldest daughter, Esme, was now living. I'm pretty certain that Frank wasn't my great-grandfather, considering that Nanny Libby was born on 21 March 1941, long after he had left Newport to fight in the war and long before he would have returned. Unless this was the greatest miracle since the Immaculate Conception, it seems highly improbable. The dates weren't the only giveaway. Nanny Knott had ten children and my grandmother was her fifth. With her dark hair and olive skin, Nanny Libby stood in stark contrast to the fair complexions of the rest of her brothers and sisters, with the sole exception of her sister, Judy, who was also born during the war years and whose complexion was even darker. My real great-grandfather's identity remains a mystery, except for one vague admission dropped by Nanny Knott that he was an Australian serviceman who found himself in South Wales during the war.

Nanny Knott would never marry or enter into another relationship again. 'I wouldn't have a man if his arse was hanging in diamonds,' she would say, with such frequency that it's become one of our family's favourite sayings. She had a whole stock of witty phrases apt for every occasion with the lilting Welsh accent she never lost. Along with her quick wit came a sharp tongue, which no one was safe from. Not even the late Queen ('She's a public servant, she should bow to me') or God almighty ('I'd rather go to hell anyway, I know more people there').

Wherever Nanny Knott lived, it would always be the epicentre of our family. Her four-bedroom flat next to Nan's in Bengal House was no exception. It was cramped living with five family members – including three of her children, one grandchild, Amanda, and Nanny's great friend, who everyone called Uncle Nicky. And, if that weren't confusing enough, other children and grandchildren, as well as kids from the estate, would be coming and going at all hours of the day and night. But most incredibly of all, a menagerie of animals occupied such a privileged status that they were given their own bedroom.

I kid you not. In a hugely overcrowded four-bedroom flat, with far more occupants than there were bedrooms, one whole room was dedicated to the pets that Nanny Knott accumulated, housing budgerigars, canaries, doves, mynah birds, a giant brown poodle and even a spider monkey. Like an East End Doctor Doolittle, Nanny Knott would take in any animals that came her way, injured and neglected, and nurse them back to health.

Each animal had its own distinct personality, which created plenty of problems. Coco, the giant brown poodle, hated adults and was fiercely defensive of the children. One night, he effectively barricaded the door to Amanda's bedroom where she was sleeping and refused to let anyone in to check on her. Mum had to be woken up in the flat next door and brought in to coax Coco out of the way as the dog refused to budge for anyone else. Judy the spider monkey loved Nanny Knott and the children, but heaven help anyone she took a dislike to – she may have looked sweet, but her glistening, pointed fangs could give a nasty nip.

The family loved the mynah birds best because of their wicked tongues. Of all the ones Nanny Knott had over the years, the family favourite was George: a beautiful black bird with an orange streak around his eye. His unerring timing would have everyone in fits of laughter. Whenever there was a knock at the door, he'd shout out, 'Quick, Nan, the Old Bill's at the door!' And when Nanny Knott got one of her dreaded visits from the loan collectors – the 'Provy' men – George would squawk, 'We're out! We're out!'

Nanny Knott's home was always a fun place for children. Mum would be jealous of the kids sleeping over next door when she was a child, but whenever she asked if she could stay at Nanny Knott's, her mum would reply, firmly and resentfully, 'No. She's already got one of my children; she's not having any more.'

But for all the good times, the fun and the laughter, the family was living in gut-wrenching, grinding poverty. My grandparents' flat was minuscule and sparsely decorated. Whatever furnishings they had were stolen goods. In their pokey little kitchen, they didn't have a modern washing machine, just a bucket and an old-fashioned wringer. They would fiddle with the electricity meter by putting camera film in to stop the dial from turning around, but eventually, the electricity company grew wise and came around to fit a new meter. Still, as the technology evolved, so did the fiddle. A hole was drilled, and a wire put in to stop the meter from turning. This worked perfectly until one day it blew up. Nan phoned Grandad in prison to ask what she should say when they came around to inspect the damage. 'Tell them it was me,' he said. 'They can't lock me up twice!'

Nanny Knott never did a day of paid work in her life, as she raised all her children on her own. The money she received in benefits didn't stretch far, and there were always lots of mouths to feed. Sometimes when food was scarce, she would take the labels off the tins she had left in the cupboard and invite the kids to play pot luck to decide who got what. If you were lucky, you got something you liked, like beans for toast, or some soup. If you were unlucky, you ended up with a tin of mushy peas or some custard, which might sound nicer than some of the alternatives but hardly constituted a decent evening meal.

The family would help each other out as best they could. It didn't matter if they'd had a huge row and fallen out; if some-one was in trouble or needed a bob or two, the family would take care of it, and when there was nothing left to share, Uncle Nicky would go shoplifting or nick stuff off the back of the delivery vans on Mile End Road to cater for the kids. It wasn't just food. When the kids needed new coats and clothes for the new school year, Uncle Nicky would take them up the Roman Road. The kids would pick out their coats, try them on, and Nicky would say, 'You go and wait outside while I sort all these out.' Moments later, he would come dashing out of the shop laden with coats and shout, 'Quick, kids, run!' before they all scarpered into the bustling throng of the customers and traders of market day. The rest of the family never batted an eye – stealing what they needed but couldn't afford to buy was, unfortunately, a way of life. It was the only way they thought they could get by.

When Grandad Pops wasn't serving at Her Majesty's pleasure, he would sometimes put his driving skills to good use as an HGV driver, but even when undertaking legitimate lines of work, he would put his criminal mind to inventive use. When he worked for a fishmonger, the whole family enjoyed crates full of king prawns, Dover sole, mackerel and other spoils he helped himself to and delivered around the family. Nanny Knott was delighted. Every inch of every freezer in every home was crammed full of seafood – the entire family ate fish for weeks. When he was doing deliveries for a wine merchant, he would come home with cases of wine. Anything he didn't need, he would sell on – he was a cheerful benefactor, remarkably generous with other people's money and property, like the good-quality doormats he stole from his employer to sell around the pubs and estates. The front doors of the East End had never provided a finer welcome!

Believe it or not, Grandad Pops apparently did have an ethical code, even as an armed robber. He would never rob his own, meaning other working-class families. He would steal from businesses and wealthier people and justify it to himself and to others on the basis that they had insurance or could absorb the losses. But, of course, his crimes were not victimless, and his logic for excusing them was sometimes hard to fathom.

Mum remembers one occasion when Grandad Pops came home in fits of hysterics about the day he'd had. 'What are you laughing at, Dad?' she asked her father innocently. He could hardly control his laughter for long enough to answer but just kept on saying, 'Only a woman! Only a woman!' It turned out that it was 'only a woman' who'd outwitted him. He had marched up to the front desk of a post office with a shotgun and demanded that the cashier open the till and empty its contents into his bag. As her hand reached for the police panic button under the counter, he held the shotgun in her face and threatened to shoot her. He described her reaction as calm and stony-faced as she boldly pressed the button then looked him in the eyes and replied: 'Go on then, do it.' But he didn't. He stared at her, baffled, for a moment, and then he quickly turned tail and ran all the way home. 'Only a woman could have done that,' he said. He found her cool response hilarious, but I very much doubt his victim returned home that evening laughing about the day's events.

Grandad's armed robberies would become notorious in the East End, thanks to the distinctive rubber mask he wore, which he named Claude. Claude had longish grey hair, a contorted face and a giant nose. It was a hell of a disguise. On one occasion he went into a pub wearing Claude and had the customers roaring with laughter at what they thought was just a practical joke, until he produced his shotgun and started to fire warning shots into the ceiling. The *East London Advertiser* carried the headline, 'Claude has them in fits . . . of fear!' The police never caught him for that one.

Occasionally, his crimes would be acts of revenge. Late one sunny afternoon, when he'd come into some money, he took Mum to a fancy restaurant on Mile End Road. It was to be a lovely treat, but as they arrived, they could see the chairs already stacked on the tables and the staff arms deep in washing up. The proprietor emerged shaking his head, 'Sorry, we're closed,' he said firmly. But my grandfather wasn't to be deterred. 'We're only after a quick bit of lunch, and I'll make it worth your while,' he pleaded. 'No, we're closed,' came the emphatic reply. Bitterly disappointed, they had to settle for another, much less fancy place. His plans to treat his daughter had been scuppered, so with simmering resentment, Grandad later took himself to Tesco on Bethnal Green Road, bought himself the women's leather gloves that fitted his slender hands perfectly and returned that night to rob them.

Mum asked him once if he had ever thought about his victims or worried about the impact of his actions on their lives. 'Nah,' he replied. 'They live such boring lives; I've given them something to talk about.'

Grandad Pops certainly gave his own family plenty to talk about. When he was in with some money, he'd love taking my nan, my mum and her siblings on day trips to the seaside, or to funfairs, swimming, or fishing in whatever vehicle he'd stolen for the purpose: one day it might be a nice saloon car or a Mini Cooper or, for a bigger crowd, it would be a large van that everyone would bundle into.

At night, there would be parties until all hours in the flat. I'm told my grandparents would give ten shillings to Nan's younger sister, Angela, to borrow her little blue Dansette record player and blast out reggae, blue beat and old ska music. Mum might be able to stay up a little later, and Grandad would pick her up and dance with her until it was time to go to bed. All the wine, beers and spirits, probably stolen for the occasion, would then flow, and all their friends would pile into the little flat for a good time, including the villains Grandad knew from all across London.

I've often been asked over the years whether Grandad was in with the East End's most notorious gangsters, the Krays. My answer is always that yes, he knew them, but he wasn't in with their crowd. Even Grandad's skew-whiff moral compass pointed him away from their more sinister methods.

One of Grandad's closest friends was another famous gangster, Johnny Bindon. The son of a London taxi driver, Bindon came to prominence as an actor, after Ken Loach spotted him in a pub in 1966 and cast him as the tough husband in the 1967 film *Poor Cow*. In a case of art imitating life, Bindon would later be cast in a number of roles as a thuggish mobster. Off-screen, he was known for his violent temper and involvement in a number of protection rackets. What he lacked in professional training as an actor, he made up for in his experience as a gangster. When he wasn't rubbing shoulders with the aristocracy through his girlfriend, the baronet's daughter-turned-actress Vicki Hodge, or reportedly entertaining Princess Margaret on the Caribbean island of Mustique, Bindon was partying with my grandparents in Bengal House with a cast of other criminals. Among his many nicknames, Bindon was known as 'Big John' on account of his 'party trick' – hanging five half-pint glasses by their handles from his erect penis!

Then, as now, there was a certain type of glamour associated with the likes of the Krays and John Bindon, a notoriety that made them, and anyone who knew them, more interesting. For my family, however, Grandad's criminality and its consequences were far from glamorous. Away from the parties, the day trips and the spoils of his jobs, my grandfather, like so many of the criminals he associated with, was not a good husband or father. In so many respects, he could count his family among the victims of his actions.

When he wasn't in prison, he would be out all hours of the day and night, and Nan would have no idea where. She would wait up into the small hours and sometimes pop her head around the door and ask Mum, barely a teenager, to look after her brother Billy, and sister Eve, who arrived in 1972, while she toured the pubs and streets looking for him. Once, Mum was bundled into the back of a car in the middle of the night and taken on a three-hour round trip to Aylesbury to look for him. He had been out with his close friend and associate, Vince. Vince's wife, Val, had picked up Nan and Mum and, along with her own daughter, Sharon, had gone 120 miles there and back to collect their roving husbands. They'd found them, eventually, drunk in a cemetery making ghost noises. Given the character of the two women who stood over them, thoroughly unimpressed, they were lucky not to have been buried alive.

That journey had been a lot safer than some of the drives Mum used to take with Grandad. He was a heavy drinker and would regularly drink-drive, as he claimed it made him a better driver. On one occasion, when Mum was just twelve years old, he was so drunk that he asked her to do the gears while he steered and did the pedals. Mum had to point out that she wouldn't know when he had his foot on the clutch.

Mum's home life would manifest itself in her behaviour at school. She would be distracted, disruptive, unruly, insubordinate and argumentative. That was when she was there. At primary school, she wasn't beyond climbing out of windows and doing a runner back into the estate. Her first school-teacher at primary school recognised that, while Mum did not respond well to authority, she did respond well to being given responsibility. From the moment she was put in charge of the Wendy House in the classroom, her behaviour and engagement improved.

Mum had the same reputation on the Ocean Estate. From the age of eight she was taking care of her newborn baby sister, Eve, preparing her bottle for feeding, rocking her to sleep and even changing the old-school fabric nappies she wore with a safety pin. When Eve arrived, she was the light of Mum's life, and Mum enjoyed the responsibility she was given for caring for her. By the time she was eleven, Mum had earned the nickname 'Little Mum' for taking care of other kids around the estate. During school holidays she would even be given money by their parents to take kids from the estate on days out on the buses to London Zoo and other destinations across the city.

At primary school and at her secondary school, Mum found herself the leader of the outsiders and misfits. At home, she had picked up a violent temper, but she had also picked up an appreciation for the underdog and a hatred of any form of discrimination. It came from Nanny Knott's open door. Despite the social attitudes of the time, Nanny Knott counted black and Asian people among her circle of friends. Uncle Nicky was gay and accepted in the family long before homo-sexuality was decriminalised in 1967. Mum wasn't afraid to use her temper in defence of kids who were being picked on because of their skin colour, their nits, their visible poverty in their hand-me-down clothes and moth-eaten uniforms, or whatever else it was that made them a target for bullying.

Mum grew up feeling battered and unloved, so some people in the family feared that I would grow up to be a battered child in turn. But Mum was determined to make my childhood better than hers. It is hard for me to reconcile the Nanny Libby of Mum's childhood with the Nanny Libby I grew up with and the mother–daughter bond I saw between two of the most important women in my life. The difference between the two was that, throughout Mum's childhood, Nanny Libby loved my grandad and stood by him in spite of everything. Not only was he a shocking father, but he made Nan miserable, and she took this misery out on the people around her. By the time I was born, she had divorced him and he was out of her life, which made her much happier and much nicer to be around.

It is also hard for me to reconcile the Grandad Pops I knew – funny, kind, clever, the one who made me stuffed animals by hand, or the one who called me 'Welly Boots' when I was small and gave me big bear hugs when he was home – with the armed robber who held guns to the faces of his victims and beat his own wife. The joker and the prankster who was also a gangster. So institutionalised was he in the criminal justice system that each time he landed himself back in prison, the prison guards, or 'screws', would greet him like an old friend with a friendly 'Back again are ya, Bill?' or a disapproving 'Oh, Bill, what have you done this time?'

He would later talk about the routine that borstal, approved schooling, and then prison would give him and even the status he enjoyed behind bars as an armed robber – top of the villains' pecking order in those days. It wasn't unusual for him to take the rap for other people's crimes, especially in his younger years. Not just because he wouldn't grass on his mates, but because he knew that he could handle prison better than some of them. Even when he was arrested he would treat the experience as a bit of fun, using his double-jointed wrists and fingers to remove his handcuffs behind his back, before reaching up to the coppers with a cigarette in his hand, asking, 'Have you got a light, mate?'

Though the unspeakable abuse and tumultuous childhood Grandad Pops experienced doesn't excuse his life of crime, it does explain it. I can't help but wonder what kind of life he might have led if he'd had some of the same support I'd enjoyed: a loving family, great teachers, and the opportunity to build an honest career for himself and his family. Later in his life he admitted he regretted all the bad choices he had made and the hurt he had caused, but the damage was done – to his victims and his family, who would have to overcome the additional hurdles created by his life of crime, on top of those they already faced living in poverty in one of the most deprived parts of the country.

CHAPTER FOUR

Bill Streeting

Grandad Bill Streeting with Mum and Dad. Early 1980s.

GRANDAD POPS, BILL Crowley, and Grandad Bill Streeting shared a first name, but that was about all they had in common. Whereas Grandad Pops served at Her Majesty's pleasure, Grandad Streeting served King and Country. In his upbringing, his career, his politics and his parenting, Bill Streeting couldn't have been more different to Bill Crowley.

The Streetings had been a nuclear East End family for as long as anyone could remember. My great-grandparents, James and Emma, raised their five children in a small two-up two-down terraced house they rented on 46 Armagh Road in the heart of Bow, around the corner from the hustle and bustle of the market traders on the historic Roman Road.

They had no bathroom, just an outdoor toilet shared with neighbours, and a pokey kitchen that could barely accommodate two people at a time. The small garden out the back was like a jungle of assorted potted plants; some were fruit and vegetable crops, others decorative flowers. They also kept some chickens, and even a goat to provide milk after the birth of their lactose-intolerant daughter.

Grandad was the fourth of the five Streeting children, born on 9 September 1923. But if this was the 'Roaring Twenties', it was passing the Streetings by. Contrary to the spirit of the age of post-war optimism and economic recovery in the early 1920s, the East End was still gripped by poverty. My great-grandfather, who served in the Royal Navy during the First World War and worked as a crane driver on the railways after the war, instilled firm discipline and a hard work ethic in my grandad, as well as an expectation that, when he was old enough and had finished his education, he would go out to work to provide for his family just as his brothers, Ernie and Harry, had before him.

When Britain declared war on Germany, Grandad joined his two older brothers in the Royal Navy – just as their father had done during the First World War. I have a photograph of the three brothers together in their freshly pressed uniforms, Grandad in the centre, grinning from ear to ear, flanked by his brothers on either side. His white sailor's hat indicates he was serving on HMS *Fowey* at the time, a Shoreham-class convoy escort vessel, and the insignia on his arm identifies his rank as 'Stoker 1st Class', which would have seen him on engine-room duties.

By a stroke of good fortune, all four of the Streeting boys survived the war, although one of Grandad's brothers had a near-miss when a Nazi U-boat struck his vessel and the ship began to sink. By pure chance, it was Grandad's ship that mounted the rescue and, to his enormous surprise, he found himself pulling his own brother from the icy water.

After the war, Grandad returned to his family home on Armagh Road, which was now a little less crowded with just his parents and younger brother Harry living there. Ernie and John had left home to start their own families; my grandad's sister, Vi, and her husband, Michael Barrett, were still close by, just up the road at number 38 Armagh Road, with their two children, Rita and Mick.

Grandad was proud of his military service and enjoyed the routine, the discipline and the camaraderie of the Royal Navy, so after the war, he wanted to remain in the uniformed services and applied to join the City of London Police. Unfortunately, at five feet and ten inches tall, he was an inch too short for the minimum height requirement and so put his Royal Navy engineering experience to good use with the Port of London Authority instead, working on the boats that policed the docks along the River Thames.

Alongside the strong work ethic and respect for law and order that had been instilled by his father, Grandad carried with him a deep Christian faith, the result of his upbringing, which guided him throughout his life. Unlike Grandad Pops, each of these qualities ensured Grandad Streeting kept on the straight and narrow – he never so much as received a parking ticket. He did, however, find himself behind bars once in the late 1950s. Unlike Grandad Pops, however, Grandad Streeting was innocent of the charges made against him.

He had left the Port of London Police to work for Balfour Beatty as an engineer and found himself posted to the Suez Canal at the time the Suez Crisis erupted. When the Egyptian president, Gamal Abdel Nasser, nationalised the Suez Canal Company in the summer of 1956, which controlled access to the route between the Mediterranean Sea and the Red Sea, Britain, France and Israel mounted a military campaign to regain control of the canal. Civilian workers, like my grandfather, were arrested as spies and taken captive as prisoners of war.

The conditions in the camp were harsh, with extensive exposure to the glaring heat of the Egyptian sun. His family were given little information on his welfare and whereabouts during his captivity, until they received a telegram not long before Christmas that year that informed them that Bill was missing, presumed dead. It came as a devastating blow to the family, who were left stricken with grief by this sudden, untimely loss, with no explanation as to what had happened to him. So you can imagine their enormous shock and relief when, on Christmas Eve, Bill arrived on the front doorstep, shivering and dishevelled, but very much alive. He was still wearing the shorts and short-sleeved shirt that he had been wearing in Egypt before he was despatched home at short notice, but the ice-cold breeze of the English winter's night against his exposed arms and legs was a small price to pay for being reunited with his family.

The Suez Crisis was a miserable chapter in Grandad's life, made worse by the fact that his first wife had left him while he was held captive in Egypt. He kept the details of his marriage and the subsequent divorce a secret from Dad and me, no doubt due to his devout faith. It must have been a real source of shame and embarrassment for him – I didn't even discover that he had been married before he met my paternal grandmother until I was researching our family's history for this book.

Following his separation from his first wife, Grandad found himself living back at home with his parents in his thirties. By this point, my great-uncle Harry had flown the nest, too, which meant that Grandad had his own room, at least. He landed himself a new job as a civil engineer with City & Guilds, the educational association established by the City of London to develop a national system of technical education. His career began in the boiler room on the lower-ground floor, but he was hardworking and incredibly likeable, so he eventually rose through the ranks of the organisation to become head of maintenance. On the occasion of the Duke of Edinburgh's visit to the new City & Guilds headquarters on Portland Place in 1958, his qualification to maintain and repair the lifts meant that Grandad was placed on escort duty. If he was impressed by Prince Philip, he never let on. Despite Grandad's staunch support for the monarchy and love for the Queen, he would always refer to the Duke of Edinburgh as 'Phil the Greek', a common name for the Queen's husband in the East End, and not an entirely complimentary one.

It was at City & Guilds that Grandad met my grandmother, Heather, who worked as a clerk for one of the directors. A romance blossomed between them, and although she was eighteen years younger than Grandad, they married in July 1960 when she was nineteen years old, and he was thirty-seven. Grandad was dapper as always in his sharply cut suit, hair slicked back with a side parting, and a beaming smile that was topped with a thick, meticulously groomed moustache, which was far less grey than it was when I knew him. He was a terrible chain-smoker, and nearly every photograph from the wedding captured him with a cigarette in his hand as if it were his own take on a wedding bouquet. Nan looked beautiful, but nervous, clutching a more conventional bouquet of mixed flowers, wearing a smart white dress that came down to just below her knees, and horn-rimmed glasses. Perhaps the anxiety her face betrayed was an early clue that their marriage wouldn't last.

Far from newly wedded bliss, the early years of my grandparents' marriage were the beginnings of a tumultuous time for the Streetings. My great-grandfather was diagnosed with throat cancer and was in and out of the Royal National Throat, Nose and Ear Hospital in St Pancras. His deterioration was slow, painful and distressing for the family, especially his wife, whom everyone called 'Little Nan'. After his death in 1963, Little Nan insisted on wearing black for a mourning period which spanned an entire year. Nan, and Grandad's sister, Vi, took her up to the C&A department store in the West End to kit her out with all the black attire she would need to keep to her word.

Shortly after my grandparents' wedding, they rented a house in Stroud Green in North London to start a family. They spent the next four years trying, unsuccessfully, to have a child of their own, which took its toll on the already unhappy marriage. They weren't at each other's throats in the same way that the Crowleys were, but Grandad had a very traditional view of a woman's role and responsibilities within the

74

home. He expected that he would go out to work to provide for the family and his wife would stay at home to raise children as a housewife. But Nan was young, bright, and of a generation who had grown up in the aftermath of a war in which women had made a significant contribution to the home front. She wanted to have a career, as well as children, which put a remarkable strain on their relationship. But still, they tried for a baby, and after what seemed like an eternity, Mark Ian Streeting was born on 2 February 1965 at the Whittington Hospital in Islington – ten months after Mum was born in the same hospital under very different circumstances. Whereas Mum spent her first six weeks in prison before being sent off to live with her grandmother until Nanny Libby's release from Holloway, Heather was dressing Dad in some of the finest outfits, given to her by a friend who also made clothes for Prince Charles.

The much-anticipated and longed-for arrival of Dad might have been a picture-perfect moment in their lives, but my grandparents' marriage didn't improve. Not long after Dad was born, they moved down to Bexhill-on-Sea in East Sussex, nearer to my grandmother's family, to a little flat above a furniture shop with a view of the sea and the busy seaside town below. But despite the change of scenery, it had become clear that the differences between my grandparents were as large as their age gap and irreconcilable. In October 1966, my grandad's mum, Little Nan, passed away. She never recovered from the loss of the love of her life, and on top of the loss of his parents, Grandad found himself grieving the end of his second marriage. My grandmother suffered a breakdown and moved closer to her family in Hailsham, East Sussex, so

Grandad took Dad with him back to Armagh Road, hoping that the extended family would be better placed to help him care for the baby. For my grandmother, the separation was unimaginably painful, but she feared that she would not win custody of my father after her illness and so she had to let him go.

At number 38, Grandad's sister, Vi, lived upstairs as a widow after the death of her husband Michael in 1956, as a result of injuries he had sustained during the war. Downstairs lived her son, Mick, his wife, Sue, and their son, Stuart. At the original Streeting house, number 46, lived Vi's daughter, Rita, and her three children: Paul, Kamala and Tina. Rita had the difficult task of bringing up her three children alone after ending her marriage to their father – a task made even more difficult as a result of the racism that the children were subjected to because of their mixed-race heritage.

Grandad moved in with his cousin Rita and the children at number 46. Dad was now growing up in the same house that his father had, and the conditions weren't much different. Forty years on, there was still no bathroom and only an outside toilet. It was still a pokey two-up two-down, so Dad shared a bedroom with Grandad and Rita, and her children occupied the two other bedrooms. But at least now they had a living room at the front of the house.

For more than a year, when Dad was still a baby, his mum took the train to central London and went across to Bow Road station before making the short walk to Armagh Road to see her son during the evenings. She knew he was well cared for, but every night saying goodbye was painful. She maintained regular visits, but her relationship with Grandad remained strained and deteriorated further after he overheard her saying, 'If I ever get hold of that child, I am never ever going to let him go again.' The question of custody became a growing sore. Grandad was anxious that my nan might try and seize custody, and my nan regretted her unguarded comment within his earshot.

The distance between my grandparents grew even further when she fell in love with and later married a man named Robin Hill. Robin was a graduate of the London School of Economics and was building a successful career as a management consultant. When he was given the opportunity to travel to West Africa for work, she joined him. This was a difficult choice for my nan and proved to be equally difficult for Dad, who was so young when she left that he didn't recognise her when she first returned from a stint living overseas.

The tragedy of my grandparents' divorce was the distance it created between mother and son, which took decades to recover from. Growing up, I had a strong and loving relationship with Nanny and Grandad Hill. Dad always made an effort to take me to visit them down in Cuckfield, in West Sussex, where they later settled. The times he spent with his mum as a boy were memorable, but few.

Despite the losses and the setbacks they'd experienced, the Streetings and the Barretts – sharing the house and sharing the childcare – continued in the same spirit they had always done: making the best of it. Like Mum's family, everyone mucked in, albeit with less ducking and diving and bobbing and weaving from the police. Dad's family were always on the right side of the law. Grandad was still working at City & Guilds, Aunt Vi and Rita worked as machinists in a shop above the Roman Road, and Sue worked in one of the shops below, so between the four of them, Dad and his cousins were well looked after. Everyone played their part with the childcare, getting the kids washed and dressed, doing the laundry and taking care of the school runs. Dad found himself shuffling between numbers 38 and 46, day by day, sometimes hour by hour, but it was a stable routine and having the support of Aunt Vi, Rita and Sue made life as a single father a lot more manageable for Grandad.

By all accounts, Dad was a happy child. In fact, compared to Mum, his childhood was pretty idyllic, even though they didn't have much money or the standard nuclear family. He went to a charming little primary school that was only a short stroll from his house, and he made the daily journey with his three cousins, who also attended. He was good at school, never a problem child, never caused a fuss. He spent most of his free time after school with his dad, who even volunteered as a leader for the local Cubs so that they could spend more time together.

During Dad's final year at primary school, Tower Hamlets Council made the decision to clear the substandard council housing on Armagh Road to make way for more modern housing developments. It was a long time coming, but incredibly disruptive for a child to be uprooted and moved once again. Armagh Road, which had been the epicentre of the Streeting family for decades, was no more. For Grandad and his sister, Vi, it was sad to say goodbye to the houses where they'd grown up and where they had, in turn, raised their children, but the move was an opportunity to get a better lot for themselves and their children and, in Vi's case, grandchildren.

The family were dispersed across East London, and some were luckier than others. Dad's Aunt Rita and her kids were moved out to the Becontree Estate in Dagenham, a place which was a big step up in the world for families like ours. Becontree houses had front and back gardens, indoor bathrooms and toilets and new public amenities like schools, libraries and doctors' surgeries constructed to support them.

Grandad wasn't so lucky. He and Dad were moved to a place called Verity House, to a ground-floor flat next door to Aunt Vi that made Becontree Estate seem like Mayfair in comparison. It was so poorly constructed that the top-floor flats had water leaking through the ceiling and walls so damp that the wallpaper would peel off. The ground-floor flats weren't any better; in fact, in the winter, the cold and damp was so bad that mushrooms grew on the carpet.

The three of them suffered through at Verity House for over eighteen months with the misery of their squalor and the bad chests the damp and mould created. Eventually, the council relented to protests from the residents about the horrific living conditions, and they were relocated once more. Having their fate in the hands of the local council was a horrible experience. The waiting, the uncertainty, the fear that – even if they ended up somewhere better – they might be separated. Grandad was heavily dependent on his sister to help with childcare. Thankfully, he and Aunt Vi were kept together on account of their shared care of Dad and moved to Bancroft Road in Stepney Green in 1976. Grandad was relieved to be given his two-bedroom maisonette on the third and fourth floors of Walter Besant House at number 18; Aunt Vi lived across the road on the ground floor of a three-storey block of one-bedroom flats. She had a little front yard and a square back garden, which she mostly paved over, except for a border where she kept rose bushes that she would tend to every week like clockwork. She could see the Streetings' front door from her back garden and would continue to be on hand to support Grandad in bringing up his son for years to come.

*

Grandad took the same approach to parenting as his father had, instilling the work ethic he had learned from his own father into his son. He would make sure that Dad was provided for in terms of the things he needed, but if there was something Dad wanted, he would have to work for it. If Dad wanted more fashionable trainers or school shoes, Grandad would give him the money he was planning to spend on a more basic pair and Dad would have to earn the rest from odd jobs or part-time work on the market or a paper round. But he didn't resent it. Quite the opposite. By the time Dad left school with a handful of O levels at sixteen, Grandad wasn't just his father, but his best mate, the person he would confide in and share everything with. Even when Dad was off out with his mates on a Friday night, he would make the time to pop into the Three Crowns on Mile End Road for a pint or two with Grandad – a tradition he started when he was about fifteen, well before he was legally entitled to. It was probably one of the few times Grandad looked the other way when it came to the rules and providing discipline during Dad's upbringing. He wouldn't even swear in front of his son – except on one occasion when Dad paid an unexpected visit to his office at the City & Guilds only to find, to his horror, Grandad effing and blinding at the top of his voice to his colleagues about something that had gone wrong.

There was something about keeping up appearances with Grandad. He would always wear a suit and smart, perfectly polished shoes wherever he went. Occasionally, in hot weather, he might wear an open-collar shirt and trousers, but he never owned a pair of jeans in his entire life, and the only time he wore a tracksuit or trainers was if he was doing outdoor activities with the Cubs and Scouts or coaching the Scouts' swimming club on a Friday evening. In his retirement, he occasionally wore a vest and trousers to smoke on the landing outside his flat, but otherwise, he was immaculately turned out.

Grandad's conservative personality was reflected in his political views – he was a lifelong Tory voter. The only exception was in local elections when he 'voted Liberal to keep Labour out'. This wasn't unheard of. In Grandad's day, a sizeable share of the working class traditionally voted Conservative and while Grandad didn't grow up with much and was reliant on council housing, he worked his entire life, paid his own way and took pride in never taking a penny from the state in benefits. When Mrs Thatcher came to power in 1979, her brand of politics appealed to him. He associated the Conservative Party with reward for hard work, patriotism, defence and law and order. He associated the Labour Party with welfare for those who couldn't be bothered to work, mismanagement of the economy and what he described as the 'loony left', which had taken control of the Labour Party in the 1980s. Although he never took advantage of the 'right to buy' his council house, introduced by the Thatcher government in 1980, many of our family did, and it consolidated the support that many of the Streetings and the Barretts gave the Conservative Party.

I often wonder what he would have made of his grandson becoming a Labour MP. I wish he had been alive to see it, just as I wish I had had the chance to talk politics with Nanny Libby. On the occasions when Dad's dad and Mum's mum met, the debates could be explosive and entertaining at the same time, but they had a mutual respect and admiration for each other, nonetheless. Both of them had strong convictions, integrity, and a devotion to their grandchildren.

Grandad also loved Mum. After my parents separated and Dad moved back home, he was always there for her to lend her a sympathetic ear, to offer advice – even when it was unsolicited – and to provide some extra shopping, some money if she was in need or some unscheduled childcare if some work became available, or she made plans with friends. In some respects, he was the father she never had.

My grandad was more than a chip off the old block. For me, and for Dad, he was the rock upon which our family was built and the single biggest influence on my life to this day.

CHAPTER FIVE

East End Boy

Me at home in Clichy House, 1986.

FOR AS LONG as it has existed, the East End of London – where Grandad Streeting grew up, where Grandad Pops ran riot, and where Nanny Libby campaigned tirelessly for social justice – has been synonymous with poverty, deprivation, overcrowding and crime. It has always seemed to exist as a world apart from the rest of the city – the historian John Strype's 1720 *Survey of London* described London as consisting of four parts: the City of London, Westminster, Southwark, and 'That Part beyond the Tower'. It was in that part beyond the Tower that the East End was born.

The roots of London's East End can be found beyond the walls of the ancient city of Londinium, along the road built by the Romans out to Camulodunum, modern Colchester, the first major city in Roman Britain. Along the route of the Roman road grew several villages and hamlets, which over time became the modern London Borough of Tower Hamlets.

Over the centuries, the Manor of Stepney, first recorded around the turn of the millennium in AD 1000, covered the area across East London that now encompasses the London Borough of Tower Hamlets and the London Borough of Hackney. By the time John Strype produced his survey of London in the 18th century, the East End was playing host to the noisy, dangerous, or foul-smelling industries that the wealthy inhabitants of the City of London were no longer willing to tolerate under their noses. These included the tanning of leather, which required the processing of urine, the manufacture of gunpowder and the proving of guns, which was noisy and dangerous, and the manufacture of clothing and textiles, which required large areas for tentergrounds.

Further growth was driven by the construction of the Georgian docks in the early 19th century, which would drive Britain's trade across the world, and the displacement of London's poor, caused by the clearance of slums in the City of London to make way for the great new railway stations that would ferry people and cargo across the land. The overcrowding of the East End saw the departure of the few wealthier residents of the area for more pleasant conditions elsewhere in the city, leaving the rest of the inhabitants to live in substandard conditions, which had only marginally improved by the time of my birth, some one hundred years later.

Throughout the 20th century, the destruction of homes by the Luftwaffe in the Second World War and the clearance of more slums in the 1960s meant that residential streets were replaced with huge, looming tower blocks and endless rabbit-warren housing estates. Once again, London's poor were displaced across the east of the city. In the square mile between Commercial Road and Mile End Road that makes up Stepney, hundreds of pokey flats and high-density, poor-quality council housing had been constructed to house those grappling with poverty, including me and Mum.

The East End's story has always been one of migration, since Oliver Cromwell's decision to allow the resettlement of Jews in 1655, followed by other Jewish people in the 1870s and 1880s. The Huguenots arrived in the 18th century, mainly weavers concentrated in Spitalfields. Chinese communities established Chinatowns around Shadwell and Limehouse, until their destruction in the Blitz and relocation to Soho in London's West End. The docks became home to freed American slaves who had fought on the side of the British in the American War of Independence, as well as sailors and freed slaves from the colonies of the British Empire in the West Indies. From the late 1950s, Bangladeshis began to arrive from the new Commonwealth, working in the local docks and within the fashion and textile industries that had been built by East London's Jewish communities. Today, the East End remains a melting pot of different cultures, who aim to follow the well-trodden path out towards the wealthier London suburbs and into Essex. For all its poverty, it is a place where people aim to get on, whether through wheeling and dealing as Grandad Pops did, or working hard and playing by the rules like the Streetings.

Ironically, the East End is now a destination for people on the up, too. Sandwiched between the City of London and the glittering lights of Canary Wharf, many young professionals see Tower Hamlets as the place to be, which is ironic, given how determined I was to escape it.

Of course, the poverty of the East End made it synonymous with crime. The docks were a target for theft. Prostitution was rife. A series of high-profile villains, from Jack the Ripper in 1888 to the Kray twins in the 1960s, gave added notoriety to the reputation of the East End and its inhabitants. Everyone in the East End claims to have known the Krays, and although in Grandad Pops' case, it was true, I find the exaggeration of this family connection in the press, and the glamorisation of the Krays in film and television, somewhat baffling and unedifying. It's not something to aspire to!

The social conditions gave rise to a radical political tradition. Nanny Libby's activism was preceded by a century's worth of likeminded East Enders fighting for justice for the poor and downtrodden: the Salvation Army was born in Whitechapel in 1865; the matchgirls went on strike against their brutal working conditions in Bow in 1888, an event that served as a forerunner to the modern trade union movement; 1914 saw the establishment of the headquarters of the Suffragette movement on Old Ford Road; and the march of fascism was halted in the infamous Battle of Cable Street, where East Londoners forced back Oswald Mosley's Blackshirts in 1936.

For much of the history of the East End – indeed, the poorer areas of London in general – its residents have felt the need to take matters into their own hands to draw attention to their suffering and campaign for change. But those in power also made positive changes of their own accord. For example, on account of the high levels of deprivation in Stepney in particular, and the high proportion of mothers who would necessarily be out at work to provide for their families, the borough was chosen by the London County Council as one of the two pilot sites for preschool nursery education. When Old Church Nursery School opened its doors to the local community in 1930, the head teacher estimated that, of the eighty-eight children on the roll, a third had rickets, a third had problems with their tonsils or adenoids, and four in ten were suffering malnourishment. When I attended the nursery just over fifty years later, the diseases may have changed, but the underlying poverty remained in families like mine. Even today, despite being home to one of the richest places on earth in Canary Wharf, the London Borough of Tower Hamlets has some of the highest rates of child poverty in Britain, with children going hungry, their parents skipping meals, living in substandard, poor-quality housing or temporary accommodation in bed and breakfasts and bedsits.

Old Church Nursery, situated on Walter Terrace, just off Bromley Street, was warm and welcoming, despite occupying the same single-storey building for half a century. It had just four classrooms, as well as bathrooms with child-height sinks and tiny toilets, a medical room, and a small number of offices for the staff. One of the benefits of the building's size was the large open space at the front and back of the nursery, which gave kids like me who lived in flats the chance to run around like maniacs at playtime on what seemed like a vast green space to little three-year-old legs.

Going to nursery was the highlight of my toddler day. The only time I would cry in the morning would be if I had been staying with Grandad Streeting and he was dropping me off. I would cling to his hand for dear life and sob my little heart out as my teachers tried to entice me inside with the promise of fun games and milk at break times. I always hated saying goodbye to Grandad – why would I want to play at nursery when I could stay at home with my best friend in the world?

I had all sorts of adventures at nursery school that I just couldn't have at home. In the corner of the room sat a battered wooden dressing-up box, the contents of which spilled onto the floor and rails on either side. The possibilities were endless – we could let our imaginations run wild as pirates, cowboys, princes and princesses. I loved dressing up and could usually be found playing a wizard or witch. When not in costume, we would play in sandpits and build water fountains in big trays that stayed in the middle of the classroom, but my absolute favourite thing to do at nursery was paint. Standing at a minia-ture table, wearing a big red apron which, although child-sized, reached down to my ankles, I would splodge primary colours over an expanse of paper using paintbrushes that were definitely on their last legs after years of use. We painted so often that I remember Mum buying a little wooden bench with a chest under the seat for my bedroom, where piles of my 'works of art' would go. Occasionally, the finished pieces were vaguely recognisable, like the butterflies I would make by slapping mounds of paint onto the middle of a sheet of sugar paper before carefully folding it shut, smoothing it down and then eagerly peeling it open to reveal what I thought were beautifully symmetrical butterfly wings. In reality, it probably looked more like someone had made the unfortunate mistake of sitting on wet paint.

Old Church Nursery had a huge collection of books that sprawled across the shelves of each classroom. By the time I arrived, I was already a keen reader or, at least, was read to enough to know certain books by heart, which allowed me to give the impression that I was reading along with the teacher at story time. By the time I was three, I had been read the entirety of the Ladybird 'Well-loved Tales' series, which were proudly displayed on the little bookshelf in my bedroom at home. The classics from my early years had later been added to with the more modern Ladybird books that cashed in on my favourite television series, like *Thomas the Tank Engine* and *He-Man and the Masters of the Universe*, which I would watch on the small black-and-white television set – assuming we could get ITV after fiddling with the tuning dial for a good twenty minutes to get a clear picture.

When I was small, I rarely felt self-conscious or particularly aware of the poverty I was growing up with. It was all I knew. But the exception was my fourth birthday. I wish I could remember the names of the staff at Old Church Nursery School; I may have forgotten them now, but I have never forgotten how they made me feel, especially on 21 January in 1987. Usually, on someone's birthday, there would be a cake and a little party. Parents would send their children in with fun-sized sweets to share with the class. But when it came to my birthday, Mum hadn't sent me in with anything. I knew she hadn't forgotten. She didn't have the money to spare for the cake and sweets, but the other children expected that there would be a celebration. Admittedly, my memories of nursery are sparse, coming back to me every now and then as colourful yet slightly out-of-focus flashbacks, but the memory of that birthday is as clear as day. I can still feel embarrassment like a hand twisting my stomach. It was, I think, the first time that I had felt the humiliation of poverty – that Mum wasn't able to provide something other parents could, that we were the exception because we were poor. It wouldn't be the last time, but on this day, fortunately, it would be short-lived, thanks to one of the staff who went across the road and bought a Victoria sponge. It was only a small cake, in a little cardboard box with cellophane wrapping, but it meant the world to me that day. When the time came, everyone gathered around the table, sang 'Happy Birthday', and I blew out the candle to make my wish.

I know I thanked my teachers at the time. So did Mum, who was touched by the gesture. It was the first birthday party I ever had, and it has stayed with me ever since. I spoke to Mum recently about this episode and how it made me feel, and she was taken aback. As she pointed out, she could have asked Grandad Streeting or Nanny Libby or Dad to contribute to a cake or some sweets, to spare the embarrassment, but it never occurred to her because her birthdays hadn't been celebrated in the way that other children's birthdays were either.

Every day, even now, in classrooms across the country, there are teachers performing similar acts of kindness: having some cereal bars on hand because someone's turned up to school hungry, giving a quid to the kid on the school trip whose parents couldn't afford spending money for the gift shop, making someone's birthday special. If you're one of those teachers reading this, thank you. Those kids, like me, may not remember your name in the decades to come, but they will never forget your kindness.

Each day at three o'clock, Mum would be there to collect me. With the other parents and carers, she would come into the nursery, ask me how my day had been, collect my coat from the coat peg in the hallway and we would make our way home in time to watch my favourite TV programmes. As the other kids piled into the little shop opposite the entrance on Head Way, I would plead with Mum for us to join them so I could buy some sweets. The answer would always be no, to my disappointment. It was a luxury she couldn't afford. Besides, on Sundays, my Grandad would always spoil me with some chocolate for the week ahead.

Our daily routine was so fixed that when Mum arrived to pick me up one afternoon, slightly worse for wear, it was highly irregular. Mum was never a big drinker anyway. She may have had a couple of vodkas on a weekend night out at Stepney's nightclub – a place made famous by the appearance of its 1970s illuminated dance floor in the video for Pulp's 1995 hit 'Common People' – but I can count the times I have seen her hammered on one hand.

I'm sure she was trying to be discreet, but unfortunately, my precocity at the age of three or four dropped her right in it. With my hands on my hips, I let out a deep, theatrical sigh of disappointment. 'Oh, Mum, have you been drinking again?' I asked, shaking my head like a disapproving parent.

I watched as my mother turned a deep shade of fuchsia, trying to laugh my question off. She protested her innocence at effectively being labelled a drunken old lush in front of all the other parents. One of the teachers turned from washing her hands at the sink to laugh along sympathetically, but there was probably more than a hint of judgement, too.

I had been unfair, but her inebriated state that afternoon had taken me aback – she was definitely half-cut and smelt like a brewery. The culprit? My grandfather – Grandad Pops.

This is my earliest memory of my 'other grandad'. He was not long out of prison and, true to form, leading my mother astray. They had spent the afternoon down at the Artichoke pub, a dive of an East End boozer, a stone's throw from where we lived in Clichy House. As we went back to meet him there, Mum could barely walk in a straight line.

On the outside, the Artichoke didn't look too bad. It was a three-storey townhouse, with a little balcony elevated at the front and a smaller two-storey annexe on one side. In the summer they would make it look more presentable with some hanging baskets and flower planters around the front of the pub. But no amount of cosmetic improvement could change what it was on the inside: dingy, well worn and full of eye-watering cigarette smoke. It was the sort of place you would go for a right old cockney knees-up. Cheap and cheerful – the pints and the punters.

Grandad Pops fitted right in there, with his flat cap covering his balding head, gaunt cheeks, and a mischievous, slightly goofy grin. He would always greet me with "ello, Welly Boots!' – until I grew out of the nickname – and he'd give me a big hug with his skinny arms. That sort of quality time – if you can call it that – with Grandad Pops was rare. I didn't see him from one year to the next as a kid – he was usually up to no good and would wind up back in prison. His being there was never hidden from me. He'd been in and out for so much of his life that it was almost normalised in our family, although I always felt a sense of disappointment in him when he once again landed himself in trouble. But when he was about, he was great fun to be around. He was just like any other grand-parent: loving, caring, tickling. He had a good sense of humour and saw the funny side of it when I asked if he would take me to the London Dungeon on Tooley Street. I'm not sure he was that keen to find himself back behind bars again, but he took me anyway.

After a particular stint in prison, when I was still a baby, Grandad Pops landed a job as an official receiver through a friend. I'm sure he couldn't quite believe his luck – he was being paid to legally take people's possessions from them. For a while, this new job worked rather well for him. A lot of it was corporate work, seizing assets from big businesses that were going bust. But then he would find himself sent to families just like ours, struggling to make ends meet, and having to look women like my mum in their bloodshot, grief-stricken eyes as they saw family possessions they could no longer afford to keep or replace, being carted out of their already mostly bare homes. My grandad couldn't bear to take from people who couldn't afford it – he felt as though it went against everything that he stood for. So, he packed it in and returned to his regular line of work as a criminal. He said it felt more honest.

Thankfully, we never had the bailiffs round to our house, even when times were particularly tough. Even from a young age, I could always tell when Mum was really struggling financially, as it would inevitably involve a trip to Chrisp Street Market in Poplar. There wouldn't be enough money for bus tickets for us both, so it was an hour and a half's walk to and from Chrisp Street, along Stepney Way, past Stepping Stones Farm, through the grounds of St Dunstan's Church, down the whole length of Salmon Lane crossing the Regent's Canal and the Limehouse Cut, then just as it felt we were getting closer, when we arrived at East India Dock Road, I would start to remember just how long the stretch up Canton Street and Grundy Street would be. We would do this lengthy walk of shame so that Mum could go to the pawnbroker's to pawn whatever jewellery she had for some cash in return and a slip of paper outlining the deadline for her to return the money she had borrowed, with an additional fee, in return for her jewellery. Sometimes we would traipse down to Chrisp Street Market just so that Mum could pay the fee and take out a new pawn agreement, with a new fee attached, so that she didn't lose the jewellery. I remember her stress and anxiety about whether she would have enough money in time to meet the deadline. It wasn't just the sentimental value she was worried about, but also how she would explain the absence of her jewellery to Nan. I was under strict instructions not to tell any of the family, especially Nanny Libby, that Mum had pawned her jewellery. It was ironic, really, as Mum only knew what a pawnshop was because Nanny Libby had taken her on the exact same journey when she was a child.

When I wasn't at nursery, I would go up to the hustle and bustle of the busy Whitechapel Road with Mum every Monday, where she would take her 'signing on' book to claim the benefits she was entitled to. In 1985, this would have been just over £120 a week in unemployment and housing benefits, child benefit and the additional lone parent supplement. The

Whitechapel post office was a huge, miserable, grey hall, and we would often face a long queue of equally miserable, grey faces. I would wait patiently without complaining because I knew what was coming immediately afterwards. Once Mum had signed on and collected her money, we would go across the road to the Wimpy, where I would be treated to a big, greasy burger and chips. It was our thing that we did together. That was always the way with Mum. She never had much, but she made sure that I was fed and clothed, and if there was money spare for a treat, I'd have one. If she didn't have it, I would go without, and I generally wouldn't complain either.

There was – and still remains – stigma and shame attached to signing on for benefits. I know Mum already found it humiliating, but the most degrading and dehumanising experience Mum had took place at the local DSS Office. The Department for Social Security was the government department responsible for the administration of pensions and benefits. Just the mention of going 'up the social' with Mum would fill my heart with dread. The wait, governed by a ticketing system, was always so long and boring. Occasionally, I would entertain myself by discreetly taking a handful of tickets to annoy the clerks behind the counter, who would grow more and more frustrated, calling out numbers to no reply.

The offices were sad, soulless places, and it seemed that the people who worked in them had hearts as hard as the plastic chairs in the waiting room. This particular day, I was at nursery when Mum collected her ticket and waited along with everyone else, many of them also anxiously awaiting the impending inquisition. When Mum was called in, after what felt like an eternity, she was taken by a stern-looking woman to a back room, which was unusual. Any other time she had the unfortunate need to visit the office, she would have been seen at one of the booths with a perspex screen.

As they entered, the DSS official locked the door. 'Why have you locked the door?' Mum asked nervously.

'Just for privacy, don't you worry about that,' came the matter-of-fact reply.

Mum took a seat on the cold, uninviting chair and nervously smoothed her jogging bottoms and T-shirt.

The official proceeded to interrogate Mum about her employment status and about my father. The experience had been degrading enough before the bureaucrat leaned over the desk and sneered, 'Do you know that *we* have to pay for *your* son out of *our* taxes?'

Mum was gobsmacked. Even by the standards of the DSS, this was unlike anything she had ever experienced before. She was also incredibly hurt – she had recently taken up a leisure and recreation course at Tower Hamlets College, which had really built her confidence and given her opportunities that she hadn't had at school, like an outdoor residential course in Wales, where she had the chance to do horse-riding, abseiling and other outdoor pursuits. She had begun to dream of a career as a fitness instructor – one that would help her, and me, build a better life. She finally felt good about herself in an educational context, which she never had before. She was trying to better herself, to make herself more employable, and she was enjoying it, too.

Quick as a flash, she snapped back: 'Oh no you don't! *My* mother pays for me out of *her* taxes, and her taxes are much higher than my benefits!'

Horrified at what she deemed to be insolence, the stony-faced woman threatened to deduct twenty per cent from Mum's benefits and spat that she was 'impertinent'.

By now, Mum had had enough of the insults. Crossing her arms and lifting her chin up with classic Corrina defiance, she looked her straight in the eyes and said: 'Well, you're the most obnoxious bastard I've ever met!'

And at that, the interview was terminated. Mum stormed out of the dingy office and marched straight home in a state of panic about what she'd said to the DSS officer. Her fears were allayed when we got home and opened the dictionary.

obnoxious – adj. extremely unpleasant; e.g., 'obnoxious odours'.

She breathed a sigh of relief. 'That's her to a tee,' she told me. She hadn't worried about calling her a bastard, she was more concerned that she'd used the wrong choice of word by calling her obnoxious!

Having checked her English, Mum went straight round to Nanny Libby's. Offering Mum a cure-all cup of tea to calm her nerves, Nanny Libby provided some small reassurance. 'Don't worry, love,' she said, 'they're doing that to a lot of people.' Nan was doing a lot of work for the tenants' union at the time and helping local residents who, like Mum, were having trouble dealing with the DSS and the local authorities.

I wish I could report that the culture has changed more than thirty years later. What happened to Mum in that office was an extreme case, but the underlying dehumanisation that people experienced in the DSS offices in the 1980s is replicated today in branches of Jobcentre Plus, with the portrayal of benefit claimants as scroungers, and punitive sanctions that are far worse now than they were then. It is one of the reasons why, even as a Labour politician who believes strongly in public services, I have always been conscious of the fact that many people feel more like victims of the state than supported by it. That was certainly the case for Mum. Fortunately, that hard-nosed jobsworth didn't follow through on her threats. Mum's benefits were never docked.

However short of money we were in the family, the one thing I was never short of was love, whether I was with Mum during the week or Dad and Grandad at the weekends. If ever Mum was short of anything, we'd walk half an hour from Stepney to Wapping to raid Nan's fridge and cupboards. Nan gladly obliged so often that I used to ask Mum if we were going to Sainsbury's or Nanny's to go shopping. Dad and Grandad, only a twenty-minute walk away, would always be willing to help, too.

When it came to childcare, Mum was similarly well supported, which was especially useful when she started silver-service waitressing. Nan was often occupied in the evenings attending meetings of the local Labour Party, tenants' association or whatever other rabble-rousing she was involved with. I would always be keen to stay with Grandad, but Mum knew she would face a job persuading me to come back home. I also loved going to stay with my Auntie Mandy and my Uncle Kevin at their flat on the thirteenth floor of Lewey House, the looming tower block on Bow Common Lane, which dominated the East End skyline before the days of Canary Wharf. I could watch *He-Man*, *Transformers* and *SuperTed* on their colour television, and Auntie Mandy let me put sugar on my Weetabix – a five-star experience for a little kid.

CHAPTER SIX

Mrs Dodd

Me as Ebeneezer Scrooge.

JUST BEFORE I left Old Church Nursery School, Mum and I were moved from our flat on Stepney Way around the corner to 23 Jamaica Street on the Exmouth Estate. I don't remember the move, but it was a step up for us both, literally and figuratively – it was a ground-floor maisonette. It had a back garden that was about five metres by three metres, which backed onto the two double bedrooms downstairs. The kitchen upstairs was a decent enough size to fit a small table with a couple of chairs; the living room next door had room for a sofa and an armchair, with space to spare. There was even a little balcony that overlooked the big area of grass in the middle of the estate, inconveniently set on a slope – presumably to prevent

99

kids from playing ball games – which was surrounded on three sides by six-storey blocks of flats and at the back, a complex of small shops and the estate office. The new flat also had central heating, which was a real improvement on the little gas heater we had in our living room in Clichy House, and would save Mum a fortune during the winter. Even the solitary slide in the middle of the estate beyond our back garden felt like a real upgrade, compared with the miserable strip of grass that lined the pavement at the bottom of Clichy House. It's amazing how much fun I could extract from going down the same slide over and over again.

When the time came to leave nursery for primary school, Mum had hoped I could attend our local school in Stepney, St Mary and St Michael Catholic School, which was a few minutes from our new flat. But places were in short supply, and since we weren't Roman Catholics, they were unlikely to take me. As a result, I was sent to St Peter's, London Docks, a Church of England primary school in Wapping, which was a twenty-minute walk away from where we lived.

There were tears when Mum dropped me off, all of which were mine. After prying my little clammy hands from around her waist, she bent down to give me a kiss on the top of my head, ruffled my hair and gently pushed me into my new classroom, as she looked on from the doorway, smiling in encouragement and no doubt feeling the same combination of pride and anxiety that every parent feels on their child's first day at school. I wonder how many of us have the same recollection of being told to go and sit on a carpet full of little strangers, looking back to our parents with watery eyes and sniffly noses, just as I did with Mum?

I was a bag of nerves in a strange, new environment. My brand-new school uniform – a burgundy red V-necked jumper, white shirt and grey trousers – was a little oversized so that I could grow into it. The shirt cuffs almost touched my knuckles and I had plenty of room to breathe in my too-big collar. The burgundy jumper wasn't the correct bright red shade of the school uniform code because Mum had bought a cheaper version from British Home Stores. But the school didn't make a fuss about it. Uniforms were expensive, especially for families like mine. Throughout my time at primary school, I remember Mum receiving school uniform vouchers to spend at a local supplier. She always tried to buy uniform to last, and Dad and Grandad Streeting helped out with the costs. Money was still sparse. Just over £100 a week didn't get Mum very far once the rent and bills were paid and the shopping was bought, which meant that any unexpected expenses were a real struggle. But Mum always made sure that I was well turned out for school, and if ever my black shoes lost their shine in the rough and tumble of the playground, Grandad would notice when he picked me up from school on a Friday. By the time I was returned to Mum on Sunday night, they would have a shine almost good enough to see my reflection – what Grandad called a proper Royal Navy polish.

The old cliché that you never forget a good teacher is true. I still remember mine all these years later, but it was the head teacher at St Peter's, Mrs Dodd, who made the biggest impression. She was a formidable woman. Short and stout, with dark hair in a short bob, big glasses with a thick rim, and a stern voice that would have been well suited for military discipline. She ran a tight ship and demanded high standards of effort from her pupils. At times, she could be terrifying. The last place you would want to be sent was Mrs Dodd's office. Not even the cheekier children dared to mess about when she led the weekly hymn practice in the school hall. But beneath her hard exterior was a big heart and a determination to get the very best out of her pupils and staff. She was utterly devoted to us.

St Peter's was smaller than the average-sized primary school, with just one class in each year from reception to year six. It was a tight-knit school community, where every child received close attention, and no one was allowed to slip through the cracks. This was important in a school that served a community with high levels of deprivation and child poverty. Children didn't leave their problems from home at the school gates. Whether it was hunger, domestic abuse or violence, parents with drug or alcohol addiction, or family breakdown, those challenges would manifest themselves in pupils' behaviour.

The first time I was summoned to Mrs Dodd's office wasn't on account of bad behaviour. In fact, I can't recall ever being sent to Mrs Dodd for a telling-off – I was always eager to please. Polite and helpful. Doing as I was told. On the rare occasion I found myself in trouble, as I did one afternoon for not sharing a pair of scissors, even the mildest rebuke from my teacher ended in floods of tears. I did not like being in trouble.

As I had arrived after the start of the school year, on account of Mum's late application and difficulty in finding a school place, Mrs Dodd had called me in to assess my reading level. In her small square office overlooking the playground, where she could keep our behaviour in check under her watchful eye, she sat me down on one of the smaller chairs at the coffee table, placed a huge stack of brightly coloured but slightly tattered books in front of me and asked me to start reading from the top of the pile. They were short reads from the 'One, Two, Three and Away' series, written by Sheila McCullagh, centred around the Village with Three Corners and the alliterative people who lived there: Roger Red-hat, Billy Blue-hat and Johnny and Jennifer Yellow-hat.

I read the first book effortlessly from cover to cover. And then the second. Then the third. As I looked up to grab another book from the rapidly shrinking pile in front of me, Mrs Dodd's eyes were wide, and her preened eyebrows, usually knitted together to reinforce her stern persona, were raised to form an expression I hadn't seen on her face before. I carried on reading one book after another until she was running short on time and books. She told me, as excitedly as her serious disposition would allow, that my reading age was years ahead of where it was expected to be. Although I hadn't been at St Peter's long by that point, I knew that Mrs Dodd wasn't the type to give praise willy-nilly. I remember feeling the warm glow of pride fill my chest as she told me I was a star reader. I also fell in love with the characters of the Village with Three Corners and was more than a bit disappointed when I outgrew that particular reading scheme.

I needed little encouragement to read at school. I'd already had all the encouragement I needed at home. I enjoyed class story time on the carpet with our teachers, but I was equally happy reading to myself. In those early years at St Peter's I started off with books like *The Very Hungry Caterpillar* by

Eric Carle and *Not Now, Bernard* by David McKee and quickly progressed to books by Janet and Allan Ahlberg, like *Cops and Robbers* and the 'Happy Families' series, including *Mr Creep the Crook, Mrs Wobble the Waitress* and *Master Money the Millionaire*.

My parents and grandparents might not have had much money, but reading was one of the greatest gifts they gave me. Children from the poorest backgrounds arrive at school at the age of five already behind their peers. With a good education, they can make up the difference, but despite all the progress made in state schools, the gap remains stubborn. Thanks to my family, I arrived with a head start, and with a love for learning that would change my life.

At the end of my reception year, Mum and Dad both came to my first parents' evening, where I received my first school report. I will never forget the opening words because Mum read them to me over and over again, beaming with pride, as Dad drove us back to our flat that night. 'Wesley is a bright, intelligent pupil . . .' she read through tears of joy, taking her time to enunciate the words 'bright and intelligent' for maximum effect. She said she had never seen a report like it when she was growing up – I suppose she mustn't have hung around with many swots like me. In so many ways, it was her report as much as it was mine. It was a validation of her parenting, of all the sacrifices she had made to raise me the best way she could. Her investment in that little library she curated when I was a baby and didn't even have a cot to sleep in had clearly paid off.

But Mum's outpouring of pride that night caused a minor dispute between her and Dad – he complained that it would 'give me a big head' and breed arrogance and complacency. It may sound harsh, but this was the start of a parenting dynamic that would serve me well. Dad kept my feet firmly on the ground. Whenever I protested, he would say: 'Your problem is that your mum puts you on a pedestal so high that it's my job to bring you back down to earth.' Looking back, it was the perfect combination of challenge and praise, but at the time, I didn't appreciate the lesson Dad was teaching me.

One of St Peter's great strengths as a school was its diversity. In my class, roughly half of the pupils were from Bangladeshi families. Their parents and grandparents had been coming to the East End since the 1950s and lived in the flats on Prusom Street, which backed onto the school premises, and in Shadwell on the other side of the Highway, which ran from Limehouse down to the Tower of London. The remaining fifty per cent or so were from white families and these were divided between the kids from the council estates, like me, and those who were from more middle-class families, the 'yuppies' – young urban professionals – who were moving to the area as part of the regeneration and gentrification of London's Docklands. Although St Peter's had a strong Christian ethos, the diversity of the school was celebrated. We were taught how to write our names and count to ten in Bengali. In the playground, Kabaddi, the national sport of Bangladesh, was played alongside football, skipping, tag and hide and seek. We would learn about different faiths and celebrate religious festivals from all the major world faiths: Chanukkah, Diwali, and Eid. We only felt jealousy when our Muslim friends were given the day off for Eid and would come and show off their brightly coloured party clothes by the school fence while we were cooped up in the classroom.

One of my favourite things about St Peter's was the weekly church service. St Peter's was a majestic grade-one-listed Anglican Church built in 1866, with grand red-brick arches, beautiful stained-glass windows and a ceiling so high it seemed to reach the heavens. Even from a young age, I adored the smells and bells of high Anglicanism and the lessons about loving our neighbours as ourselves and being good Samaritans. I had inherited my religion from Grandad Streeting, but it was through these acts of collective worship at St Peter's that I developed a strong Christian faith of my own, attending church and reflecting on the lessons we were taught during services and school assemblies. It was something special that I could share with Grandad, who would come along to our church services on a Friday afternoon to collect me, suited and booted as he always was.

When I was about eight years old, I was chosen to serve in the church as an acolyte, also known as an altar boy, donning a black cassock and white linen surplice over my uniform to perform my main duty of parading a tall candle in a brass candlestick holder around the church. Like Mum and her Wendy House in primary school, I enjoyed having a role to play, being trusted with responsibility and dressing up in the uniform that came with the role. I gradually progressed through the junior school, firstly as a thurifer, the person who waves the incense around the church during mass, and finally as the Master of Ceremonies, who coordinates the other servers to make sure they're in the right place at the right time during the service. But it wasn't always plain sailing. During my first outing as a thurifer, I was overly generous when filling up the incense burner, so the service was marred by coughing and spluttering children before they emerged into the daylight with red, bloodshot eyes from all the smoke. After a mild rebuke from the priest in charge, Father Peel, I didn't make the same mistake again.

Alongside the theatre and ceremony of our weekly church services, I discovered a love for a different type of performance, on the school stage. Like our country's well-known private schools, St Peter's understood the value of the arts and activities for our development and made sure these were part of the school day. Things like learning to play a musical instrument, taking part in drama, visits to museums and galleries, and trips to the seaside or the countryside, were part and parcel of the school curriculum. They may seem like basic components of a normal childhood, but lots of us at St Peter's were experiencing abnormal levels of poverty and would have been deprived of those opportunities without the investment of Mrs Dodd and her teaching staff. Although Dad and Grandad would make an effort to take me on trips to places like the Science Museum or the Natural History Museum, or on holidays to places like Devon, where Dad's cousin Rita had a bed and breakfast, or on caravan holidays to the seaside, Great Yarmouth or Lowestoft in East Anglia during the school holidays, my family didn't have the money to spend on things like after-school clubs or music lessons. That these opportunities were provided as part of the school day gave me a powerful foundation for the development of my education and well-being.

This is where my love of school drama began. Every year, the school would put on a Christmas concert with a series of plays performed by pupils, and from my first starring role as the Nutcracker in year one, dressed in a tunic made of red and gold foil and with a tinfoil sword to do battle with King Rat, I was hooked. Whether I was playing percussion in the music section, acting as narrator or playing Ebenezer Scrooge in *A Christmas Carol*, I lapped up every minute. I enjoyed the dressing-up, the escapism, and it gave me a self-confidence that I otherwise lacked.

Reflecting back on my time at St Peter's, I really believe it was a school whose teachers were determined to do everything in their power to broaden our horizons. I'm sure that's why Mrs Dodd made a point of playing classical music every morning as we entered the school hall for assembly and again as we left. She would tell us who the composer was and occasionally test our knowledge to see whether we were paying attention. It worked. When I was nine years old, I cajoled Grandad into buying me a magazine series called *The Classical Collection*, which came with a free CD. I knew the greatest hits of Tchaikovsky, Beethoven and Handel just as well as I knew chart-toppers like Whitney Houston, Queen and Mariah Carey. When Mrs Dodd asked if we could name the composers of the music she played at the start of our morning assemblies, my hand would shoot up as I inevitably knew the answer. I had a love of learning outside of the classroom that Grandad nourished at the weekends, and Dad, though bemused by my love of classical music, encouraged.

I always felt the guiding hand of Mrs Dodd behind me, pushing me to succeed. She gave me the chance to take up cello lessons, when I was about eight or nine, as part of a programme being run for Tower Hamlets schools, and I relished the opportunity of being one of just eight St Peter's pupils chosen to play. My parents were very proud, although lugging the cello I was loaned to and from school made me wish I had been given the violin to play instead, and I'm sure the noise of my rehearsals was an unwelcome disruption to Mum's religious commitment to watching *Emmerdale*, *Coronation Street* and *EastEnders*. I kept it up for three years, with rehearsals on Tuesday afternoons and the chance to perform at a concert in the vast surroundings of Christ Church in Spitalfields at least once a year. The grand church made St Peter's look small by comparison and the sight of the packed pews of proud parents, including mine, made for an impressive, if slightly intimidating, audience. Still, how many kids from Stepney could say they had played the cello in a concert?

Occasionally, Mrs Dodd pushed a little too hard. She persuaded my parents that I should skip a year at the end of infant school. I found myself, as a seven-year-old, in a class full of kids aged eight and nine. It doesn't seem like a big age gap now, but it felt like a leap at the time. I didn't struggle with the work, but I did miss my friends. I knew some of the kids in the class from playing games in the playground during break, but in many respects, it felt like my first day at a new school. We didn't have the bonds of friendship or familiarity built over years of shared class time. One or two of the kids seemed to resent a younger, obviously clever kid being fast-tracked to their level. Even those that were more welcoming had friendship groups that were already well forged. I stuck close to one boy whose sister had been in my class for the first three years, and we became friends, but I still felt lonely and longed to return to my old class. So after some protests and tears, I was allowed to return to my old classmates in year three. Undeterred, the following year, Mrs Dodd had me take a maths scholarship class after school with pupils two years older than me. This time I did struggle to keep up academically, and this was a deeply uncomfortable experience for someone who was used to being top of the class. I always left the class feeling defeated and out of my depth. I didn't have the foundational knowledge to keep up, so I conceded defeat, as did Mrs Dodd.

I didn't realise it at the time, but everything Mrs Dodd did was part of a grand plan to get me a scholarship for what she deemed to be a 'good' school. She was evidently determined that I wouldn't end up in one of our local secondary schools. During the 1980s and 1990s, London's schools were a byword for educational failure, and Tower Hamlets schools had among the worst reputations of the lot. Most families in Tower Hamlets couldn't afford extra tuition after school and certainly couldn't afford the fees charged by private schools, which were more than Mum's entire income for the year. Mrs Dodd was one of the people in my corner who was determined that the circumstances I was born into were not going to dictate my future. Sometimes, I look back and wonder just how different my life would have been if I hadn't had her there, helping to forge my path.

Mrs Dodd wasn't the only one plotting my escape from Tower Hamlets during those years. It didn't take long at St Peter's before I became painfully aware of how poor we were relative to some of the other children in my class. It's a difficult feeling to describe if you've never experienced it – a combination of shame, envy and disappointment. I became more aware of how other people lived their lives, how some people didn't have to traipse for half an hour in the cold to sign on at the benefits office or keep candles in the cupboard when the electricity ran out and they couldn't afford to top it up. I can't remember when it was that I first decided that I wanted to escape our council flat on Jamaica Street, but it was a feeling I kept long after I did. I knew a better life was out there, and I wanted it badly, for myself and my family.

I had a glimpse through a window into that better life through friendship. From my very first day in primary school to the very last day of my GCSEs, my best friend at school was a boy called Luke. Luke was bright and well-spoken with soft and spiky blond hair. He was a bit taller than me when we were five and considerably taller a few years later. Luke lived just up the road from our school on Garnet Street in a two-bedroom apartment on Newlands Quay, overlooking Shadwell Basin in Wapping. The development was one of many springing up across the Docklands. They were smart, with royal blue railings on the balconies that overlooked the water, red cladding and window frames set against the brown brick and cream columns and archways along the promenade. We hadn't been friends for long when I was first invited to Luke's home to play after school. It wasn't much bigger than ours, but it was well furnished and had the smell of new carpet and fresh paint that comes with a new-build development. His mum and dad, Jacky and Colin, were always welcoming, kind and generous, which always made me feel at home with them. They weren't necessarily rich – Colin was a London taxi driver and professional photographer, and Jacky worked at an estate agent for a time – but they earned enough to own their apartment and provide a middle-class upbringing for Luke.

Luke and his family were the first well-off people I had ever met, and the stark contrast between their trendy new-build and Mum's maisonette on the Exmouth Estate was often too much for me to bear. While I would be regularly invited to play with Luke and some of my other friends at their homes, I never felt comfortable returning the favour and would make excuses about Mum being too busy. I was too embarrassed to admit that I was ashamed of where we lived.

Even though our home on Jamaica Street was an upgrade from our previous flat, it was still bleak. When we arrived, there were no carpets in any of the rooms, just bare, dark-green, standard-issue tiling covering the floors. This was a peculiar trait of our council – whenever they handed over a new tenancy, they would strip the property of absolutely everything inside, including the carpets. It made no sense. Surely any carpet was better than none? Not to mention that the expense of furnishing a property was a cost that few families in need of council housing could afford – Mum and me included. Our garden – as fortunate as we were to have one – was empty: barren soil, covered in rubbish that had been thrown over the fence. We started off with our beds, a small second-hand sofa and armchair from Grandad, and a colour TV from Nan. We did at least have a cooker, a washing machine and a fridge freezer, but that was about it. We weren't posh enough to pass it off as minimalism.

Over time, Mum would add to the flat with the help of our family or a loan from the council. Throughout the seven years or so that we lived in that flat, there were no carpets on the floors of the hallways, downstairs or upstairs, which made the floor unbearably cold, especially in the winter. But Nanny Libby offered to buy us some carpet for the bedrooms and the living room, so Mum was summoned to meet her at the carpet shop next to the ABC cinema on Bethnal Green Road. She insisted that Mum should bring her best friend, Cheryl, with her. The reason for Cheryl's invitation soon became clear. As soon as Mum picked out a practical grey roll, Nan's response was, 'If you want it, you can have it, but you two will need to carry it home.' She wasn't daft. There was no way she was going to pay for a carpet *and* lug it for a mile back to its new home. Instead, she marched down the street alongside Mum and Cheryl, barking out instructions. Her days in the Salvation Army back in Liverpool were being put to good use!

To complement the new carpet, Mum wallpapered the entire living room by herself and one of her friends donated his mother's old flowery three-piece suite in exchange for some vodka – a fair trade. Mum got her resourcefulness from Nanny Libby, I think, who managed to fit some tiles on the kitchen floor – although the walls in there remained bare, except for the remnants of scraped-off layers of wallpaper left behind by the previous tenant.

Trying to furnish the place wasn't the only challenge Mum had with our house. Our flat's electricity meter was relatively modern, which meant that, unlike Mum's days at Bengal House, when they put a wire in the meter to stop it from counting accurately, there wasn't a fiddle we could use to keep the electricity running when the money ran out, which it often did. All the lights would go out; the TV screen would switch to black, or the stereo would cut out mid-song, leaving us in pitch-black silence, with only the sound of police sirens in the distance or ambient noise from the neighbours above, below and either side of our flat. Then the fridge would start to warm, and the freezer would begin to defrost, which made the kitchen stink. The first time it happened was a frightening experience for a young boy. I didn't know what was happening or why. It was confusing, and I was afraid of the dark! But over the years I got used to it, sadly. Depending on Mum's financial situation, this could happen from month to month, but also throughout the week. I would first run downstairs to the meter and put the key in to activate the emergency supply. On a good day, if we were lucky, power would return, buying us extra time to get the key topped up with some more money from a machine in the wall on Cambridge Heath Road, near Bethnal Green, which was a forty-minute round trip – a nightmare when it was cold and wet, as London so often is. But sometimes the meter had already been running on the emergency supply, so we were plunged into utter, inescapable darkness. Mum would frantically rummage around the kitchen cupboards, looking for candles before she had to call around the family to borrow enough cash to keep the meter running for another few days. For our first five years in that flat, we didn't have a phone line, so we'd have to walk down to the telephone box at the end of the street to ring Nanny Libby or Grandad Streeting to see if they were in, either using up any spare change we had lying around or, more likely, reversing the charges. Even when we did have a phone line, we'd go through periods where it was cut off because Mum couldn't pay the bills.

But despite these hardships, I wasn't a miserable child suffering through a miserable childhood. I was happy, contented and made the best of any situation. If I had my toys and my books, my imagination could do the rest. Mum often says I had some of her best years, and I think she's right. Having a young mum was fun. She could make a chore as boring as walking from our flat in Jamaica Street to Nan's house in Wapping fun, leapfrogging the bollards on the long stretch along Cable Street, laughing our heads off past the famous mural to the Battle of Cable Street. Not many other mums would do cartwheels and handstands in the park with their kids, even if they knew how to, and I doubt many of my friend's mums would blare out everything from 80s pop to acid house on the stereo at home like mine did as we danced around the living room like lunatics. For a while, Mum came into St Peter's to teach short tennis (tennis for children) to some of the other kids as part of her City & Guilds course, which made her, and me, very cool. 'I wish my mum was like yours,' the other kids would say, which left me feeling pretty proud.

Because we spent so much time together, Mum and I would talk for hours about anything and everything: what I'd been learning at school, what we'd seen on *Coronation Street* or *EastEnders*, or the latest drama to darken our door in the form of one of her friends seeking advice or a shoulder to cry on. Mum could often be found sitting at our small table in the kitchen, dishing out advice. Just as she'd kept in with the 'outsiders' at school, Mum tended to befriend people who carried troubles or baggage of their own: difficult childhoods, illiteracy, alcoholism, drug addiction, and mental health issues. I didn't hear all of it, but probably more than I should have. Mum treated me almost as an equal, which gave me a vocabulary beyond my years and a self-confidence, bordering on precociousness, when talking to adults. So my education was not only from Mrs Dodd and St Peter's. It was also from Mum.

*

Although Dad and Grandad Streeting weren't exactly made of money and were also living in a council flat, staying with them at the weekend was definitely a step up from my quality of life during the week. They were both working full-time – Dad still in shipping, first in Stratford and then in the Docklands, and Grandad still at City & Guilds – so between them, they had disposable income in a way that Mum simply didn't. My poor dad, I'm sure he so looked forward to spending as much time with me as he could whenever I came to stay, but I'll confess that he struggled to get a look in. I was very much Grandad's boy and spent almost every minute of those three days with him. On Friday, he would collect me from primary school and take me home for dinner with Dad, unless he was having a night out with his friends. Some Saturdays, Dad would take me to the suburban East London shopping centres of Stratford or Ilford, but more often than not, I would go 'down the Roman' – round to the Roman Road Square Market – with Grandad. I would trot along beside him, holding his wrinkly, well-worn hands until they were laden with big, sturdy, checked laundry bags full of fruit and vegetables for the week ahead, as well as some extra for me to take home to Mum. We'd pop into the butcher to pick up some bacon and some meat for Sunday lunch, and I'd be allowed a pot of Wall's coleslaw, which I would devour there and then with a little plastic fork. Then we would visit Fryatt's, the newsagent, stationery and toy shop, where I would try and persuade Grandad to buy me another *He-Man* action figure or, at the very least, some *He-Man* jellies. Finally, to show Mum how much I loved her, I'd ask Grandad if we could pop by Joanne's florist, so that I could buy a small bunch of freesias to take back home, and because he was such a gentleman, he would always oblige.

If I was really lucky, we'd go across the road to the Victoria Fish Bar, an old chippy as battered as the fish in it, run by a lovely Italian couple. They always knew what I wanted: a wing of skate and chips. Grandad first introduced me to skate, which must have set him back an arm and a leg over the years, as it cost a few quid more than cod, and I insisted on having it every time unless they'd run out, in which case I'd settle for a Peter's minced beef and onion pie. Grandad would scrape the batter and fish off the bone into a pile on the plate next to an equally big mountain of chips smothered in salt, malt vinegar and onion vinegar. It was my favourite and remains so all these years later. Every time I sit at home with a wing of skate and chips from my local chippy, I always think of Grandad and the times we had together on the Roman Road, setting the world to rights over fish and chips and a can of Coke.

On Sunday afternoons, Grandad made sure the three of us would sit down together for a roast dinner. We'd sit around the table with the square twenty-four-inch colour TV on in the background, usually *On the Record* or the *EastEnders* omnibus, and tuck in. I loved Grandad's roast dinners – the meat was always juicy, the crispy potatoes always swimming in gravy – but the star of the show was always the Yorkshire pudding. Not that anyone from Yorkshire would recognise it as such. He would make the batter and pour it, not into the individual moulds you might expect, but into one big roasting tin, which led to a tall, thick, crispy crust and a sloppy, squidgy centre. It certainly wasn't anything to look at, and it might have been an acquired taste, but it was one that me, Dad and Grandad truly loved.

When I wasn't with Dad or Grandad, I would be playing with Christopher, the boy next door. Chris was a few years older than me, but we got on well, and his parents just about tolerated the racket I would create when I went in to play on Chris's Nintendo console. He was a couple of school years above me, and spending time with someone a bit older definitely pushed the boundaries of my learning, especially when he got me into *Star Trek: The Next Generation*. This is where I must out myself as a Trekkie. A proper Trekkie. The sort of Trekkie who started swapping *He-Man* toys for *Star Trek* figurines. Chris had episodes of *Star Trek* recorded on VHS cassette, and those he didn't have, he rented from Blockbuster video on Mile End Road. For younger readers, this was the 90s version of Netflix. We lacked the immediacy of streaming films on the internet, which had yet to become a thing for the vast majority of homes, but Blockbuster's unique selling point was that you could keep the cassette for three whole evenings. It was revolutionary for its time!

Fortunately, the playground at St Peter's wasn't the sort of place where you got picked on for walking around with the technical manual for the Starship Enterprise, although my teachers did start to raise eyebrows when their creative writing tasks were returned with my own original *Star Trek* plotlines and scripts complete with references to quantum singularities and the space-time continuum. In my defence, and in defence of Gene Roddenberry's creation, it was hugely beneficial to my education. But it wasn't just a learning experience. *Star Trek* fed my active imagination and provided an escape from the challenges of life at home.

I loved being in and out of so many people's houses as a child, from Dad and Grandad's, Aunt Vi's – who always had the latest Argos catalogue and a gold-coloured chest of toys and colouring books – Christopher's, Luke's and, in between, all of Mum's extended family across the East End. There was never a dull moment. At Nanny Libby's, I watched *Knight Rider* with my Uncle Billy – his favourite – and fell into fits of hysterical laughter with my Auntie Eve when she stole the Daim bars Nan was saving to make a cake. Nanny Libby did not see the funny side of it, but luckily Eve bore the brunt of her verbal assault as she was the oldest! I loved spending time with Nan but going round there wasn't as fun as going to Auntie Mandy's, where I had three cousins close in age, or to Nanny Knott's, where there were always loads of kids, something tasty cooking in the kitchen, and cable TV with the Cartoon Network. Plus, Nan was often in and out of the house, going to and from Labour Party meetings or the local tenants' association, working on some latest cause or project.

My preference for Auntie Mandy's, or Nanny Knott's, over Nanny Libby's, caused a terrible upset one evening when I was about eight or nine, which still mortifies me to this day. I was in the flat with Mum, expecting to be picked up by my

Uncle Kevin and taken to Bow to stay with him, Auntie Mandy, and my three cousins, Ashley, Arran, and Peryn, at their flat on Fairfoot Road in Bow. So when I overheard Mum on the phone to Nan in the kitchen making arrangements for me to go to her house instead, I threw a massive, screaming, stomping, red-faced tantrum. 'I don't want to go to Nanny's. I hate going to Nanny's. It's boring!' I yelled at the top of my voice. Despite Mum's best efforts to silence me with her hands and arms while balancing the phone receiver under her chin, Nan heard every word. When the receiver went down, my exasperated mum explained I was only going there for a few hours until Uncle Kevin picked me up on his way home from work. I was placated, but the damage was done. When I arrived at Nanny Libby's, waiting awkwardly at the front door, I got the silent treatment from the moment I walked in. She was acting tough, but it was obvious that she was really hurt by what I had said. I did my best to apologise, sheepishly following her around the flat, trying to get her attention, but aside from a curt acknowledgement of my attempts, she didn't say a word from the moment I arrived to the moment I left. She didn't even look at me.

Of course, she forgave me eventually, and when I next saw her, we were back to normal, but this episode, and the guilt I felt, have always stayed with me. Going to Nanny's wasn't as exciting as playing with cousins my own age, but I loved Nan and our times together, which were about to become a lot more frequent, but entirely different. Things would never be the same again.

CHAPTER SEVEN

Love and Loss

Nanny Libby.

RAISING A CHILD as teenagers can't have been easy on my parents, and it must have been difficult to carry the baggage of having a child from a previous relationship when they began dating other people. Not that I was ever made to feel like baggage; it's just a simple statement of fact that being single in their twenties wasn't made easier with a young son in tow. Few people their age wanted to jump into the role of step-parent.

Thankfully, the abusive Lenny, who had terrorised my mother, was a horrific anomaly that I was too young to remember. Neither of my parents had many partners – or if they did they weren't serious enough to be introduced to me – though the ones they did have were always good to me. I remember a fairly brief relationship Mum had with a super-market manager called Barry, whose only fault, as far as I was concerned, was that he smoked Hamlet cigars, and I hated the smell of them even more than I hated the smell of Mum's cigarette smoke that wafted around our flat. Then there was Rob, a glazier from Forest Gate. The downside with Rob was his working hours. I grimly remember having to go out with him on out-of-hours jobs fixing broken windows, which at best left me sitting awkwardly enjoying the hospitality of a stranger's living room, or worse, sitting bored in his white van for hours on cold, dark nights. Whether he thought the excursions would give us a chance to bond or just give Mum a break for a few hours, I don't know, but it wasn't exactly the best way to entertain a seven or eight-year-old.

He did, however, earn a big plus in my books when he took Mum and me on a drive through the countryside to visit an old friend of hers. It wasn't so much seeing the friend – though he seemed like a nice enough guy – as the surprise in store. When we arrived at his house, Mum pointed excitedly to a curled-up ball of golden fur outside the front door. 'What do you think, Wes?' she asked, struggling to hold her emotion. My stomach did a somersault.

'Are we getting a dog?' I squeaked, grinning so much that my cheeks began to throb. It was like all of my Christmases had come at once.

I was now the proud owner of a golden cocker spaniel. Mum's friend was a dog breeder, and they wanted to give me one of their puppies. It was such a generous offer that my mum gratefully accepted. Despite my protestation, Mum called her Mishka. It was a stupid name for a dog, I thought, but Mum was pretty unconventional with names, which is how I ended up being called Wesley.

I carried Mishka on my lap in the car all the way back to Stepney, stroking and comforting her as she whimpered at her unfamiliar surroundings. She was still a puppy, and in the weeks and months that followed, Mum and I spent time training her to go to the toilet on her walks, to give us her paw in exchange for treats and to sit and lie down as instructed.

She was a happy, friendly dog, and we took Mishka everywhere with us: visiting family (luckily for Mishka, Nanny Knott's menagerie of animals was long gone by then), on long strolls around nearby Vicky Park, and out for regular walks around the estate. She was always the first to greet me when I returned from school and was a hit at the school gate and a draw for the crowds on the school sports day in Wapping Gardens. In fact, she became more of a permanent fixture in our life than Rob, whose relationship with Mum eventually fizzled out.

The only one of Mum's partners I've ever regarded as a stepfather – although they never married – was Pat. Pat came into our lives after things with Rob didn't work out, when I was about eight years old. Fairly tall at six foot with blond hair and blue eyes, he was a police constable with London's Metropolitan Police, based in Hackney. They'd met in a pub on Mile End Road. It was such an unlikely pairing, the copper and the convict's daughter. My Grandad Pops and Pat never quite knew what to make of each other. They were always civil, amicable even, but as for the characters that determined their chosen professions, they were like chalk and cheese.

Mum and Pat's relationship was always a bit 'on again, off again' in nature. Their lives were different – in many respects, his outlook reflected my Grandad Streeting's: Pat also served in the Royal Navy – and they bickered quite a lot, so in the beginning, I wasn't really sure if he would be around for very long. But I was wrong. Pat's entry into our lives was about to change ours quite dramatically. It was late 1991. I wasn't far away from my ninth birthday. Mum and Pat hadn't been together that long, barely a year, and I'd just got home from school. I can't quite remember what I was doing, probably watching TV or reading that week's library book from Grandad, but I do remember Mum calling me into the kitchen, where she was sitting at our little table, and saying she had something very important to tell me. She sat with a cup of tea and had a little smile on her face. I couldn't tell whether she was nervous or excited, but before I could figure out that it was both, she dropped the bombshell. She was going to have a baby. I was going to be a big brother for the first time.

I jumped up and down cheering, as though Arsenal had won the league. I had wanted a brother or sister for as long as I can remember. I liked the idea of being a big brother and having someone around to play with – I would ask Mum if we could get a baby from Sainsbury's when we did our weekly shop together, much to her amusement. Finally, my wish had been granted.

But not everyone was as delighted by the news as I was. It is fair to say that Pat hadn't expected to become a father yet, given that their relationship was still quite new. I now realise I had a window into my own past and the sorts of arguments Mum and Dad must have had when Mum fell pregnant with me. This time, however, there was no need for a fry up and no termination appointment on the calendar – by raising me, Mum had proven to everyone around her that she was capable of being a good mother. Nanny Libby was delighted by the news and looked forward to being a doting grandmother to Mum's second child.

I enjoyed the visits to the hospital with Mum during her pregnancy. I was in awe of the whole thing. Watching the ultrasound scanner sliding across her bump to reveal grainy images of the growing baby was mesmerising. I'd never been brought up to believe that babies arrived carried by storks like they did in cartoons. I can't remember ever having the 'birds and the bees' chat, partly because Mum normalised conversations about biology, answering any questions I had without any awkwardness or embarrassment, so it didn't stand apart from any other conversations we had. Even so, I couldn't quite believe that what looked like an inflated, grey kidney bean was going to be my long-awaited little brother or sister. Mum opted to wait until the baby arrived rather than have the hospital reveal the sex. I couldn't wait for them to be born – I started using my pocket money on the weekends to buy rattles, teething aids and soft toys.

I anxiously awaited the arrival of the baby, who I hoped would be a built-in best friend. At least, until that day came, I had Mishka – she was a more-than-adequate stand-in. Every moment I spent with her, I would think about all the things I would show my new sibling – how she could sit, roll over; how she could play fetch with her ball in the park for hours if you let her; how she would run to greet you the moment you walked through the door and how she would lick your ears and face wet if you lay on the floor and let her. She was a hugely affectionate dog, and she somehow made our flat feel brighter, warmer, and more like a real home.

Then one night, just a month or two before the baby was due to arrive, I was awoken by the sound of the front door closing and whispers coming from the downstairs hallway outside my bedroom. I immediately recognised one of the hushed voices as Mum's, but I couldn't tell who the others were. She hadn't mentioned any evening visitors.

My curiosity got the better of my heavy eyelids, and so I got out of bed to investigate. As I opened my bedroom door, Mum's surprised reaction and her guests' nervous expressions made it quite obvious that my presence wasn't welcome. 'What's going on?' I asked with a trepidation that grew to panic as I surveyed the scene like a detective about to solve a crime.

My gaze fell to the hands of the strangers. They were holding Mishka's basket, lead and toys. 'Mum, what's going on?' I repeated anxiously. Mum glanced at the strangers and then looked at me, her eyes brimming with tears. She didn't really need to respond; I already knew the answer. They were taking Mishka away, and it was clear this was no dog-napping. Mum had decided that trying to look after a dog, as well as a newborn baby, would be too much for her to handle. The news came as a bolt from the blue – no one had thought to consult me about it. Mum thought it was the best way to cushion the blow and prevent causing me too much upset. In truth, there really wasn't a good way to handle the situation. Although I understand Mum's decision now, there was no way she could have convinced me back then.

If Mishka was unaware of what was happening to her, my crying, sobbing and shouting in protest at Mum's decision surely told her that something awful was happening. Until that point, I don't think I had ever been so angry or distressed.

This wasn't just any temper tantrum. That was the first time in my young life that I had ever felt betrayed. My presence at the handover wasn't planned. Had I remained asleep, I wouldn't even have been afforded the opportunity to say goodbye. At that moment, I wanted to keep my dog more than I wanted a baby brother or sister, but I was powerless.

I couldn't bear to see my best friend taken away from me. I called out to her and hugged her the way we always did: her front paws on my shoulders as she stood on her hind legs. She licked my tear-stricken face as I gulped breaths between quiet sobs, trying to calm myself enough to be able to say goodbye. Mum put her hand on my back. 'Come on, Wes, she has to go now,' she said gently. Seeing her now belonging to someone else was just too much for me. I furiously shrugged past Mum and ran straight back into my bedroom, curling up under my well-worn Teenage Mutant Hero Turtles duvet and cried myself – freely and louder now – back to sleep. But before she left, Mishka pushed my bedroom door open with her nose and padded over to my bedside, carrying the squeaky toy cake that I had bought for her with my pocket money just days after we'd brought her home. She hopped up and placed the toy next to me on the bed, sniffed at my face, and then hopped down and trotted back out the door. It was as if she knew what was happening, and that was her way of saying goodbye.

Mum felt terribly guilty seeing how upset I was. She loved having Mishka, too. I was told she was being taken to a good home – to live with a lady who had recently lost her own dog. But it was of little comfort. In the weeks and months that followed, I would see a golden cocker spaniel that looked just like Mishka on the way to and from school. The first few times I saw the dog, I called out her name, hoping she would come running over to be reunited. But it wasn't her. I would imagine that she would mount a great escape from wherever she was and come back home to me. But these were pipe dreams that only served to prolong my sadness. We would never see each other again. I had to let go.

It was my first experience of loss. Real loss, like a bereavement. I cried for weeks after Mishka left, taking the squeaky toy cake she left me everywhere I went. Except for the memories, it was all I had left.

As the baby's due date moved closer, Mum decided she was going to have a home birth. In fact, she was adamant. I thought it was bizarre. I couldn't imagine why she wouldn't want or need to be in a hospital surrounded by doctors and midwives. But her hospital experience when I was born had been an ordeal, to say the least. She hadn't felt at all supported by the midwives. Worse still, she had felt judged, ignored, and then imprisoned when they kept her in for a week after the birth. She told anyone who would listen that she wasn't going to go through that again. The living room floor was more appealing to her than the clinical surroundings of a hospital bed.

Mum's carefully laid plan kicked into action early in the evening of 22 July 1992. The first call was to the hospital to arrange for the midwife to be dispatched; the second was to Grandad Streeting's house, where I was to be dispatched. I had been with Mum throughout her pregnancy journey, but I was happy to give this last part a miss.

I was giddy with excitement at Grandad's that evening. It took multiple bedtime stories before I finally gave in and fell asleep. Then, at around four o'clock in the morning, the phone rang with the news: I had a baby brother. I was delighted, as I would have been to have a sister too.

Jordan's arrival on 23 July coincided with the birthday of one of my friends who was having a party at the St George's swimming baths on the Highway. My first meeting with my newborn brother would have to wait a few hours, though if I had been given the choice, I would have gone home in a flash. Instead, I found myself surrounded by all my friends from school, who were patting me on the back, rubbing my hair and congratulating me on becoming a big brother. I felt on top of the world and fit to burst with pride.

With a belly full of sweets and party cake and eyes still itching with chlorine from our playtime at the pool, I made my way home with Grandad to see my brother, Jordan. The house was busy when we arrived, but I can't remember exactly who was there. I was only interested in one person. The baby boy I held in my arms for the first time, with unconditional love and an absolute terror that I might drop him.

My family wasn't only expanding on Mum's side. Dad had finally got over the hurdle of dating as a young father. He'd been introduced to a woman called Karen by my grandad, who was apparently trying his hand at being a matchmaker. She worked part-time in his local pub, where he was a regular. He said he thought she would be a great match, and he seemed right.

The first time I met Karen, her arrival was shrouded in mystery. I was patiently awaiting my weekly Sunday roast – complete with soggy, rectangular Yorkshire pudding – but I was told by Grandad that we had to wait a little while longer because a guest was joining us. I had become accustomed to a weekend routine with just Dad, Grandad and me. There'd been no warning that the guest might be a new girlfriend and a major new addition to our group. So when the knock at the door came, and a short woman with dark hair and a big smile walked in, I just greeted her formally by saying, 'Hello, guest.'

Karen was introduced as Dad's new girlfriend. We hit it off straight away. Karen had an infectious laugh and seemed interested in the things I liked doing. She became a happy part of my weekend routine with trips to Vicky Park, shopping in Ilford or Romford on Saturdays, and Sunday lunch with Grandad.

Things were looking up for Dad. He was progressing with his career in the shipping industry in London's Docklands. With a lot of hard work and saving, he put down a deposit for a house in Dagenham with Karen. Not long after, he proposed, and they began planning their wedding for the following year. I would be a page boy, and I was absolutely delighted for them.

Dad's new house on Digby Gardens seemed like a real step up in the world, even though it was a small two-bedroom ex-council terraced house just off Dagenham Heathway – a stone's throw from the Ford Motor Company plant. But Dad was now a homeowner, and I had my own bedroom, a back garden I could play in, and a sense, at last, that there was life beyond Tower Hamlets. Dagenham was hardly a leafy suburb.

It still had its own issues with poverty and deprivation, with lots of terraced council housing built after the war, but compared to where we lived in Stepney, it was a step up in the world. The back garden wasn't particularly big, but it was well-kept and a place where I could play. The streets felt a lot safer, and I could play out happily unsupervised on the cul-de-sac where Dad and Karen lived. I could see where Dad's hard work and income were getting him: out of the East End. Moving up, not just moving on.

Dad's new beginning meant a change to my weekend routine. Once the move to Dagenham was complete, I still spent my treasured Friday nights with Grandad on Bancroft Road, but then Dad would collect me in his gold Austin Metro on Saturday morning to take me on the half-hour journey to Digby Gardens. Although this new routine meant less time with Grandad, I so looked forward to having a whole crowd of new kids to run around with in Dagenham. Of course, next door to Grandad's, I still had Christopher, *Star Trek* and Nintendo, but this was the first time I had a group of friends to play with on my own street. It was quite a contrast to life during the week on Jamaica Street, where Mum was always reluctant to let me play with kids on our estate. There'd been one summer when she let me out to play, and the kids from around us had taken a little children's tool kit I'd been given as a birthday present and used the tools to scrape almost all the bark off one of the trees in the middle of the estate. It may have only been a small act of vandalism, but Mum was furious and decided they were a bad influence, so after that, she kept me in. It was another reason I had loved having a dog and now enjoyed having a baby brother at home. Stuck indoors, I was otherwise left to my own imagination, and it could be boring, especially during the school holidays.

The weekends in Dagenham were a release from the confines of Tower Hamlets. Once Dad and Karen got to know my friends on the street and their parents, we were trusted to venture further afield, to Old Dagenham Park, which had huge trees that were perfect for climbing, and to Goresbrook Leisure Centre, which was a twenty-minute walk away down the side of the A13, but with a huge fun pool with a slide and a wave machine. On Sundays, I was even able to join my friends at the Sunday school in Dagenham Parish Church. I'd never been to church on Sunday before, only my weekly visits to St Peter's during the school week. Sunday school was fun. We only sat through part of the service before being taken to the church hall for some orange squash and activities.

During the months leading up to Dad's wedding, our new routine was punctuated with suit fittings and shopping for the occasion. I was going to wear a little tuxedo with tails, which I was told would be complemented by a peach cravat that matched the colour of the bridesmaids' dresses. I had no idea what a cravat was, but I was looking forward to dressing up and playing my role in the ceremony.

When the wedding day came around, just a couple of weeks after my baby brother Jordan arrived, I took my responsibilities as page boy very seriously, even pompously. The posh suit and peach cravat – I was a little disappointed to learn that it was just a fancy tie – seemed to make me stand a couple of inches taller. I was delighted for Dad and Karen, who was now my legal stepmother, although she had already become like a second mother to me.

Once the ceremony was over, we headed over to the reception at the Mill House, a social club in Dagenham just off the A13, where a sit-down lunch was to be followed by a DJ. My spell in drama at school had already given me a taste for the limelight, and although there was no karaoke planned, I managed to persuade the DJ to let me take to the mic for my own a cappella performance of Buddy Holly's 'Heartbeat'. It was a song I loved from when it was covered by Nick Berry as the theme tune to the ITV series that I'd watch religiously every week with Grandad. It came as no surprise to my family that I enjoyed performing – they'd seen me perform regularly at school – but although I thought my singing was a highlight of the day, no one was putting money on me having a career in music after what I later learned felt like a lengthy two minutes of monotonous wailing.

After the wedding, Dad and Karen jetted off on their honeymoon to Spain, and I spent a couple of weeks in Dagenham with Grandad, who was house-sitting while they were away. The long, balmy summer days staying with Grandad meant later curfews, friends in and out of the house, and junk food on demand. It was the best summer I had ever had. A new brother, my parents in happier relationships, and a stronger sense of security than I'd ever had. Things were looking up.

The year 1992 had been great, one of the highlights being the great-grandmother of all parties – Nanny Knott's eightieth birthday. A huge surprise party had been planned at a hotel just outside London for the occasion. There had never been an event like it in our family, and there never would be again. Nanny Libby's youngest brother, Alan (who had worked with the Norwegian state oil company Statoil), had paid for the whole thing: the venue, the catering and the coaches. Needless to say, he had done pretty well for himself compared to the rest of the Knotts. The whole family was going to be there, not just the East End regulars – distant relatives had come from Ireland, Canada, Norway, and even Australia. Everyone was going to make the trip, except, I feared, Mum and me.

We were late. We always seemed to be late. Grandad Streeting used to expect us at least an hour after the agreed arrival time when we had plans together, but even that often proved to be optimistic, such was our loose relationship with timekeeping. It used to drive Grandad potty, and although I used to hate waiting for Mum to get her skates on, it was a bad habit I picked up, too. It would take me twenty years or so to break the habit of bad timekeeping myself. But this time, we couldn't afford to be unpunctual. There were a couple of coaches waiting to drive us to the party venue, and we all needed to arrive in good time in order to land the big surprise with Nanny Knott. If we didn't make the coach at the agreed time, we'd be left behind.

As we hurtled down the streets between our flat and the rendezvous point, as fast as was physically possible, Mum's patience was wearing thin at my breathless complaining that she had left it so late and left me running my little legs off to keep up with her, which only ceased when we reached the coach. Fortunately, there it still was, ready and waiting to whisk us off on the twenty-six-mile journey to Brentwood in Essex.

Nanny Knott thought she was off for a quiet birthday lunch at a hotel in the countryside with Alan, so when she wandered into the entrance to the function suite, she was oblivious to what lay ahead. Minutes prior to her arrival, we had been ushered into position and told to wait in silence. Silence has always been a stranger to Mum's side of the family. Wherever the Knotts are, there's usually a chorus of lively conversation, raucous laughter or loud disagreement. But somehow, our gathering of over a hundred children, grandchildren, great-grandchildren and an assortment of cousins, second cousins, nieces and nephews managed to contain the nervous excitement into a near-silence of quiet whispers punctuated by impatient shushes.

Looking back, it probably wasn't the best idea to scare the living daylights out of an unsuspecting eighty-year-old, but fortunately, the surprise had the desired impact: Nanny Knott, who rarely left her council flat in Bow, was moved to tears by the sight of the family she was now seeing all together, many of whom she hadn't seen for years, and none of whom she'd expected to find waiting for her.

The scale of the gathering was clear from the moment we entered the party room. It was a pretty standard hotel function room that had been simply decked out with pink balloons, but to my nine-year-old eyes, it was the most spectacular thing I had ever seen. Nanny Knott was seated at the centre of a long table that stood at the top of the room, alongside her sons and daughters, and facing four more columns of tables where the rest of the family sat down for the start of a three-course lunch. It says a lot about my sweet tooth that I remember my first taste of profiteroles just as well as I remember the novelty and spectacle of our huge extended family being in the same place for the first and last time in my life. There were speeches from Uncle Alan and Nanny Libby, both of whom were accustomed to public speaking, albeit in very different settings. I could imagine Alan, a stout Welshman with distinguished grey hair, addressing a boardroom or a conference of businessmen. I needed no imagination at all to picture Nan at a protest or a picket line. It was a special moment, a chance for all of us to thank Nanny Knott, the matriarch of our family, and to show her how much she was loved by all. No one else in our family carried the affection and connection to bring the entire clan together.

We kids were in our element. The open bar meant bottomless Coke or lemonade and as the tables were packed away and the dance floor opened, we put all that sugar to good use. While the DJ belted out classic 70s and 80s hits, we turned the floor into a racetrack, skidding across what had been freshly buffed wood on our increasingly blackened knees, now thickly covered with dirt, to the horror of Mum, who had put me in cream trousers for the occasion.

The joy of that evening was still fresh in my memory when the phone rang at Mum's a few weeks later. It was a weekday morning, and I was just getting ready for school. As usual, I reached the phone before Mum did. It was Nanny Libby, and I could tell from her voice that she had been crying. She asked softly, 'Can I speak to your mum, please?' I didn't know what was happening, nor did Mum, but we knew it was serious, so we dropped everything to answer her call to go round. Mum even rang for a minicab, which was as unusual as it gets.

My suspicion that Nan had been crying was confirmed by her wet, bloodshot eyes as she opened the front door. We followed her into the kitchen, where her voice shook as she revealed the tragic news. 'Alan's died.' She could barely utter the words as she fell onto Mum's shoulder. I could scarcely believe it. Uncle Alan had been the life and soul of the party just weeks before. He was only forty-seven years old and had died of a heart attack.

I'm not sure Nanny Libby ever recovered from the death of her brother. Not knowing Alan well, it didn't affect me quite so deeply. But I knew how close Nan was to him and how often she'd visited him over the years at his home in Norway. As Mum and Nan stood in the kitchen crying, I almost felt guilty for not sharing in their tears. This was my first experience of death in the family, and I wasn't sure how I was supposed to react. But it wouldn't be long until I learned my lesson the hard way.

*

It was a few months later, in the spring of 1993, that she was admitted to the Royal London Hospital with fluid on her lungs. It had been giving her chest problems. I remember visiting her there for the first time, weaving through the labyrinthine corridors and up the ageing wooden staircases with their metal railings to find the ward she had been admitted to. She was pleased to see us, and we made our way down to the smoking area together. Looking back, I'm not sure what is more shocking – the fact that there was a smoking area at all or that Nanny Libby, sitting there in her hospital gown, was still smoking.

The news wasn't good. A scan of Nan's lungs had shown a shadow that required further investigation. I didn't really understand what that meant at the time. When the shadow was diagnosed as lung cancer, I didn't really know what that meant either, but I knew it was bad. Really bad.

Mum was always honest with me, but even though she told me about the cancer diagnosis, she held back just how bleak the prognosis truly was. She told me that the doctors would do their best to treat Nan, but that there was a chance that they would fail. Nan had contracted pneumonia, and the hospital gave her just two weeks to live. Worse still, it became apparent to Mum and the family that the hospital hadn't checked to see if she had eaten or had a drink for two days. At this stage, it was the pneumonia that was killing her, not the cancer. It took a huge protest from my Aunt Amanda to cause the hospital to relent and treat the pneumonia.

Over the subsequent weeks and months, we would follow her progress almost daily. The regular trips to and from the hospital after school were draining, especially for Mum with the baby in tow. If Pat was at home, he would take care of my brother and me while Mum made the trip to the hospital. Occasionally, I would grumble about being made to go, before receiving a firm rebuke from Mum reminding me that supporting Nanny Libby through her treatment was far more important than whatever I was missing on Children's BBC. She was right, of course, and I would sheepishly follow her through the streets of Stepney carrying my guilt on my shoulders as we trudged along to the hospital. She was worried sick about her mum. The last thing she needed was a complaining ten-year-old worried about missing cartoons.

As her health deteriorated, the gravity of Nan's illness dawned on me. We never knew what condition we would find her in when we arrived. On some days, she was cheerful and upbeat. On others, she looked tired and forlorn. The treatment was evidently taking its toll, and she was losing weight rapidly. She didn't think much of the hospital food either, which didn't help. If we found she hadn't been eating, Mum would often go down to Whitechapel Road to pick up some fish and chips, a burger from Wimpy or some cakes from the Percy Ingle bakery and sneak them back in, to Nan's obvious delight.

This went on for months. For as long as she was in the hospital, Nan didn't want to be left alone. She was never short of visitors, but all the bedside care and love in the world from her children, her grandchildren, her brothers and sisters and her mother, couldn't alter the painful fact that her treatment wasn't working. In the early 1990s, only around one in five women with lung cancer could be expected to survive longer than a year. The survival rate for five years was around one in twenty. Nanny Libby was a fighter, but this wasn't a fight she could win. The odds were stacked against her. People don't die from lung cancer because of a lack of fight. They die because medical science can't save them.

When Nanny Libby moved from the Royal London Hospital to St Joseph's Hospice on Mare Street, in Hackney, it confirmed the suspicions that were already growing with me that her diagnosis was a death sentence. Even as a ten-year-old, I knew that hospices were places where people went to die. I visited Nan as often as Mum would allow. I would spend time at her bedside, holding her hand and talking to her and occasionally taking myself off to the chapel to pray. The chapel was a light, ornate space, with wooden chairs and desks facing the altar and cross at the far end of the hall, although when I visited, it tended to be dark as the evening light had given way to the gloom of night-time. There was never a soul in there, except on one occasion when a nun took pity on the young boy crying in prayer on his own and gave me an apple.

Death can be a testing time for faith. No amount of prayer could change the fact that my grandmother was dying and what a terrible injustice it was to see a woman who was only fifty-two with young grandchildren being taken in the prime of her life by such a cruel and painful affliction. The loss of her eldest son to a car accident had crushed Nanny Libby's own faith all those years ago and she'd left the Salvation Army behind. Now that she was on her deathbed in the hospice, preparing to meet her maker, she had started the process of making peace with God and rekindling her Christianity through prayer and visits from the chaplain.

Nan was also beginning to worry about the fate of the family she would be leaving behind. She asked Mum to move back to her house at 47 Crofts Street with me and Jordan. She thought Mum would look after the house she'd put so much work into, and I think she still, even as the cancer ravaged her lungs, held out hope that she might be able to return home for her final days. Mum obliged, although she didn't entirely give up our flat on Jamaica Street and allowed a friend to stay there instead, just in case she wanted to move back later.

I was happy to be in Crofts Street. It wasn't exactly the escape from Tower Hamlets that I'd been hoping for, but it was still an upgrade from Jamaica Street. As well as being bigger, it was more homely. Nan had put a lot of work into making it a nice place to live over the years. She had fitted her own kitchen and bathroom and kept it nicely decorated. Also, although the walk to school took the same time as it did from Stepney, it meant I was finally living in Wapping like all the other kids I went to school with and could join them on the way in.

But our home life was difficult. As well as dealing with the pressures of a newborn baby and the deteriorating health of her mother, Mum's relationship with Pat continued to be volatile. There would be regular arguments, raised voices and harsh words. Sometimes when we were visiting the hospice, instead of going straight home, Mum and I would take refuge in Cafe 67, a greasy spoon across the road, just so Mum could avoid another fight with Pat. The arguments weren't violent, but they were constant. I hated the fighting and seeing the impact it had on Mum. It made me feel nervous and on edge, as if I was treading on eggshells, not knowing what to say or what mood Mum would be in. It made an already painful situation much worse.

When I arrived with Mum at St Joseph's in November 1993, I knew it was to say goodbye. The person I was looking at barely resembled my grandmother. As she lay there curled up on her side, her skin was clammy and yellow, and she was barely conscious. She was reduced to skin and bones. The fighter I had known all my life was now just fighting for every breath she took.

So many members of the family were there too. This was really it. The woman who had been there from the moment I was born was entering her final hours. I took her tiny, skeletal hand and leaned over to kiss her goodbye, fighting back the tears until I couldn't hold them in any longer. I shuffled into the corridor with Mum and hugged her tightly. We stood there sobbing as the world continued to turn around us.

It all became too much for Mum. When we got home to Crofts Street that afternoon, she immediately arranged for me to be taken to Grandad's in a minicab. She was devastated and couldn't cope and she knew that it was the right place for me to be.

Nanny Libby died that evening, and so her mother, Nanny Knott, faced the unimaginable grief of losing a third child. Nan was only fifty-two years old. It seemed so desperately unfair that she should be taken so soon.

As the rest of the family still with her at the end stepped out to the dark hospice corridor, they caught sight of another, unexpected, visitor approaching. With her brown shoulder-length hair and pronounced cheekbones, the woman could easily have been mistaken for Nanny Libby in the dim light. But, as she got closer and the light of Nanny Libby's room caught her face, there was no question who it was.

Christine Keeler was older but still unmistakable. When she heard the news that she had just missed her chance to say goodbye, she was crestfallen. 'I'm so sorry,' she said sombrely. 'Libby and I were the dearest of friends and the closest of sisters.' At least, now, her friend for all those years was at rest.

Back at Grandad's, I was struggling to get to sleep. It was my first experience of bereavement, and frankly, I was afraid. 'What if Nanny comes to see me as a ghost in the night?' I asked Grandad, who was sitting at the foot of my bed. 'I'll be frightened,' I whimpered, clutching at my duvet.

'You don't have to be afraid,' Grandad replied. 'Your nan would never do anything to scare you. But if you are frightened, just say the Lord's Prayer and you'll be OK,' he added. Reassured, I drifted off to sleep, as the feelings of fear and anxiety gave way to sweeter dreams.

CHAPTER EIGHT

Living with Grandad

Me, St Peter's, 1993.

'A LIGHT HAS gone out in the East End', read the Tower Hamlets freesheet, *East End Life*, when it reported Nanny Libby's death. Our family always knew that she was well-known and respected in the local community, but this recognition meant a lot to us. There was some comfort in knowing that we weren't alone in our grief.

A crowd of family and friends had gathered outside Nanny's house on Crofts Street ahead of the funeral. My eyes were sore and swollen from crying that morning, so I refused to make eye contact with anyone for fear of starting again. I had a job to do. Mum asked me if I would give one of the readings at the church service, and I was determined not to let Nan or my family down, so I positioned myself on the outskirts of the swarm of people, keeping my eyes fixed firmly on my shoes – the black ones I wore for school, which had been given their best possible polish and shine by Grandad for the occasion.

Mum appeared beside me, having squeezed through the crowd. I still wouldn't look up, but I could see her hand outstretched towards me. 'Come and see Nanny,' she said softly, taking my arm and gently leading me towards the house, where Nan was resting in her coffin on her large kitchen table. I looked at Mum in shock, and I saw her eyes were as puffy as mine and wet with tears, too. I resisted, pulling back against her grasp. 'No, no, no, please . . . I don't want to see her,' I protested, 'I'm scared.' I had never seen a dead body before and had no desire to see one now, especially not this one. But Mum persisted, and I could see it meant a lot to her. 'I promise you'll be OK,' she insisted. 'She looks peaceful. You need to say goodbye, Wes.'

I found myself being dragged through the throngs of people outside the garden gate into the house and straight through to the kitchen. 'Look, darling,' Mum urged gently. I had scrunched my eyes shut in protest, but with Mum's encouragement, I opened them slowly, one at a time. I'd been terrified, but as soon as I saw her, I knew there was nothing to be frightened of. My shoulders dropped and my tightly balled fists loosened. I felt an odd sense of calm. There she was. Lying peacefully at rest, as Mum had promised.

Mum took me to the side of the coffin so that I could see Nan properly. I kissed my hand, placed it delicately on her cold cheek and said, 'Goodbye, Nanny.' That was it. The dams in my eyes burst, and the tears flooded down my face as Mum wrapped me in a tight hug.

I felt Mum shaking, and assumed she was sobbing with me. I squeezed her tighter, thinking that we were sharing a tender, mournful moment together. But when I looked up at her, I couldn't believe it. She wasn't crying. She was laughing. Not just laughing – shoulder-shaking cackling. I must have looked horrified, which only made her laugh harder. It took a moment for her to catch her breath long enough to explain herself.

'Her hair,' she laughed, 'look at what they've done to her hair! She'll haunt us for letting her go to her funeral looking like that.' Puzzled, I looked back down at Nan. Mum was right. For whatever reason, the funeral directors had given her a 1970s comb-over side parting. Nanny would have absolutely hated it. I joined Mum in an uncontrollable fit of giggles, our tears of sorrow giving way to tears of laughter.

This wasn't the first round of hysterics beside the coffin in the kitchen. Mum had arranged for it to arrive the night before the funeral, so Nanny Libby had been there all night while Mum and Eve prepared food for the wake. They were chatting away to her and chuckling at all the good times they'd had together. 'You should've been here,' Mum said to me as she recounted the night's events with a big smile on her face, 'we've had a good laugh and a good cry with her.' I can't think of anything more typical of my family – somehow, we always manage to find something to laugh about, however tough or difficult the situation, and this was one of the hardest in my life so far.

I am so grateful to Mum for giving me that final opportunity to say goodbye. In the days that followed Nan's death, I had been haunted by the harrowing image of her dying in the hospice. It had been replaced with a more peaceful image, albeit complete with a dodgy side-parting.

When I think of Nanny Libby, I don't dwell upon how she died, but rather on how she lived. In every single one of those memories, she is full of energy and drive. Rushing out the door to a Labour Party meeting. Walking at a hundred miles an hour, forcing me to run to keep up. Sleeves rolled up and tools in hand, fitting her own bathroom. Doing jobs around the house for Nanny Knott. Cooking casseroles and pies or baking a Daim cake. Yelling up the stairs at Eve, demanding that she turn her music down. Passionate arguments and debate about the state of the country and how much she wanted rid of the Tories. Only death could silence her. Even now, I still hear her voice, imagining what she would say about a particular challenge or situation, her sense of right and wrong guiding my own values and politics.

We all accompanied the hearse on the short drive up the Highway to the church. St George-in-the-East is a magnificent church, one of six in London designed by Nicholas Hawksmoor, a contemporary of Christopher Wren. Its tall white stone tower cuts an imposing sight on the Wapping skyline. It was intimidating for a ten-year-old, walking up the long path towards the grand entrance archway, where the doors were already open and the vast interior already packed to the rafters with hundreds of mourners.

I had given many readings at St Peter's Church during our weekly school services, but this was by far the hardest. Grandad Streeting had helped me practise to make sure that I was word-perfect and projecting loudly enough to carry across the congregation. During rehearsals, my voice had reverberated around the empty church, but this was now a full house. It didn't feel like a burden or a pressure; if anything, the discipline of trying to maintain my composure before the reading helped me get through the service. It was a privilege to play a part in giving Nan the send-off she deserved.

The reading was from the Book of John – the same reading that former Prime Minister Liz Truss gave at the funeral of Queen Elizabeth II. When I heard it again, it made me smile, knowing that I had given Nan a reading fit for a queen. I still have my copy of it, taken from the Book of John, chapter 14, verses one to six, with Grandad's underlining for emphasis.

Do not let your hearts be distressed. You believe in God; believe also in me.

There are many dwelling places in my Father's house. Otherwise, I would have told you, because I am going away to make ready a place for you. And if I go and make ready a place for you, I will come again and take you to be with me, so that where I am you may be too. And you know the way where I am going.

Thomas said, 'Lord, we don't know where you are going. How can we know the way?'

Jesus replied, 'I am <u>the way</u>, and <u>the truth</u>, and <u>the life</u>. <u>No one</u> comes to the Father <u>except through me</u>.

As I returned to my seat, a ripple of applause turned into thunder, but I thoroughly disapproved. Clapping was not the 'done thing' in church and would not have been tolerated at one of our weekly services at St Peter's!

The service was uplifting, reflected in the choice of hymns, including one of my favourites: 'When the Saints Go Marching In'. The congregation gave a rousing rendition, as though we were all letting the saints know she was on her way.

Once we'd been to the crematorium, and it was all over, there was a proper East End knees-up at the community centre on the Royal Mint Estate. In keeping with our family's tradition of being able to look on the bright side whatever the circumstances, there was a lot of laughter. I had never been to a wake before and given the jollity, I couldn't understand why there wasn't a DJ like there had been at Dad and Karen's wedding a year earlier. But smiles, the reminiscence, and the reforging of friendships and connections that had been lost over time was exactly what Nanny Libby would have wanted.

Even Grandad Pops was there. After all these years and all the acrimony that existed between them, it was clear he still loved Libby. He had visited her in the hospice, and she had welcomed him as an old friend. He wanted to be at her funeral to say goodbye, but he also wanted to be there for his children, in the way that Libby had been, and he had so rarely been.

The trouble with funerals is that their organisation often provides a displacement activity that allows us to momentarily avoid confronting our bereavement. The following day, the laughter and levity were gone, replaced with silent grief instead. In the weeks and months that followed Nan's death, Mum struggled to cope with the loss. She has always been a strong woman in a family full of strong women. But Nan's untimely passing left her broken.

My opinion on the Crofts Street house changed. Now, it felt cold and empty, but somehow also suffocating. It was Nanny Libby's wish for us to stay there, but her absence was glaringly loud. Mum wasn't herself, either. The lights were on, but no one was home. Pat wasn't around either. They were going through a bad patch and had separated.

Not long after my nan died, maybe a few weeks, I was due to go on a school visit to Gorsefield, an outdoor residential education centre in Stansted Mountfitchet, owned by Tower Hamlets Council. The night before we were due to leave, I had pestered Mum to help me pack, but she seemed to move around the house in a daze. So, in the end, I resorted to packing my clothes myself, into plastic carrier bags. The next morning I arrived at school, embarrassed to be seen with my bags tearing at the handles and my belongings looking a mess amidst the suitcases and holdalls of the other children. Thankfully, sturdier carrier bags were brought from the school office, and my clothes were repacked. Mum was contacted, and she eventually delivered a travel bag which was to be dispatched to Gorsefield for the journey home. Once more, I found myself indebted to my teachers for their kindness and lack of harsh judgement.

But this wasn't like Mum, who always made sure I had everything I needed for school, often sacrificing her own needs to do so. I was worried for her. She was going through more than she'd ever had to cope with before in her still young life, back on her own, bringing up two kids and navigating her life without the woman who had always been her rock. She needed time and space to recover, so I was sent to live with Grandad Streeting while my brother went to live with his father in Loughton.

I saw Jordan a few times during that period. Despite the fact that Pat and Mum weren't together, he made the effort to bring my brother over to Grandad's so that we could play together and keep the bond that we had formed since his arrival the previous year. Seeing Jordan always put a smile on my face, and I was grateful to Pat for understanding that we needed each other, but those were also the moments when I felt Mum's absence most acutely. It felt wrong for us to be a family without her.

For the rest of the time, I was wrapped in the comfort blanket of Grandad's care, with all the joys usually reserved for the weekend now in abundance. As difficult as it was to be without Mum, I couldn't help but feel lucky that I was able to spend so much quality time with my best friend.

Grandad had always indulged my sweet tooth, with chocolate from the corner shop at the end of the street, or a sweet and sticky apple covered in desiccated coconut from the toffee-apple man who appeared during the week on his bicycle, and a near-constant supply of fizzy drinks that Mum refused to buy because of the high sugar content. It was only when I went through a phase of having severe stomach aches in the night and two visits to A&E that Dad put his foot down and Grandad had to regulate how much Coca-Cola or R Whites lemonade I was allowed to drink. Mum obviously had a point when she banned them at home.

But even after Dad put his foot down, Grandad couldn't help indulging me. I was the badly behaved cause of an almighty row one Sunday when I had asked Grandad for a Mars bar, not long before our Sunday dinner was going to be served. 'Ask your Dad,' came my Grandad's polite reply. Dad's answer was predictable: 'No, you're having your dinner soon; you'll have to wait until later.' I knew exactly what I was doing when I returned to my Grandad in the kitchen, barely able to tell him that 'Dad said no' as I bit back my disappointment. Sure enough, Grandad took pity on me and handed over the Mars bar. I also knew exactly what I was doing when I returned to the living room, Mars bar in hand, and gave Dad my smuggest grin as I took a huge bite. Dad hit the roof, exploding with an anger I'd never seen before, even threatening a parental strike. Only then did I feel guilty for being quite so cheeky, defiant and manipulative.

It's a universal truth that most grandparents can't resist spoiling their grandchildren. I definitely took advantage of this fact. For breakfast, as long as I asked politely, my Grandad would indulge my requests for a ham, cheese, cucumber, tomato and lettuce sandwich with Heinz salad cream, or even Birds Eye beef burgers with potato waffles – not exactly a healthy start to the day, and a far cry from the bowl of Weetabix I'd get at home. It even made Mum's treat of Coco Pops look healthy. Every night would be rounded off with a bedtime story or two, accompanied by a giant cup of hot chocolate. It was a miracle I managed to sleep at all with so much sugar coursing through my veins.

But fortunately for me, it wasn't just sweet treats and junk food that Grandad spoiled me with; he also indulged my ever-growing appetite for books, by way of my first library card. Every week, we would walk to Bancroft Road library together, browsing the shelves in search of new novels that would carry my imagination away. From the Chronicles of Narnia and the bestsellers of Roald Dahl to the escapades of the

Secret Seven, I was a bookworm transported to faraway lands and distant times. I was the sort of kid who would knock on the back of the wardrobe to see if there was an entrance to Narnia. Looking back, I can see why fantasy, sci-fi and fictional worlds all fed my growing desire to escape Tower Hamlets in search of somewhere where there were no pawnshops and DSS offices, or empty electricity meters and empty cupboards.

With Grandad's encouragement, I delved into the world of non-fiction too, to inform projects I was working on at primary school, sometimes under my own initiative, depending on what my career ambition was that week. As a child, they would change often – from a teacher to a lawyer; a doctor to a journalist; an astrophysicist to an author; and even a priest, the latter to Dad's bemusement and mild concern. Although largely alien to the professional experiences of family members, every single aspiration of mine was encouraged by my parents and heavily indulged by Grandad. If my ideas were too grand, obviously impractical, or just clearly a pipe dream, I was never made to feel as though my circumstances would dictate what I could or couldn't achieve. Never let it be said that aspiration or ambition are the preserve of the middle classes. What too many children from my background lack isn't aspiration; it is opportunity, and the sense of security all of us need in life.

I brought my love of learning home from school. Every child of the 1980s and 90s will remember the excitement of seeing a chunky television set and video cassette recorder (VCR) being wheeled into their classroom. My school showed us programmes provided by BBC Schools and Grandad would dutifully follow my instructions, checking the TV listings as to which programmes he should record for us to watch back together in the evenings, usually from the *Look and Read* series, like 'Geordie Racer' or 'Through the Dragon's Eye', or 'Music Time', which we would sing along to. Grandad loved to sing and whistle to himself in a deep, almost mock-operatic tone. It's a trait he has passed on to me!

Grandad had a VCR long before Mum and I had one at home, although his video library spoke volumes about who the main beneficiary of the investment was. Alongside a solitary video of Crystal Gayle in concert were dozens of *He-Man*, *She-Ra*, Walt Disney and family blockbuster video cassettes. When we weren't reading, talking, or playing together, Grandad would sit through whatever video I had chosen. Sometimes we would even watch the same film twice in a row, usually Whoopi Goldberg's *Sister Act* or the *Masters of the Universe* movie, which we rented so many times from the shop downstairs that we must have paid for the cassette a hundred times over.

It may sound odd, given that I was separated from Mum and without my nanny too, but although set against the backdrop of deep sadness and loss, those months with Grandad were among the happiest of my life. Although I remained worried about Mum, out of sight was also out of mind. Grandad provided insulation from the deep pain and grief that Mum was going through, and he was the only person that could have provided such an antidote to the heartbreak of bereavement.

When Mum was ready for me to return home to her, having had no real contact with me while I was with Grandad, it was back to Jamaica Street. Nan's house on Crofts Street would always be hers, and our living there would have been a constant reminder of her absence. When I arrived back in our flat, I remember the feeling of warmth when we went upstairs. With the little money that she had, Mum had made a real effort to make it feel homely again, with the heating on full blast and the scent of lavender oil filling the air. She had a big smile and an even bigger cuddle waiting for me. So did Jordan, who came toddling along to the top of the stairs to greet me with a little toothy grin. It felt good to be home, to be a family again.

With so much changing around me at home, school was a bedrock of stability. I had known my year-six teacher, Ms Eden, throughout my time at St Peter's because she was also the school's deputy head teacher. Ms Eden commanded the same respect as our head teacher, Mrs Dodd, and had the same devotion to her pupils, but she had a friendlier exterior, with her blond hair cut short, a big smile for all her pupils, and twinkling blue eyes. I had always been blessed with great teachers at St Peter's and couldn't have wished for a better teacher to see me through to the end of my time at primary school. She didn't make a fuss about it, but I knew she was keeping watch over me and keeping Grandad updated about my performance at school throughout the turbulence of life at home.

My class teacher wasn't my only guardian angel at St Peter's during that difficult year. Mrs Dodd continued her plan for my escape from Tower Hamlets. A shelf in our classroom was filled with promotional literature from a wide range of secondary schools competing for our interest. Mrs Dodd wanted to make sure I went to a good state school outside the borough. Mum was supportive and spent hours reviewing a range of options suggested by Mrs Dodd. After a visit to an open evening with Dad, they settled on Westminster City, a boys' school in the centre of London, as their first choice. But it would be competitive. There was huge demand for places, but Mrs Dodd had mentioned her success in getting one or two boys in there over the years, and one or two girls into its sister school, the Grey Coat Hospital.

Mum and Dad weren't left to fend for themselves at Westminster City's open evening. Colin and Jacky joined them and took Luke along with them. Luke's report back was as glowing as my parents'. Although most of my classmates would be applying to schools closer to home, Westminster City sounded posh. The old school building in the brochure brought to mind high ceilings and chandeliers, a studious academic environment, and a world away from life on a council estate. That turned out to be a little misleading, but nonetheless, the school had a long history and a good reputation. With Luke there, I knew I wouldn't be alone, and with some of my other friends applying to Grey Coat, the girls' school nearby, I had visions of a crowd of us East Enders jostling about on the tube into Westminster every day.

As Westminster City was a non-denominational Christian school, I stood a better chance of admission if I had a letter of recommendation from my priest. I dutifully went around to the vestry after school to collect the letter from Father Peel, who happily obliged. Earlier in the school year I had been baptised and confirmed at St Peter's by the Bishop of London on All Saints' Day. It had been a battle to secure the permission of my parents to go through with the ceremony. Although

I had regularly served in church with the school and opted to attend Sunday school in Dagenham at the weekends, they were initially reluctant to follow my judgement, questioning whether I was old enough to make such a commitment. It took several rounds of pleading, and an appeal to Grandad to advocate on my behalf, to persuade them that I was mature enough to make the decision for myself.

The process required a serious commitment of time: Bible study after school at the church and regular attendance at St Peter's Church on a Sunday. The latter posed a challenge because I spent the weekends with Dad and Karen in Dagenham. But Father Peel agreed to accept my attendance at Dagenham Parish Church as a substitute if I presented him with the order of service from each mass, which I did without fail.

Each candidate for confirmation was allocated a sponsor: a trusted adult within the church who could assist with religious instruction. My sponsor was Jane Hoyle, the wife of the other priest at St Peter's, Father Hoyle. Jane was a warm and generous person, who invited Grandad and me to their vicarage next to the church on Friday evenings for dinner. As one would expect from a vicar's wife, Jane took the role of sponsor seriously and on the day of my confirmation she presented me with a copy of the New Jerusalem Bible, which I still use today.

Whether it was down to my Christian credentials, strong support from Mrs Dodd, a good interview, or a combination of the three, I was offered a place at Westminster City. The journey to the school for the interview with the head teacher, Mr Billingham, gave me a taste of what the following year would have in store. In stark contrast to the small, single-storey, family set-up of St Peter's, Westminster City was a gigantic four-storey Victorian building, with golden brick, tall windows, and two grand arched entrances – one for pupils and one for staff. As we waited in the oak-panelled vestibule outside the school hall, I surveyed the names inscribed in gold on the wall of Old Boys who had lost their lives in the First and Second World Wars. The bell rang, and boys in uniform charged up and down the large staircases like elephants stampeding, some of them arriving through the door beside me, laughing and pulling at each other's blazers. This boisterous environment was going to be very different to St Peter's.

My parents were proud of my offer, but all too soon they would be confronted with the cost of the transition. The uniform policy for Westminster City was demanding. In addition to the white shirt, grey trousers and black shoes, I needed a black blazer with the school badge, a grey jumper, the black-and-gold school tie, a yellow football/rugby jersey, black shorts, a white T-shirt with the school logo for PE, yellow PE socks, a pair of football boots and black trainers. To make matters worse, the school badge and tie were only available from Peter Jones department store on Sloane Square. The letter offering me a place at the school came with an order form for all of this uniform and kit, which was to be returned before the summer holidays at the year-seven induction day.

This wasn't the first time in my life that school uniform had created financial stress for my parents. Although Dad worked full-time and Mum had some assistance with school uniform vouchers, spurts of growth or the start of a new school year would always create a pinch-point for them. When St Peter's introduced a new sweatshirt with the school logo on it, I wanted one to fit in with my friends, who had begun to sport them, but they were more expensive than the plain old red V-neck we'd always worn. My parents just couldn't afford the luxury, so Grandad stepped in and paid for a couple, so I didn't feel left out. Even a simple swimming cap caused anxiety because Mum simply didn't have the money. Instead, we walked all the way to Nanny Libby's, who assured Mum she had one that I could use. Unfortunately, the swimming cap she had in mind was from the 1970s – a hideous, off-white number that was held in place with a thick strap that went under the chin. During its first outing at a swimming lesson, I was a laughing stock. My friends might not have realised that I didn't have a swimming cap because we were poor, but I knew, and it was humiliating. Once more rescued by the kindness of a teacher, I managed to borrow a more appropriate cap from Mr Lee, who taught PE, for a few weeks until Mum could scrape together the money for a new one.

As induction day at Westminster City crept closer, I began to dread the same shame and embarrassment of explaining why I wasn't wearing the right uniform. Neither I nor my parents wanted anyone – student or teacher – to know that they weren't going to be able to get the money together in time for induction day; that they needed the extra time over the summer to buy the uniform piece by piece, even with more help from Grandad. So, to spare all our blushes, Mum phoned the school to tell them I was unwell and wouldn't be attending that day. While the rest of my year explored our new stomping ground, I sat bored at home, wondering what I was missing out on.

All that was left was for me to enjoy my final weeks at St Peter's. For seven years it had shaped and supported me; it was a constant, stable presence whenever my home life was tough, free of judgement and full of warmth, kindness and fun. Leaving it behind was a wrench. But Mrs Dodd had achieved her ambition for me. I was leaving Tower Hamlets for the bright lights of the inner city. She had done all she could to give me the best possible start to my education – to the rest of my life, really. I will be forever grateful to her and to all the wonderful staff at St Peter's.

CHAPTER NINE

From East End to Westminster

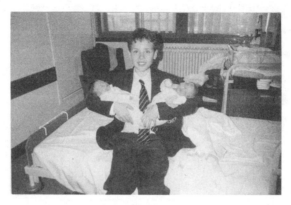

A proud big brother: with my newborn twin siblings, 1995.

I HAD SPENT the summer holidays excited about going to secondary school in the big city and all the opportunities I had hoped it would provide. It was still pitch black when I woke up for my first day at the new school. As my eyes adjusted to the darkness of my bedroom, I could just about make out the shape of the brand-new blazer that was hanging on the front of my wardrobe. It was black, woollen and probably from British Home Stores and if I squinted, I could make out the school badge that Mum had sewn onto the breast pocket. It was done neatly enough, but I was nervous that it might make me stand out compared to the kids whose parents could afford to shop at Peter Jones in Sloane Square. The school logo looked as posh as Westminster City sounded. It had two oval-shaped golden shields sitting beneath a golden crown. Beneath it was the school motto, in Latin, *Unitate Fortior* – strength in unity.

Thankfully, the rasping alarm call of my red digital clock interrupted my train of worried thoughts, and I shot out of bed before the second mechanical buzz, anxious not to disturb my baby brother who was sleeping in the same room. After wolfing down a bowl of Coco Pops, I raced back to my bedroom to get changed into my slightly too big school uniform. The boxy blazer and too-wide trousers made me look rather rectangular – not unlike most first-year children, who look as though they've been dressing up in one of their parent's suits.

Dad had arranged to take me to school, and he was coming over early to help me tie my tie because I didn't know how to – I'd never needed to wear one before. Standing in front of the living room mirror together, he showed me how to loop the striped black-and-gold fabric into a full Windsor knot just as his father had shown him. A 'proper knot', as my Grandad would call it.

I had also never taken the tube by myself before, so Dad was going to make sure I didn't get lost in the web of the London Underground. The seating on the District Line train I'd be taking to St James's Park was upholstered with a well-worn pattern of orange, yellow and brown rectangles. I had to dart onto the carriage quickly to grab a seat and avoid being squashed between all the city workers or, worse still, having to stand on tiptoe to try and reach one of the black spherical handles that hung from tightly coiled springs like baubles.

As we emerged at the other end it was as if I was stepping into a different world. Now there were commuters dressed in suits carrying briefcases and expensive-looking handbags walking briskly past each other, and crowds of tourists with heads buried in maps, probably en route to Buckingham Palace, Westminster Abbey, or Big Ben.

This is most people's typical idea of London, but it was a far cry from the London I knew. I had rarely been to the West End. Aside from occasional trips to the big museums in South Kensington, most of my life had revolved around the East End – Stepney, Bow and Wapping. My London. Even Poplar had seemed like a trip further afield, and visiting Dad in Dagenham didn't feel like being in London at all. This London, the London of city workers and tourists, the London of my life today, was faster paced and energetic. People had places to be, things to do. It was exciting.

Dad and I walked over to join the small crowd of parents who were standing by the black iron school gates on Palace Street, waving their sons off on their first day. I didn't dwell on goodbyes for long; I was too eager to go in and get started. I found Luke, who was just as excited as me, and with a quick wave over our shoulders to our parents, we joined the shoal of new pupils squeezing through the double doors into the school reception.

The school hall was enormous compared with the one at St Peter's, yet still only big enough to hold half the school for assembly each morning. Luke and I shuffled in to find our places on the first couple of rows, sitting down gingerly on the brown wooden chairs, necks craned upwards like meerkats in a zoo, inspecting our alien habitat.

At the front of the hall was a stage, on top of which stood a long, dark wooden table with a grand oak chair behind it carved with the school logo. To either side of the table were four or five more high-backed wooden chairs with a light brown leather padding. The whole scene projected the power and authority of an Anglo-Saxon court. Providing a backdrop to the stately furniture, two sweeping indigo curtains draped the rest of the stage. As I marvelled at them, I hoped that I'd soon be standing on stage behind the thick, dark velvet, anxiously waiting for them to open to reveal me, under a spotlight, in the starring role of my first secondary-school play, stealing the limelight. It looked far more impressive than the small stage at St Peter's.

We year sevens were the quietest we would ever be – small talk with strangers isn't something Londoners do comfortably. Some of the boys, like Luke and me, arrived with friendships from primary school or their council estate, so our conversation created a low murmur that echoed around the largely empty hall, which fell to silence as the headmaster appeared, flanked by other senior staff.

Mr Billingham was a stout man with grey hair in a side parting, perhaps in his late fifties or early sixties. He was suited and booted and his outfit was finished with a dramatic black gown and a white fur-trimmed hood. Marching onto the stage, he stood surveying us all from the lectern on the side of the stage, as other – important, I assumed – members of staff took their places on the wooden chairs that seemed to tower over us, leaving the wooden throne empty for the headmaster.

Mr Billingham had a voice well suited to school leadership: it was deep, rich and commanded our attention as it projected across the hall. He welcomed us to the school and referenced our grand surroundings in a talk about the school's history.

Westminster City's origins lie in five educational charities founded in the 17th century, one of which received its charter from King Charles I, which explained why the King who'd precipitated civil war and lost his head was looking down on us from an exalted position on the wall next to the stage. The 'modern' school building had stood on its Palace Street site since 1877 and Westminster City School was given its name in 1890. In 1944, Westminster City had become a voluntary-aided Church of England grammar school and in 1977 it dropped the grammar school status to become a mixed-ability school with a non-denominational Christian ethos.

Mr Billingham's extended oratory sought to connect our experience as pupils to this rich history, but in reality, his lecture was harking back to a bygone age that bore little relevance to our lives. The modern Westminster City wasn't rich in any sense, not least its pupils. The proportion of children there, like me, who were on free school meals was higher than the national average and remains so today. Like St Peter's, it was a melting pot of cultures – although a consequence of its predominantly Christian intake was that there were far fewer pupils from South Asian communities. Many of us were drawn from council estates across London, which distinguished us from *the* Westminster School, the renowned and prestigious £30,000-a-year private school just up the road. The addition of 'City' to our school name was intended to provide distinction between us – heaven forbid the two be confused – although the private school boys gave us their own, less-than-affectionate nickname to do the job: 'Shitty City'. Charming!

I had been placed in form group 7P, happily, along with Luke. The P was for Palmer's, one of the school's houses. According to the board in the school hall, the house was named after the Reverend James Palmer of the Parish of St Margaret's in Westminster. It is a happy coincidence in my life that St Margaret's Church, which serves as the church for Westminster City School, is also known as the parish church of the House of Commons. I wonder what eleven-year-old Wes would have thought if he had been told that almost twenty years later, he would attend the same church as a Member of Parliament?

We had been sorted into our form groups by a woman who would be a presence as a teacher and head of year throughout my time at Westminster City, Mrs Meadows. Mrs Meadows was a short and sharp woman of Ugandan Asian heritage. Her face was as stern as her voice, reinforced by power suits from Laura Ashley and glasses that were either planted on her nose or hanging around her neck on a chain. She was a disciplinarian, but she needed to be. The bright and shiny faces of the new intake belied the rowdy and rebellious personalities that would soon emerge, in my form group in particular. She was one of a handful of teachers able to strike enough fear into the hearts of boys to command their silence and respect.

As 7P shuffled into our new form room on the ground floor of the school, we were still on our best behaviour. We were assigned our seats on tables of two. Luke and I quickly found our seats next to each other. I felt the guiding hand of St

Peter's still wielding its influence and, sure enough, later in the school year, Mrs Meadows confirmed that St Peter's had recommended that we be kept together. I was glad of it, although we tended to be cliquey as a result.

Most of our first day was spent in our form room, doing rounds of introductions and ice-breakers, with a break for lunch. The school canteen was in the basement under the school hall and by the time my form charged down to the playground outside the hall to queue, we found ourselves at the end of a dishearteningly long line.

After what felt like an eternity, I made it through the doors of the canteen, where I realised that, to my dismay and embarrassment, I needed to join a separate queue to collect my 'dinner ticket' for my free school meal that day. So while Luke and other members of my class joined the queue for their lunch, I trudged over to the back of another pretty lengthy line and felt my cheeks flush and my stomach grumble in protest. I made an effort to keep my chin up, but I noticed a few of the other skinny boys in oversized uniforms ahead of me looking sheepishly over their shoulders at the rest of the kids in the canteen. I knew exactly what they were thinking – wondering if the other boys were looking, if they were being judged for not being able to afford to pay for a hot meal by themselves. At St Peter's, school dinner money had been handed into the office by parents at the start of the week. No distinction was made at lunchtimes between those whose parents paid and those of us who received free school meals. But at Westminster City, we were marked out. If that was the intention, to pigeonhole us as the poor kids, it definitely worked. Although not small in numbers or proportion, we were officially the 'others'. Had I known what the word 'stigmatising' meant when I was eleven, I'm sure I would have used it to describe the whole experience.

The dinner ticket came with a financial value attached. Around £2, as I remember. This tended to be enough for a dish and a couple of sides with a small bottle of Panda Pop. Usually something unhealthy like pie, beans and chips, or two of my favourite Bernard Matthews turkey drumsticks with more chips and beans. That was if they were still there. The delay in getting our tickets meant the popular dishes had often gone by the time we reached the top of the food queue so we'd be left with the untouched sandwiches and salads. I was more fortunate than a lot of the other 'poor kids' because I usually had a bit of pocket money from Grandad to top up my lunch voucher or to get a KitKat on the way home. For some kids, that school lunch was the only hot meal they would receive on any given day.

After lunch, the first day flew by. Luke's dad, Colin, picked him up in his black cab and offered me a lift home, as he often did. We'd made it through and so far so good. But the following weeks at Westminster City would prove to be much more difficult, and I felt like a very small fish in a big pond. Lesson changes were boisterous and noisy – the older kids would think nothing of shoving weedy year sevens like me against the wall to get to class.

The comparative haven of St Peter's had provided me and Luke with an excellent start to our education, but it had also insulated us from the coarse language that was bandied around our class. From misogynistic language like 'pussies' to homophobic abuse like 'batty boys', I had never heard terms like these at St Peter's. This was not the image that the school had projected during open evenings or Mr Billingham's retelling of the school's proud history. I suppose we were beginning to learn the hard way the difference between marketing and reality.

Luke and I had marked ourselves out as different from the offset, which didn't exactly make our school experience an easy one. Luke was one of the most well-spoken pupils in the class and the tallest, so there was nowhere for him to hide. We also always got high marks on our tests and homework, and our close friendship meant we stuck together as a sort of high-achieving – I'll admit, probably quite arrogant – double act, which didn't exactly endear us to some of our classmates. It didn't take long for Luke and me to become the butt of the 'batty boy' attacks. Looking back, it feels a particularly cruel irony that those kids seemed to know I was gay some time before I recognised it myself.

My school bag and socks were the subjects of the bullies' jibes for the first few weeks. Grandad had bought me a mint green satchel that wasn't a well-known or cool brand like Nike or Adidas and some white socks that had baby pink and blue stripes around the ankle. Luckily, my stepdad came to the rescue. Pat's relationship with Mum was back on and, seeing the sadness that the bullying at school was creating, he gave me some black socks and his leather Nike sports bag, which was almost as big as me but looked better slung over my shoulders than the alternative.

At St Peter's, I had enjoyed PE and games. Whether it was rounders in the playground, swimming lessons at the local pool, or climbing the apparatus in the hall, it was always fun.

I was never a great footballer, but my friends had egged me on to take part and didn't mind if I messed up. But at Westminster City, any form of physical activity struck fear in my heart.

For first years, games took place on Thursday afternoons. We were let out of our lessons slightly early for lunch so that we could eat in time to board the coach for the eight-mile drive down to Tamworth Lane in Mitcham to the school playing fields. After being pushed and shoved off the coach, we would head to the changing-room pavilion to put on our games kit and football boots, and each time we crossed the threshold of that pavilion, rules, respect and common decency seemed to get left behind. Beyond the watchful eye of a teacher, bullies had free rein to level unprovoked abuse, wallops and kicks on whatever unwitting victims they had chosen as punching bags that day. Some days it was me, some days it was other kids in the class, but it happened every single week, except when Luke and I would hide down some stairs until we could hear the rumble of the coach engines pulling away down Palace Street. There would always be consequences for missing the coach to Mitcham, in the form of a detention, but we calculated that this punishment was far more bearable than the corporal punishment dealt out by our peers in the pavilion.

But if the intention of the bullies was to put us back in our box, it didn't work. Luke and I brought our larger-than-life characters and friendly rivalry to throwing ourselves into our classes and extracurricular activities. Westminster City had a system of incentives and rewards for good behaviour and performance through credits. Credits were awarded on A6 pieces of yellow card, and whoever got the most credits in a term received a merit badge, which pupils could display on their lapels as a sign of their achievement, but also, of course, as a magnet for abuse. Nothing said 'Bully me! I'm a swot!' as much as a merit badge, but undeterred by the risk, I set about trying to collect as many credits as I could during my first term, acutely aware that Luke was doing the same.

When one of Westminster City's two deputy head teachers, Mrs Finucane, announced in assembly that auditions would be held for a Christmas production of Charles Dickens' *A Christmas Carol*, Luke and I signed up for the audition immediately – I was going to turn my first-day fantasy of standing centre stage under the spotlight into a reality. Auditions were held after school one afternoon in the drama studio.

I walked in full of confidence. Although we were the new kids on the block, I had been in every school play since the age of five and had even played the lead role of Ebenezer Scrooge when I was eight, so I thought I had a leading role in the bag. We sat around tables and read from the script as directed by the drama teacher. I was initially pleased when the parts were announced the following week, and I was cast as Tiny Tim; it wasn't the lead, but still a significant character. Then I received a copy of the script and discovered, to my horror, that all I had were two identical lines: 'God bless us, every one.' Worse still, I had to deliver my two miserable lines with real enthusiasm. I bristled at the under-appreciation of my talents and only now can I laugh at the arrogance of my eleven-year-old self.

As well as drama, I tried to keep up with the religious and musical interests that had been nurtured at St Peter's.

Westminster City didn't take part in weekly worship, but did hold a monthly Eucharist in the school hall. My Religious Studies teacher, Martin Lloyd, signed Luke and me up to serve or to read at the Eucharist and, although this involved arriving at school for 8 am, it was rewarded with a much-sought-after yellow credit slip.

I enjoyed sharing news of my credit slips with Grandad. I wasn't able to see him as often as I used to and now our Friday nights and Saturday mornings just didn't feel long enough, so on Monday evenings, I would go to his house after school, under the guise of needing a quiet place to do my homework. This was partly true, as my baby brother Jordan was prone to making a racket, but it was also because I wanted more quality time with my best mate. Having spent so much time together after the death of Nanny Libby, I missed him terribly.

After I finished my homework, we'd eat dinner together, and then, depending on the weather, Grandad would either walk me back home to Jamaica Street or we'd go together in a minicab. It was quite unnecessary really. I was perfectly able to get myself to and from school in Westminster, travel to Grandad's and then make the ten-minute walk back home by myself, but I never told him that. We both enjoyed the extra conversation about anything and everything on the walk home or – as was more likely as the nights grew dark, cold and wet – in the cab. I was also greedily taking in as much of Grandad's undivided attention as humanly possible, as I wasn't going to be his only grandchild for much longer.

By the end of 1994, Dad and Karen were also expecting their first baby together. Grandad was so excited about being a grandfather again that he gave up a lifetime habit of chain-smoking. This was no mean feat – he was rarely without a cigarette in his hand. But he had suffered some minor heart problems, and although he assured us it was nothing for us to worry about, he decided that it was in the best interests of his health and his grandchildren's to quit. I was both impressed and relieved. I hated the smell of cigarette smoke as a kid – it was everywhere. Mum was a smoker, Dad and Karen were smokers until the pregnancy, and I was convinced that Nanny Knott's wallpaper was held to the wall by tobacco smoke. But it wasn't just that I didn't like the smoke; I held cigarettes responsible for the long, slow and painful death of Nanny Libby, and I didn't want to see anyone else I loved go the same way.

On 21 October, my second brother was born – Dad and Karen's only child together. He didn't have the easiest start in life as he was born with severe jaundice, but he recovered well enough for Dad and Grandad to take me to the hospital to see him and Karen. They had planned to call him Nathan, but after he was born decided instead that he looked more like a Liam, which was a lovely nod to Grandad, as it was short for William. He was delighted. There is a great photograph of Grandad holding baby Liam, smiling down on him with his trademark gleaming-white dentures. I was going to have to share him with my brother now, but I knew that there was enough love for the both of us. In fact, I couldn't wait for all the memories we would make, just the three of us – Grandad and his boys.

Life, however, was to take another turn. Eleven days after my new baby brother was born, I was on my way home after what had been a fairly good Tuesday – I'd done well in my classes and managed to avoid being physically or verbally tormented. All in all, it had been a great day. On the walk home, I was still reflecting on my new baby brother and how much I was looking forward to seeing Grandad again on Friday. I was also famished after a long day at school, so my stomach was rumbling as I trudged through the entry door to our flats and into the corridor where we lived. As I entered the flat and slung my backpack onto the hall floor, I was suddenly aware that the voices upstairs had fallen quiet. I wasn't sure whose they were. I knew it wasn't Pat, who'd still be at work, so I assumed the hushed tones and hurried whispers were those of a friend of Mum's bending her ear about a confidential problem. Curious, I made my way up to the kitchen.

Now the voices had hushed completely, and the only sound was the soft pattering of my brother Jordan, two years old and waddling along to greet me at the top of the stairs.

Sure enough, there was an unusual visitor sitting at our kitchen table, one I really was not expecting to see on a Tuesday night. It was Dad. 'What are you doing here?' I asked, perplexed. I was at once pleasantly surprised and a little confused. I couldn't recall a single occasion when I'd arrived home from school to find him waiting for me.

Dad didn't answer; instead, he shot a look at Mum that I couldn't quite decipher. He seemed tired, his face was paler than usual, but maybe that was normal for the father of a newborn. Or was he angry? His brow was furrowed, and his lips were pressed tightly together. Perhaps he and Mum had had an argument? But they barely saw each other anymore, so what would they have to fight about?

'Come and sit down,' Mum said, breaking the silence and interrupting my train of thought. 'Do you want a cup of tea?' she asked gently. She looked upset. Something was off – Mum knew I didn't drink tea and she was usually the one asking for it, not offering to make it. I knew then that there was bad news. I understood what a sombre offer of tea meant in a British household. My mind began to race.

'What's wrong?' I asked, the fear palpable in my voice as I sat on Dad's lap. 'You're being weird.'

Anguish was etched on his face, and by now, my heart was beating furiously.

'Last night, after your grandad dropped you off . . .' he took a breath to steady himself, but as soon as he began to speak again, I knew where this conversation was going. I looked up at Mum, whose eyes were filled with tears. I could tell from the way Dad began that his voice was drained from crying, too. 'He got back in the cab, and he had a massive heart attack,' Dad continued. I couldn't hear the rest. It was as if his words were lost in the sound of my world collapsing around me. I cried. Harder than I have ever cried in my entire life, before or since. 'I'm so sorry,' Dad was saying over and over through his own tears, as Mum held her hand over her mouth and sobbed. We sat like that for a while, squashed together in Mum's tiny kitchen, weeping for the loss of the best man the three of us had ever known.

It was impossible to take in. The night before I had been at Grandad's as usual. I had done my homework, we'd had dinner, and he had taken me home in a minicab. There was no sign of anything being wrong. When we arrived at Jamaica Street, he left the cab waiting, walked me to the entry of our block of flats, we hugged, and he waved me off from the doorway to our block as I opened the second door and walked into the corridor. I can still see him as I write this nearly thirty years later, standing at that door, seventy-one years old, suited and booted, smiling and waving. Saying goodbye.

It was only a matter of seconds later, once he'd got back into the cab and begun his return journey, that the heart attack struck. I don't know exactly what happened and I try not to think about it. The driver acted fast, put his foot down, and rushed him straight to the Royal London Hospital in Whitechapel.

Dad was at home that evening in Digby Gardens when a knock came at the front door. When he answered it, he was met with the sight everyone dreads – a sombre-faced police officer. The delivery of the news was solemn, but gentle: 'Mr Streeting, I've been asked to inform you that your father has been taken ill in a minicab. He's been sent to the Royal London Hospital in Whitechapel, you'll need to get there as quickly as possible.' But however quickly the police had arrived, and however fast Dad drove, there was no way he could have reached the Royal London in time. It was a ten-mile journey from Dagenham that would have taken about half an hour. Grandad was already gone.

That I was the last family member to see him was some consolation for my broken heart. It was as if his heart refused to give way in my presence and was holding on just long enough to give me the chance to say a final goodbye.

I decided I wanted to be with Dad that evening, and so he took me back to Digby Gardens, where Karen was waiting for us. The three of us cried together for a long time that night.

When I finally got to bed, I woke up repeatedly, each time hoping it was all just a bad dream, before reliving the loss all over again. Dad was up throughout the night consoling me, even though his loss was far greater than mine.

Dad let me take the rest of the week off school. I phoned Luke to tell him what had happened, but he already knew. Our form teacher had told the class. Usually, my days in Dagenham were spent playing out with my friends. This time they were all at school, and I was in no mood for company. I just wanted to be alone with my own thoughts, memories and grief.

Dad began making the arrangements for the funeral, all the while dealing with his own earth-shattering grief. He decided that it would take place at the City of London Crematorium and that he would ask my priests from St Peter's, Father Peel and Father Hoyle, to conduct the service, as they both knew Grandad well. It felt comforting to know they were involved.

I agreed to do a reading at the funeral, just as I had done for Nanny Libby. But this time, the one person I needed to help me prepare was the one person who was no longer there. When the funeral came, I could barely hold myself together. The room was packed and seemed to echo with sobs. I stood at the front of the crematorium and clasped Dad's hand tightly until it was time for my reading. I don't remember what it was, or even how I delivered it, or how it was received. I just remember the feeling of release as I returned to my seat with Dad, finally able to cry my heart out, or at least what was left of it.

As we left the crematorium, Father Peel and Father Hoyle were waiting at the doors to bid people goodbye. I gave Father

Peel a hug and cried again, soaking the front of his cassock with snot and tears until he was rescued by my Great-Aunt Vi.

A wake was held back at Grandad's flat. Our whole family was there, as were many of Mum's family, too. I nearly had a heart attack of my own when I came downstairs to find a tall, sharply dressed man with slicked-back grey hair and a thick moustache standing in the hall. The resemblance to Grandad was so uncanny that for a moment I truly believed I was seeing his ghost. It turned out to be his brother, Harry, whom I'd never met because they'd fallen out years before. He was the spitting image of him. As irrational as it was, my heart broke once more that day. What wouldn't I have given to walk down those stairs to find it really was Grandad there waiting for me one last time?

CHAPTER TEN

Chaos

Grandad Bill Streeting with baby Liam, October 1994.

WHEN NANNY LIBBY died, Grandad's flat had been an escape from suffering. A sanctuary. But in the weeks that followed his death, 18 Walter Besant House became a punishing reminder that he was gone. Weekends, which I had once looked forward to, became a source of dread as we sorted through all his belongings.

Grandad was a hoarder. The cupboard under the stairs was filled with years of treasure and trash, and distinguishing between the two was a painful process. It felt like sacrilege. I felt a connection to Grandad in every object, and I hated to see anything thrown into bin liners, but there simply wasn't the space in Dad's house for it all, and much of it was of little real sentimental value.

From Friday to Sunday, every hour was filled with decisions on what to do with Grandad's possessions. On top of
the dresser in his living room were models of old sailing ships
he'd collected, beautifully crafted with meticulous detail on
the masts and the rigging. But they were held together now
by dust and cobwebs, and it was time they were decommis-
sioned. Dad kept Grandad's war medals but passed his own
grandfather's medals to his Uncle Harry.

I was prolonging the agony by moving at a glacial pace
when clearing out my own bedroom there – I spent more
time reading and reminiscing than sorting and binning. I
was told to be ruthless because there wasn't much space in
either of my bedrooms at Jamaica Street or Digby Gardens,
especially as our families continued to grow. Despite their
tumultuous relationship, Mum and Pat were expecting twins
in April. The new arrivals were unplanned. It was already a
tight squeeze with me, Mum and Jordan.

My poor dad had to tie up all of Grandad's loose ends. The
bills, the bank accounts, and the council flat. My one responsibility was to return Grandad's library card. I went along to the
Bancroft Road library on my way home from school one
Friday afternoon, just as I always used to with Grandad. It was
a place we had both loved visiting together, with its grand
Victorian facade and beautiful patterned ceiling, but this time
it was acutely painful. It was made even more difficult by the
librarian behind the counter looking at me sternly over her
glasses and asking, 'Doesn't William want his library card
anymore?' Her curt tone made my cheeks flush. 'No, he's dead,'
I almost said. But it wasn't her fault really. She didn't know,
and I was still struggling to find the words. 'No, he doesn't,' I

replied softly. 'That's a shame,' she said flatly. 'Yes,' I whispered as I placed it on the desk in front of her. Wiping a couple of tears from my eyes, I trudged back down the grand staircase to the entrance hall and back out onto Bancroft Road. I never returned there again. It didn't feel right without Grandad.

Now I would have a new Friday evening routine. Terry and Sheila, Grandad's next-door neighbours and Christopher's parents, offered to take my bed into their flat so that I could stay over and keep up my friendship with their son. Each week would be the same. I'd arrive, we'd play some Super Nintendo, then watch Friday evening TV in his kitchen or bedroom whilst playing board games or cards. Of course, it wasn't the same without Grandad, but I appreciated the effort they made to try and make me feel even a tiny bit better.

On Saturday mornings, I went down to see Grandad's sister, Aunt Vi, in her ground-floor flat in Barber Beaumont House, opposite Grandad's block of flats. Grandad had always been close to her, and now, each week, she would cook me a fried breakfast and her best friend, Anne, from the flat upstairs would come and join us to hear all about my week, just as I would have told Grandad. Then they'd send me off to Dad's on the District Line with five pounds' pocket money. It was a lovely gesture, and not one I took for granted, but my full belly and pockets could do little to fill the emptiness I still felt in my heart.

My whole family knew how hard Grandad's death had hit me and they were doing their best to look out for me. That Christmas, Pat bought me two tickets to see Arsenal v Aston Villa at Highbury on Boxing Day. I was really chuffed. Football tickets weren't cheap. He had taken me to see Arsenal a few times over the years, to my delight and Dad's dismay. I'm not sure which of my two red teams caused my Tory-voting, West Ham-supporting Dad more distress – Labour or Arsenal!

It turned out that Pat had to work on the day of the match, so Grandad Pops offered to take me instead. I had seen a bit more of him since Nanny Libby died. He was only fifty-four, but he wasn't in the best of health and had severe problems with his back – what a life of sleeping on prison mattresses will do to you, I suppose. We had to set off extra early for the match so that he could hobble along to the tube station, but even then we were late. Not that it mattered much. It seemed like every time I went to Highbury, it was nil–nil. But I have no doubt that following the death of Nanny Libby and Grandad Streeting, Grandad Pops was making an effort to be there for me, and I appreciated it.

Other major changes to my routine were afoot. Grandad had left some money behind for Dad. Not much, but enough to enable him and Karen to embark on a career change. Neither of them was particularly happy in their jobs – Dad was due for promotion at work, but wasn't really enjoying his office job in shipping. Karen had an admin job at the Dudley Stationery factory in Bow but much preferred the interaction with customers in her old bar job. So, they were going to leave their jobs and retrain as publicans with the Scottish and Newcastle Brewery. Becoming publicans would allow them to run their own business, which Dad had dreamed of, in a family pub, where Karen could get back to the bar work that she loved, at the same time as bringing up my brother, Liam. It was an opportunity they couldn't have imagined, and without the money Grandad had left them, they wouldn't have been able to afford the career change. It's one of the things that can often be taken for granted by people who are more well off: it's a lot easier to build a successful career when you already have money.

But there was one big catch. They would have to go on residential training courses followed by placements in pubs all across the country. The entire process would take months, and they would be paid substantially less than they were currently earning together. To make it work, their house on Digby Gardens was going to be let to tenants, while Dad and Karen would live with Karen's parents in Bow, who would take care of Liam while they were training until they were given a pub of their own. My weekends with Dad were over for now, and I feared they might never return.

As Dad and Karen contemplated their big move, more changes just kept coming. On 3 April 1995, Mum gave birth to the twins – Kira and Callum. I was thrilled to have a sister for the first time, as well as Mum's third son and my third brother. Twins would be quite the handful for Mum, on top of me and Jordan, who was by now nearly three. But whatever challenges they might present, I was just excited they had arrived.

The arrival of my two new siblings meant that our flat in Jamaica Street was officially overcrowded. I was already sharing a bedroom with Jordan, which had its own challenges. I had been sleeping on a futon on the floor, which I didn't mind except that it was now at the perfect level for an almost-three-year-old to climb in next to me and wet the bed. Kira and Callum's cots were placed in with Mum initially and then moved to the living room. It really was a full house.

Clearly aware that a two-bed maisonette was no place for a family of five, Pat offered to buy a house for us to move to in

Epping, in Essex, closer to his own one-bedroom flat in Loughton. I was initially more enthusiastic than Mum. I had been given a taste of suburban life with Dad and Karen in Dagenham – a house with a garden and space to ride a bike. The thought of staying crammed into a tiny flat with two brothers and a sister while we waited for years to be rehoused to God knows where on the Tower Hamlets housing list was not appealing.

But Mum was very reluctant. She had spent almost her entire life living in East London. It was where her friends were, where most of our family still were, and it was closer to my school. The council flat was also in her name. Whatever its shortcomings in terms of space, decor or occasional cockroaches, it had given us stability and security. If we were moving to Epping, she would need to give it back to the council and would lose whatever independence she had, something she might never have again.

It took some time, but eventually Pat won Mum over. We were all going to move to Epping. It just felt like so much was changing all at once. As if I were sitting inside a kaleidoscope, watching the world twisting and turning and tumbling and falling around me.

With Dad and Karen preparing to leave Digby Gardens, all of my stuff was packed up to come back to Mum's with me. Dad took me down to Nanny Hill's in West Sussex, where she and Grandad Hill lived in a bungalow with a decent-sized garden and plenty of roaming ground. I was to go and stay with them while Dad and Karen were away training.

All of my friends at Digby Gardens arranged a surprise leaving party for me with cakes, crisps, sausage rolls, fizzy drinks and cheesy music. It felt as if a chapter in my life was closing. These had been my friends for four years, a third of a lifetime for a twelve-year-old.

I was also saying goodbye to Stepney. The place where I'd been born and raised. It was a strange feeling. I was leaving behind everything I knew all at once, but I wasn't exactly sad to be leaving Jamaica Street. I never liked our flat. And the familial ties didn't feel so strong anymore. Nanny Libby and Grandad had died, my Aunt Eve was now living over in Newham, and my Aunt Amanda had moved to Watford with my uncle and cousins. Only Nanny Knott remained, the constant anchor for our family in the East End, although she was beginning to show her age. Whenever we visited, the flat wasn't quite the hub of activity it had once been. She was finding it harder to stand for long on her feet, so the days of her cooking up a feast of sweet and savoury pies or chips were gone.

I was no longer an East Ender. I was moving up in the world, or so I thought. Epping is a market town in Essex just outside the M25, centred around the upmarket High Street and Station Road, and the last stop on the Central Line. Our new house was at 3 Ingels Mead, a residential street twenty minutes' walk from the tube station.

We moved in the autumn of 1995, and it soon became clear it was a disaster. The house was a fixer-upper, and it hadn't had much fixed up by the time we moved in. It did have three bedrooms and I finally had one to myself, although 'bedroom' may be a generous way to describe it. It was a 2.5-metre square box room, with a bed that gave way so regularly that I had to prop it up with books and storage boxes. My brothers and sister shared the second bedroom, which was big enough for a set of bunk beds, a separate bed and two cots, and Mum had the slightly smaller double room with Pat, who still split his time between us and his own flat in Loughton. It was all in need of new wallpaper and a fresh lick of paint.

I had just entered my second year at Westminster City. Mum agreed that I could continue commuting into school from Epping, but this was a ridiculously long journey, made worse by the unreliability of the Central Line. On a good day, this was one hour and twenty minutes each way; on a bad day, it was an hour and forty. An eternity, even by the standards of London commuting. I still had a Travelcard for zones one and two that had been awarded by Tower Hamlets Council, but as we were now living at the end of the tube network, Mum had to top up the fares. Most days this was fine, but as we drew closer to Christmas and money became scarce, I had days off school because she couldn't afford the fares.

Thankfully, our time in Epping was short. Mercifully short. My abiding memory of that house was just how cold it was. For all the faults of our flat in Jamaica Street, at least it had good central heating and insulation. As the nights drew in in Epping, the temperature inside and outside dropped. The single-glazed windows were conduits for the cold. It seemed to pass effortlessly through the glass panes and into the house, which meant that the bathroom was like a fridge in the morning and just stepping onto the ceramic kitchen tiles was like walking on ice.

I only saw the ice house in daylight on the weekends. I left for school just after seven in the morning, and by the time I got home, it was around five-thirty in the evening, even later if we had school play rehearsals, by which time it was pitch black outside, and just as gloomy inside. Even when we did have light, it wasn't much to look at. Everything was in serious need of decoration.

It was obvious that Mum was thoroughly miserable. I could tell, from the moment we arrived, that she regretted her decision. She was withdrawn and irritable. Nothing was right for her. Even the local chippy on Epping High Street put the chips in small boxes instead of chip paper, which made the chips moist and soggy. I didn't like it either. I hated the cold and missing school. I enjoyed school, and it was always an escape from the misery at home. But the flat in Stepney was gone. There was no turning back there. I know that our living situation made Mum and Pat's rocky relationship deteriorate even further. The arguments were constant, and the toxicity of their relationship soured an already unpleasant house. Mum's unhappiness was beginning to affect my relationship with Pat, too. We started to argue. On one occasion I snapped back, 'You're not my father.' It was a great shame because he had never been anything but good to me.

For weeks, the tension and sadness had been mounting, until things came to a miserable climax at Christmas. Pat was going to Lanzarote for Christmas with his parents, leaving Mum behind. This was the final straw. Mum decided that she didn't want to stay in the relationship or stay in that house a day longer. She declared that we were going to leave as soon as humanly possible. She loaded us into a hire car – me, Jordan, the twins and my Auntie Eve, who'd turned up to help – and we drove for miles the day before Christmas Eve in search of somewhere to stay. We had barely any money, few presents, and little by way of groceries for a Christmas shop, but we managed to find a caravan site near Sandwich on the Kent coast, which had a spare caravan to let. So the six of us all crammed into a miniscule caravan that was just as cold and miserable as the house we'd left behind, and, to make matters worse, the campsite had run out of gas for heating and hot water. It was shaping up to be our own nightmare before Christmas.

Thankfully, by Christmas morning some gas had been delivered, which was the best present we could have asked for. I had a *Star Trek* mug and a satsuma to open. My brothers and sister had not much else, although they at least were too young to remember the ordeal. I don't know how Mum managed it, but she used the little oven and hob to make a roast chicken, roast potatoes, carrots, peas and gravy complete with Aunt Bessie's Yorkshire Puddings, normally heresy for her. Watching films afterwards on the small TV meant we did, incredibly, manage a taste of Christmas, though it definitely ranks as the worst I've experienced.

Throughout my childhood, up until that year, I'd enjoyed every one of my Christmases. I'd spend Christmas Day with Mum and Boxing Day with Dad one year, and then alternate the following year. No matter how strapped for cash we were, Mum always made sure we had a good one. She'd enjoy getting the decorations out, putting a tree up, and making Christmas dinner. Between my parents and grandparents, they'd always club together to make sure that I got some decent presents too. I know that Christmas can be a difficult time for a lot of separated families, but I never appreciated my 'second Christmas' family dynamic as much as I did that year. My post-Christmas get-together with Dad was the main event, thank God.

Dad and Karen had finally completed their training and been given a family-sized pub to run in Hornchurch, Essex. Considering they could have been sent anywhere in the country, I was over the moon that they had been stationed so close to home. The Crown, on Roneo Corner, had two bars – a lounge, which served food, and a sports bar, which had pool tables and a big screen that showed Sky Sports. Dad and Karen occupied the flat above the pub, which had four bedrooms, meaning Liam and I could have our own rooms. When I first arrived to stay with them, I felt as if I had escaped a conflict zone. It was bliss. Sitting in the living room above the pub, I confided in them both just how awful life had been in Epping. I had never felt more hopeless or alone. I didn't have Grandad to confide in any longer, I had barely seen Dad and Karen until they were given The Crown, and I was helpless to do anything as I watched the deterioration of the relationship between Mum and Pat – so painful because I loved them both.

Needless to say, Mum and my siblings didn't return to Epping. At least I could stay with Dad. As a last resort, Mum took Jordan, Callum and Kira to live with Grandad Pops down in Orpington in Kent, but his flat was more of a hole than a home – it made the Epping house look like Buckingham Palace. The kitchen was thick with layers of grease and the air with cigarette smoke. There was never any food in the fridge, except perhaps a lump of mouldy cheese and a pint of milk that had gone off. He was always drunk, and the TV was dedicated to horse racing.

It was no environment for three small children. I can't imagine how difficult this must have been for Mum. Within the space of a few years she had lost her mother, moved three times, had twins and had now lost her own home while having three small children to care for and her eldest son separated from her. Grandad Pops was incapable of providing the support she needed and no one in our extended family had the space for Mum with the three kids in tow. In the end, in desperation, Mum felt she had no choice but to be placed in temporary accommodation in a bedsit until she could find somewhere permanent to live.

She'd dropped off all her worldly belongings at The Crown, including our television set and VCR, asking Dad to take care of it all. Then she left, promising to be in touch. If Dad and Karen were perturbed or put out by this, they certainly didn't show it, though I'm sure it wasn't what they were expecting, to put it mildly. I was just glad to be at Dad's, free of all the chaos.

Throughout the turbulence and chaos at home, school was a rock of stability. After a particularly traumatic winter, I threw myself back into my education. Despite the occasional, merciless cruelty from some of the boys, when I returned to school, most of my classmates were sympathetic and supportive.

Although I lost out in my competition for the class merit badge in the first term of my first year to Luke, which I blamed on my bereavement absence from school, by the end of the second term, I'd achieved a score draw. The school continued to push me, and I pushed myself academically. I threw myself into every extracurricular activity I could. School drama, the school newspaper, helping out at parents' evenings, anything to avoid what was going on at home.

The school also provided me with new experiences that I was unlikely to get at home. One Friday morning, in year seven, as we were getting changed for PE, our teacher, Mr

Benjamin, rather tactlessly, asked those of us whose parents were on benefits to put our hands up. Unsurprisingly, nobody obliged. Like me, no one else wanted to identify themselves as poor. The daily lunchtime queue for free meal tickets was humiliation enough. 'Don't be embarrassed,' he proceeded, with all the subtlety of a sledgehammer, 'I've got a great opportunity for you.' After a pause, a few of us reluctantly put our hands up, which was still an implausibly low number in my class. Mr Benjamin pulled us to one side and explained that one of the pupils enrolled on the school ski trip had broken an arm or leg and couldn't participate. Because it was too late for a refund, his parents asked that the place be given to a boy whose parents would otherwise be unable to afford it. There was just one catch: we would need to provide our own spending money and pay for the hire of the ski kit. That whittled the number interested down to two – myself and one other equally embarrassed but excited boy. After some pleading with Dad that evening, to my delight, he agreed to cover the cost. It might be hard for those more fortunate to fathom just how big a deal being able to go abroad on a school trip with your classmates was to a child like me, or how much pressure and shame it brings to a parent who isn't able to give them such an opportunity. I never thought it would be possible. Without Dad, it wouldn't have been, which is presumably why some of the other kids said no. Unlike Dad, who worked, their parents were reliant on benefits, and couldn't afford even a subsidised trip. It was thanks to Dad that I even had a passport, as he and Karen had taken me on a family holiday to Majorca a couple of years earlier, my first time on a plane.

A couple of months and a coach ride through France later, I was on the slopes of the French Alps. It was during that ski trip that I became particularly good friends with a boy called Ray, who was a couple of years above me, and Martyn, a cheeky chappy who sat in front of me in my form group and who were also both members of the drama club like me. The tediously long coach trip was worth it to spend time on the snow-covered French Alps. It was a far cry from Stepney, and like nothing I had ever seen before.

I wrote to thank the parents who paid for my place after the trip. It was extraordinarily generous to donate the place to someone like me, rather than simply try to sell it on. Thanks to their kindness, I had an experience that I would never have been afforded, and would never forget. I returned from the trip with a taste for travelling, a newfound confidence in school, and friendships that have lasted long after my time at Westminster City.

Moving up to my second year and living in Epping, our new form teacher, Mr Nash, proved a huge help to me, even though he was pretty formidable at first. He wasn't one to be messed with, and soon put us rowdy and unruly boys in our place from our first encounter – making us line up against the wall outside our classroom and file into the room in total silence. When the silence was broken, he made us do it again, and again, and again, until we got the message. It was the firm approach we needed, but Mr Nash was exceptionally kind and caring – one of the few people I could confide in at school about the turbulence of my life at home. He was concerned by my sporadic absence and regular lateness during the first term while I was doing the long commute, so

I gave him the background and explained what was holding me back.

I trusted Mr Nash and felt he always had my best interests at heart. From now on, I would receive a stern but understanding gaze for rolling in late. He also happened to be the head of the drama department, so our relationship was forged as much on stage as it was during our more formal form periods.

Mr Nash also ran the drama club. The previous year's performance of *A Christmas Carol* had been a success. This year, we were going to stage a production of *Ernie's Incredible Illucinations* by Alan Ayckbourn, a bright comedy in which young Ernie's daydreams, or 'illucinations', come to life. There was just one challenge: two of the main characters, Ernie's mum and Ernie's Auntie May, were women, and Westminster City was an all-boys school until sixth form.

So I seized my chance to shine. During the auditions, I had the staff and aspiring cast in stitches with a cockney version of Ernie's mum – my family gaggle of bold East Enders were, of course, excellent character references, so I had sealed my fate. I was cast as Ernie's mum, and Luke, who gave an equally funny and rather camp audition as Auntie May, was also given a female role. My friend Martyn was cast as Ernie and Ray was cast as Ernie's doctor.

Like so many young kids, I found school drama to be a glorious escape from whatever chaos was going on at home, as well as a release from the sometimes-oppressive school day. It wasn't so much the lessons I found suffocating. I was enjoying my classes and flourishing with great teachers in English as well as Maths, but the culture of bullying and 'boys will be boys' attitude both in my class and around the school was awful. I had to keep my wits about me all the time, to know when to deliver a cutting one-liner in response to a nasty comment or duck for cover from a missile thrown from the other side of the class. I realised too late that I didn't really like being at an all-boys school and would have preferred a mixed one, even if it had meant staying in Tower Hamlets. But I stuck with it as much as anything because of the friendships forged and the laughs we had during our after-school drama club.

Performances of the school play usually took place just before the end of term in the evenings to an audience largely made up of parents of the cast, school governors, and groups of pupils who came to support their mates. To generate interest, we would also perform a short preview to the entire school in assemblies.

There was no escaping and, given the homophobic nature of so much of the bullying I endured, taking to the stage in a grey wig, flowery dress, black clunky heels, and a black handbag that Mrs Thatcher would have approved of was either incredibly brave or incredibly stupid. Probably both.

As we stood waiting outside the vestibule in full costume, I had never been more terrified about walking onto a stage in my entire life. Over my shaky breathing and thumping heartbeat, I could hear Mr Nash introducing the play to the assembled crowd. The polite applause began, the lights went down, and the velvet curtains swept open. This was our cue. The moment I had once fantasised about now made me want to run for the hills, but I conquered my nerves and clip-clopped on in my black high heels behind Martyn and Ray. It took barely a second for the audience to realise it was a boy dressed up as an older woman, and then the laughter erupted. I was determined not to let it put me off – I belted out my opening line, ushering Martyn to his seat: 'Come on, Ernie! Mornin' doctor.' More laughter, and then it all died down as they started to concentrate on the play. They were no longer laughing at but with us, following the scene, applauding and cheering in all the right places. This wasn't just a relief; I felt great. Exhilarated. It was the same again for the second assembly. They lapped it up.

The only fly in the ointment was an older boy, who'd missed the play and called me a 'batty boy' on my way back to get changed in the drama studio. I'm not sure swinging Ernie's mum's handbag at his head was particularly macho, but it did the trick, and I didn't care. I was still on cloud nine.

When Luke, Martyn and I arrived back in our form class, the reaction couldn't have been better. Even one of my regular tormentors said, 'Respect, man. That takes guts.'

He was right. It really had taken guts. And I knew that it was school drama that had given me confidence in bucketloads, right from my first moment in primary school when I walked on stage as the Nutcracker. Onstage, I didn't have a care in the world, and it meant when I was offstage I was better equipped to cope with life's challenges. Beyond the school holidays, and the Christmas from hell in that caravan in Kent, there were plenty more of those challenges on the way.

CHAPTER ELEVEN

Broken Homes and Special Measures

With Dad on holiday, 1997.

IF ONLY I had been old enough to fully appreciate the bene-fits of living above a pub. My imagination occasionally wanders to how great it would have been to have free pints on demand. Unfortunately, I was just thirteen years old so the only thing I could have on tap was Coca-Cola. But still, I made the most of it, with Premier League games on the big screen in the sports bar, easy access to an endless supply of crisps and nuts, and late-night raids of the pub's kitchen stores. It was only twenty years later that I confessed to Dad that I was responsible for the stocktake issues he had with the profiteroles – I had been hooked on them since my first taste at Nanny Knott's eightieth birthday party. I would sneak down into the kitchen in the evening after it was closed to the punters, pile a bowl high with profiteroles, squirty cream, and chocolate sauce, creep back upstairs, devour the lot and then wash up the bowl to remove all evidence of the crime.

The flat above the pub was bigger than anywhere I'd ever lived. It had its fair share of challenges, like the frozen pipes in the winter, and it clearly hadn't been decorated for at least a couple of decades – the Thunderbirds wallpaper on my bedroom wall looked as if it had been there since the 1970s – but it was still the biggest bedroom I had ever had, in the nicest place I had ever called home.

I even had my own TV in my bedroom, although technically it was Mum's, and a Super Nintendo. Pat had bought it for me as a Christmas present. He always treated me like one of his own children and spoiled me without me even asking. It's another reason why I hated the arguments between him and Mum. The only games console I'd had before was a Sega Master System that I had at the weekends in Dagenham. I had begged Dad to buy me one, but he insisted that I save to buy the console, and said he would buy me some games. This was typical of Dad's style of parenting and definitely a Streeting family value he'd inherited from Grandad: if I wanted something, I would have to earn it. The great thing about step-parents is that they're often a softer touch, so Pat drove no such hard bargain.

During those early months in 1996, it was strange being apart from Mum, Pat, and my brothers and sister. I couldn't understand how or why things had deteriorated so quickly. But for the first time in my life, I was living with Dad in what felt like a 'normal' family environment. I had two parents at home, both working and earning an income and my brother, Liam, who was rapidly approaching nursery age. It was a relief from the rows and acrimony of Epping.

Mum was placed in temporary accommodation in the London Borough of Islington, where she spent a few months living in one room with my three-year-old brother and the twins, who were barely a year old. Since the accommodation was shared, the kitchen and bathroom facilities were communal, and not all of the inhabitants shared Mum's commitment to cleanliness and hygiene. I stayed over a couple of times. It wasn't somewhere I'd want to live, and I was sad for Mum that she found herself living in such cramped conditions. Fortunately, she wasn't stuck there for long. After a few months in temporary accommodation, she was given a council flat in Archway. I dread to think where she might have ended up today had she not been fortunate enough to get out of that place. As a Member of Parliament, I help a lot of people like Mum, some in far worse situations than hers. The wait for a suitable council home can take months, even years. Some people find themselves on the housing list for more than a decade, with no sign of light at the end of the tunnel. In the meantime, they're placed in temporary accommodation, often overcrowded and in conditions that are frankly unfit for human habitation. Looking back, Mum really was lucky.

Her new home was a four-bedroom maisonette over two floors in a block of flats. Its size meant that I could have my own bedroom and that the commute to school would be a lot shorter than travelling in from Hornchurch on the bus, train and tube. Great news, in theory, and to say Mum was relieved would be an understatement. She couldn't wait to have all her children back under a roof of her own. But there was just one problem: I didn't want to move.

For almost three years, my life had been subjected to constant upheaval. Moving from Mum's house to Nan's. Living with Grandad temporarily. Moving back to Jamaica Street, then to Epping, then to Dad's. For the first time in years, I actually felt settled where I was. I had a routine again, and I was anxious about anything that would change that.

I hadn't raised the prospect of staying at The Crown permanently with Dad or Karen yet, although I had dropped the occasional hint. I certainly hadn't broached the idea with Mum. I was nervous about how they would all react, especially her. How do you tell one of your parents that you don't want to live with them anymore without hurting their feelings, especially after they have gone through so much?

I also worried about whether Dad and Karen would consider me a burden, as living with them had only been a temporary measure. It was a daft thing to be worried about. I was their son, and they had never treated me like a guest or a nuisance. But I was just a kid. A kid about to make a big decision that I knew would impact the people I loved the most. I was frightened about what they might think, how they might feel, or what they might say.

When I finally plucked up the courage to tell Dad and Karen that I wanted to stay with them, it was obvious from their reaction that they had half expected the conversation. Of course, they were happy for me to live with them if it was what I wanted, but they also told me that I would need Mum's support, too. And I couldn't take the easy way out and let them break the news – I would have to ask Mum myself.

Flash forward twenty-odd years, and I've faced many a tough debate or difficult interview, but to this day, that conversation with Mum was the hardest I've ever had in my whole life. She was driving, I can't remember where exactly, but I remember my Aunt Eve was sitting in the passenger seat. I can still relive exactly how I felt as I sat in the back, staring out of the window while the guilt of my decision clawed away at my insides. I had been trying to find the right words and the courage to raise the issue myself when, out of nowhere, Mum presented the right moment: 'So, when are you coming home, Wes?' she asked, meeting my gaze in the rear-view mirror. I squirmed in my seat. My heart was pounding so hard I thought it might punch a hole in my chest. 'I was going to talk to you about that,' I began, looking out of the window to avoid eye contact through the mirror, although I could still feel the reflection of her eyes on me. 'I've been thinking and I want to stay with Dad,' I mumbled. I looked ahead to see Mum and Eve exchanging uneasy glances. I explained that I was settled and that I didn't want any more disruption. To her credit, Mum couldn't have made it easier if she'd tried. 'I thought you might say that,' she said with a sigh of obvious disappointment. 'If that's what you want . . . I just want you to be happy.'

I felt relieved and guilty all at once. I guess it's the kind of guilt that lots of children experience when their parents separate and they're asked to make a choice about who they want to live with. But this was self-imposed. No one had forced me to make this choice. I was making it for myself. Mum's priority throughout my childhood was to make sure that I was settled. It was why she sent me to stay with Grandad after Nanny Libby died and it was why she sent me to live with Dad after she left Epping. She put my interests first then, and she was doing it again now.

And so a new routine began, turning the previous one on its head. I spent the weekdays with Dad and Karen and spent the weekends in Archway with Mum. I didn't enjoy the commute. Despite the reputation of the East End, with all the folklore about the Krays and the East London gangland, I had still always felt safe leaving Whitechapel Station onto the bustling market and into the familiar back streets of Stepney. Whereas when I left Archway Station onto Junction Road, I needed my wits about me. The area outside the station was a den of drug-dealing and aggressive street begging back then. You could smell the social problems, the urine, the super-strength lager, and the pungent smell of weed. I would walk as quickly as I could down the main road to Mum's flat.

Silver Court, a red-brick block of flats standing at seven storeys on the corner of Junction Road and Bickerton Road, wasn't much to look at on the outside and there was always a faint smell of urine on the stairwell but, as she always did, Mum had made the flat her own. Although, by choosing to stay with Dad, I forfeited my own bedroom. The smallest room was now a playroom for my brothers and sister. The twins shared a bedroom in their two cots and Jordan had his own room next door. I slept on a mattress under the stairs when I stayed over. It was comfortable enough. Pat was back in Mum's life too. I wasn't sure if this was just another turn in their on-and-off relationship, but it felt as though Mum's life was back on an even keel.

At school, 'Shitty City' was living up to its reputation. At the start of year nine, our drama club began auditions and rehearsals for a production of *The Government Inspector* by Nikolai Gogol, a comedy of errors set in Imperial Russia. I played Bobchinsky, one half of a comedy double act.

There was a certain irony about the plot. Months later, the school received a visit from Ofsted, Her Majesty's Inspectors of school standards. But unlike our stage play, it was no laughing matter. The school was placed in special measures. It came as a shock to the entire school community, but it shouldn't have. Behaviour was poor, and discipline non-existent in some lessons. The school's standards were falling, and teaching quality was variable – to put it mildly.

A letter went home to parents with the outcome of the inspection, and the anxiety among the staff was palpable. One morning, once we were gathered into the hall for assembly, our relatively new head teacher, Mr Harding, appeared on stage, abruptly announced his resignation and walked off the stage again, leaving pupils stunned and confused. One member of staff, visibly distressed, was banging on the door, demanding answers as we left for our morning classes.

The consequences of the special measures were becoming clear, devastatingly so for the staff. They were told there would be a restructure and that they would have to reapply for their jobs. Some staff read the writing on the wall and started looking for jobs elsewhere. Others fought to stay.

When the proposed staff restructure was announced, the biggest casualty was one of the deputy head teachers, Mr

James. This came as a bigger shock than the initial announcement of the special measures – Mr James was one of those teachers that everyone knew. In a school that struggled to maintain order and good behaviour, he was a true disciplinarian with a bellowing voice that had results. When he yelled 'You boy!' you stopped in your tracks and feared the consequences if you were doing something wrong. He was hugely respected by staff and pupils alike. His forced departure seemed like a terrible injustice.

So I, together with other members of the drama club, hatched a plan to overturn the decision. We resolved to start a petition of the pupils demanding that the governors reinstate our beloved deputy head teacher, and so the 'Save Mr James' campaign was born.

We had the tacit, in some cases explicit, support of the staff. We gathered signatures in the playground before and after school and during lunchtime, and we were even allowed to go class to class during registration periods.

. Some of our biggest supporters were people who'd found themselves in trouble with him, but they knew that beneath his stern facade was a big heart. Kids with the worst reputations were among those who were taking the petition sheets and enlisting their form groups, which really got things moving. They weren't the sort of kids you said no to.

Within a matter of days, we had gathered more than 400 signatures, over half of the pupils, to save him. Yet, despite our best efforts, the petition didn't persuade the school governors to reinstate Mr James in his previous role. But we had made enough noise that the school offered him a position as a history teacher instead – success! Not only had we saved Mr

James, but the whole ordeal gave me a taste for campaigning. Organising that petition was my first experience of trying to rally people together to make a change – it felt good to help people, to band together for a common cause – and something in me clicked.

As the 1997 general election approached, the school decided to hold a mock election of its own. Naturally, the teachers turned to my friend Ray and the rest of our drama gang to help organise candidates. Ray was always good at corralling us into action, and we were always keen to help. We were going to run the Labour campaign, and I wanted to be the Labour candidate. I'd been following the election campaign on TV. Perhaps some of Nanny Libby's Old Labour politics had rubbed off on me, but New Labour also looked exciting and fresh. But what really sealed the deal was Ann Widdecombe. I'd seen the prominent Conservative MP attack single-parent families in the media, and it felt to me like a direct attack on Mum. It made me think that the Conservatives weren't really for people like me, despite what Dad and Grandad might have believed. Labour felt more in touch with my life, my values, and my family.

Ray proposed that our friend Martyn should be the frontman on the basis that he was one of the popular kids and so would attract more votes. That was Ray's way of politely, but not so subtly, pointing out that I was not popular. I was one of those kids who stood out as a geek, wearing my merit badges with pride. But, fortunately for me – unfortunately for Labour's chances – Martyn didn't want the job. He was a great actor, but not so interested in politics. So I landed the role. I took it very seriously. I bought a copy of Labour's manifesto from the newsagent's and contacted my nearest Labour Party office in Romford, which I often passed on the bus home, to see if they had any materials they could spare for my campaign.

When I arrived at their office after school one afternoon, to my surprise, I was greeted by the parliamentary candidate, Eileen Gordon, with her short grey hair and large, round, thick-rimmed glasses. She was warm, welcoming, and so generous with her time. She seemed much more down to earth than the politicians I had seen on the television. She looked and spoke like a normal woman from Romford. I couldn't believe she was spending her own precious time talking to me. I was just a schoolkid. She gathered a selection of leaflets, stickers and a red Labour rosette for me to wear. As I found space for the haul inside my already pretty crammed schoolbag, she asked me how my campaign was going, and I proceeded to provide her with more detail about the intricacies of my campaign and pitch than her polite question had invited. I asked Eileen if she was going to win, and she laughed. 'Oh no! I won't win here; Romford is true blue,' she said, but her obvious enthusiasm and good spirits were motivated by a belief that, while she wouldn't win, Labour was heading for government.

She was only half right. On 1 May 1997, voters in Romford went to the polls and elected Eileen Gordon as their Labour MP. Tony Blair had swept in as prime minister, but Westminster City went to the polls and elected a boy called David Dean as the Official Monster Raving Loony Party candidate. I came a close second, which was a respectable result I thought, but my challenge to pupils to imagine what kind of future they would have with a New Labour government delivering homework clubs at Premier League football grounds, and increasing state spending on education as a share of the national income, failed to inspire the masses in great enough numbers. I was one of the only Labour candidates in Britain who was not elected on that day. The mock election might not have been a winning moment for me, but it was the moment that I knew I wanted to become an elected politician one day.

I also found myself in trouble when I arrived home from school. Before I left that morning, I had plastered the upstairs windows of our living room in the pub with huge Vote Labour posters, which would have caught the eye of anyone driving around the busy Roneo Corner junction. Dad worked such long hours that he didn't see them before heading downstairs to work. It wasn't until later when one of his regulars said with surprise, 'I didn't know you were a Labour man, Mark?' that my publicity stunt came to his attention. I'm not sure what made him more angry: that I had broken the brewery's rules about political campaigning or that his customers thought he voted Labour!

*

The commute from Dad's pub almost rivalled the hellish journey from Epping and back, so Dad eventually asked if I should consider going to another school closer to home.

It took about an hour and a quarter each way, which I spent either reading a book or hastily finishing some homework. The monthly Travelcard was expensive for Dad and added to an already growing list of reasons for me to leave Westminster

City. Given the Ofsted report, it was hard to argue that the time and expense were worth the trouble. On top of that, I was still facing an almost daily onslaught of verbal and physical abuse at the hands of bullies who seemed to just despise my existence.

Dad wasn't keen to disrupt my schooling, but if there was a time to leave Westminster City, the end of year nine was it. I could make a fresh start at a new school at the same time as starting my GCSEs. But for all its shortcomings, and despite the chaos and the frequent abuse, when it came down to it, I realised I couldn't face leaving.

I didn't want to leave my teachers. Despite the Ofsted conclusions, I was really lucky throughout my time there, that I had teachers who supported me through the ups and downs of my home life and were genuinely invested in my future. To Dad's credit, and despite the financial pressures, he understood and respected that the school had given me stability during times of turbulence at home.

One of the teachers who supported me was Mr Latimer. He was my English teacher for just one year in year eight, but he made a lasting impression on me. A short, thin man with round wire spectacles, he had an air of formality about him. To us, he sounded posh, but his accent was simply middle class. At first it made him seem uptight, and I wondered if my class might judge him to be a pushover and run riot. But he managed to capture our attention and earn our respect. He was engaged, passionate and insightful, but the most powerful lesson he taught me was about the world of work. For one of our homework assignments, he asked us to find a job advert in a newspaper and to bring it in to discuss.

It led to a conversation about qualifications, salaries, and our ambitions. Mr Latimer told us that if we wanted to go to university and get a good job and be taken seriously, we would need to change the way we spoke and how we presented ourselves. He took umbrage with those in the class who wore their ties two or three inches short, or with the top button undone. We had to look the part, he said. I took the lesson to heart. My cockney accent is still there and usually emerges after a few pints or in the company of my family, but day-to-day, my accent is not the same as it was when I was at St Peter's, or even in the earlier years of Westminster City. Much as we might argue we shouldn't have to change, Mr Latimer's lesson was invaluable career advice to working-class boys like us. The truth was that we would be judged by what we looked or sounded like, whether we liked it or not. We had to be prepared to confront the world as it was, not as we might wish it to be.

I knew I really wanted to do something with my life, even if I didn't always know what that was. I hadn't formed any ambitions until one conversation with Luke during a break in the canteen. 'I think I'm going to go to university!' he exclaimed before asking: 'Are you?' He had put me on the spot. I hadn't even given it the first thought – aside from my teachers, I hadn't met anyone who had gone to uni. 'Yes,' I replied confidently, though not wanting to give the game away. Luke declared, 'I'm going to Oxford or Cambridge because they're the best. Where will you go?' I didn't know any specific universities, but I was competitive enough to know the right answer to give: 'Well, that's where I'll go, too.'

My plan was set there and then, although I knew little, if anything, about the costs or practicalities of going to university. Nobody in my family had been. But my friendly competitiveness and rivalry with Luke served me well at school. We spurred each other on to do our best, even if our constant talking in class sometimes got us into trouble. Luke and I had been best friends since the age of five. We had learned together, played together, and argued together. I couldn't imagine going through the rest of school without him – and now, I was hoping, beyond that too.

*

While I was choosing to stay put at Westminster City, Mum was on the move again, from North London to the North of England. In March 1998, Pat bought a nice new four-bedroom house in a cul-de-sac on a new development in Walton-Le-Dale, on the outskirts of Preston. It was a big call for Mum. The move to Epping had been a disaster. This time she wasn't just moving; she was uprooting from the city she'd lived in her entire life. But, unlike the place in Epping, this was a lovely house, with a front and back garden and Mum, brothers and sister were moving in with Pat. They were finally going to be together as a family and make a life for themselves up there. My decision to live with Dad had made Mum's choice easier, as she didn't have to worry about uprooting me from school, but she was anxious about moving so far away from me, and I shared her concern. There would be no more regular weekend visits and the journey time would be quadrupled, but even so, I was pleased for her and for my younger siblings. Their quality of life would be infinitely better than in their council flat in Archway.

The weekend of Mum's big move arrived, and I travelled up to Preston to meet her with Pat in a van full of Mum's belongings. By the time we pulled up at the house, 200 miles and four hours later, it was pitch black and the night sky was full of stars. The frozen, clean air of the cloudless April night hit my lungs with a shock. It felt so alien to the dirty, toxic air of North London that we had left behind. Mum looked so happy, standing on the porch of her brand-new home. It was both fresh air and a fresh start for her.

Ironically, I saw more of Mum's side of the family after she left for Preston than I did before. Maybe it was because I knew I would have to make an effort to keep in touch or risk losing contact with people altogether. I was also making sure to visit Nanny Knott as often as possible. Her flat was a short walk from Bow Road station, on the same underground line as St James's Park, so I would stop off at least once a month, sometimes as often as once a week. There was a financial incentive too as Nanny Knott would often send me off with a few pounds in pocket money, but I also just loved going to see her. She would always have an update about the goings-on in our extended family and regale me with stories from her adventures over the years. On the top of her television cabinet was a series of family photographs in frames, one of which was of Nanny Knott on waterskis in her sixties or early seventies on a visit to our family in Australia. Age had caught up with her now, in her eighties, but she still had a sharp mind and an equally sharp wit.

I spent a lot of school holidays visiting my Aunt Amanda and my cousins in Watford. My cousin Ashley was a year younger than me and we had grown up together in the East

End before they'd made the move there. We had a shared love of indie music and Arsenal, going to Highbury in 1998, the year of the double, to have our photos taken with the Premier League and FA Cup trophies. And we were even allowed to venture down to the Brixton Academy together to see Embrace in concert, about a year later, which was my first gig. They were always good times.

Unfortunately, things were less happy at home in Hornchurch. Unbeknownst to me, Dad and Karen's relationship was under strain. Running the pub together was demanding and often meant they spent little time on their own together, which was painfully ironic, given that they both lived and worked under the same roof.

If there were arguments, Liam and I were shielded from them. This made the news that they were separating even harder to understand and accept. There had been no shouting, no recriminations, no signs that their relationship was broken. Perhaps if there had been, I might have been better prepared. As it was, as far as my brother and I were concerned, the end of their relationship came out of nowhere.

It seemed like a cruel twist of fate that, just as I had become used to 'normal' family life, the rug was being pulled from under me again. I still can't recall how they broke the news to me. Perhaps I blocked that moment out. Nanny and Grandad Hill recall coming to see us at that point, though, and how awful they felt listening to me bawling on the stairs as Dad told me that Karen would be moving back to their house on Digby Gardens in Dagenham with Liam. I don't remember any of it.

But I do remember packing the car and saying goodbye to Karen and my little brother. Perhaps that was the moment it felt real. It hurt me deeply. For years, Karen had been a second mum to me. I couldn't bear to watch her leave. I had been spared the pain of my parents' separation as a baby, only to have to go through it as a teenager. This time around, I was old enough to remember the heartache.

I wallowed so much in my own self-pity that I didn't pause to think how Dad must have felt. On top of dealing with the breakdown of his marriage and a grieving, hormonal teenager, he had to cope with running a busy pub single-handed. Without Karen, he was up at the crack of dawn to let the cleaner in, stock up, receive deliveries and do the banking, and was still there at the end of the night, shooing out lingering punters who stayed past last orders, cashing up the tills and locking up. After all that, he'd get five hours' sleep before he had to do it all over again.

It was a new challenge for Dad, but I found myself once again in an all-too-familiar situation – living with a single parent, alone.

CHAPTER TWELVE

The Great Escape

On one of many nights out in the sixth form.

NO ONE EVER warns you just how hard being a teenager really is. The raging hormones, changing bodies, outbreaks of spots. Being too young to do the things that you want to do but feeling too old or self-conscious to do the things you always loved doing as a kid. The only thing that makes the ordeal even worse than it needs to be is the ruthless way in which teenagers can almost sniff out the insecurities of their peers. To be different was to be vulnerable. I already stood out because I was a self-confessed swot. But I continued to wear the merit badges I earned at the end of each year with pride, even if this bred resentment and all the extra pushes, shoves and punches that came with being a 'geek'.

I find it hard to place myself back in the school shoes of the teenager I once was, trying to make sense of the contradictions I felt at the time. I loved going to school, but I spent so much of my time there feeling afraid that the bullies would turn their attention back to me. I wore my Arsenal shirt to school on non-uniform days like a suit of armour, hoping it would shield me from abuse, but proudly brandished a copy of Tony Blair's book, *New Britain: My Vision of a Young Country*, on the coach to and from games lessons in Mitcham, knowing that it would invite ridicule. In so many ways, I was desperate to fit in, but also refusing to conform.

Throughout my adolescence, I was trying to be 'normal'. To do so, I had to bury a huge secret. A secret I had never shared with anyone. I can't remember when I first realised I was gay. I remember having a poster of England's 1998 World Cup squad on my bedroom wall because of my crush on Michael Owen, as much as my support for the Three Lions, but every time I felt gay, I also felt afraid. Afraid of my feelings, afraid that I would be rejected by my family and friends, afraid that my life would be harder than it already was. No matter how well I did in school, no matter how many merit badges I won, the pride I felt about my achievements began to be eclipsed by the deep sense of shame about who I was. What I was.

Deep down, I knew there were plenty of people I could have confided in. Luke was one of them, not just because he was my best friend. Luke came out as gay when we were about fourteen. I can't remember precisely where we were or what he said. In any case, his story isn't mine to tell, but it was an extraordinary act of courage for him to tell me and I repaid his bravery with acceptance. It would have been the perfect opportunity to share my own secret. But if I couldn't come out to myself, how could I come out to anyone else?

I was terrified that accepting who I was would only add to the abuse I already suffered in school. After all, I had been hit with homophobic slurs since I was eleven – imagine the carnage if my bullies knew the truth. But my biggest fear was of going to hell. I was afraid of God. The God of the Old Testament, of fire and brimstone and eternal damnation. I understood traditional Christian teaching on homosexuality to mean that to be gay is to be sinful, that marriage is between a man and a woman. To accept myself would mean rejecting the faith that had been such an important part of my life and turning my back on the church that I had chosen in the face of scepticism, even opposition to my baptism, from my parents. Perhaps I was even more afraid that the church I had chosen might turn its back on me. This was a secret so dark that I didn't even dare to confess it in the safe space of the confession box.

But however much I tried to hide my sexuality, I couldn't change who I was. I was one of the sensitive kids, slightly camp and effeminate. I always had been. This was a hard character to play in an inner-city all-boys school, and I had the bruises to prove it. By the time I sat my GCSEs, I felt like I had survived, rather than thrived, at Westminster City.

My exam results, four A-stars, one A, four Bs and a D, were the best in the year group. But everyone immediately asks what the D was for. The answer: Information Technology.

You never forget a good teacher. My story is a testament to that. But you also never forget an absolutely abysmal one, either. And our GCSE IT teacher was, unfortunately, truly terrible – my D grade was among the best of the year.

The end of my GCSEs also marked the end of my time at school with Luke. I was staying on at Westminster City to do my A levels with the sixth form, but he was off to the prestigious BRIT School for performing arts, which has produced some of the biggest names in entertainment. He'd decided to translate his love of drama and production into a professional career. I remained determined to continue onto A levels and then go to a top university. It's ironic in a way. I had never even considered Oxbridge until Luke had mentioned it all those years ago in the canteen. Now I was sticking to a course he'd inspired, and he was branching out to do something else entirely.

It was a bitter-sweet moment. I was so proud of Luke for winning a place there to study for a course in production. He was making a break for a highly competitive industry, but it would be the first time in twelve years that I would walk into a classroom without my best friend there waiting for me. From the very first moment I arrived at St Peter's and sat nervously on the carpet to the moment that we collected our results together, we had been inseparable. We'd supported and encouraged each other, fallen out and made up more times than I care to remember.

We've kept in touch over the years since. I visited Luke at BRIT School a couple of times to see some of the productions he was involved in, but as well as growing up, we've also inevitably grown apart. But I treasure the friendship we had during those formative twelve years, which did so much to help shape the person I am.

Luke wasn't the only one who made it after Westminster City, thanks in no small part to Mr Nash's drama club. That drama club really was remarkable. It wasn't just the plays and performances that laid the foundations for our success, it was Mr Nash himself. Although he left Westminster City in 1998, his legacy was secure as far as we were concerned. We were his success stories: his pupils, and his protégés. He saw potential in us that we didn't always see in ourselves, and my life is so much better for it.

I had hoped to spend the summer in between my GCSEs and A levels decompressing, relaxing and enjoying the sunshine of the London summer. I should have known Dad would have other ideas. 'Why don't you get yourself a summer job and earn yourself some money?' came his helpful and unwelcome suggestion while I was sprawled out on the sofa in front of the telly.

I tried to placate Dad with vague assurances that I would think about getting a job, but he wasn't convinced: 'Don't think I'm going to keep on paying for you; you've got to learn to earn your own way,' he said, in a more than usually stern tone of voice. This was straight out of the Streeting school of parenting. Dad, Grandad, and Great-Grandad were hardworking men – I wasn't going to get away with what Dad considered to be bone idleness.

Dad led by example. When he finally concluded that running a family-sized pub alone was too much, he handed in his notice and took on two casual jobs working on a building site during the day and driving a minicab at night until he landed a full-time permanent job as a car salesman with a local Nissan dealership. It was hard work for a few months, and I was worried about his long days doing back-breaking work on a building site. But one of the many things I respect about Dad is that he has always worked hard to provide for his family.

After I started my A levels, Dad found us a two-bedroom flat in the ground-floor conversion of a house in Upminster Bridge and we moved from The Crown. It wasn't much to look at, but with two bedrooms, a small kitchen that could just about fit the two of us simultaneously, and a living room that could fit the two sofas we'd had at the pub, it would do. The District Line to school from Upminster Bridge station, just a ten-minute walk from where we lived, took about the same as the commute from the pub.

Dad knew me well enough to know that I hadn't yet adopted the same work ethic that he possessed. Guessing that I wasn't putting as much effort into looking for a job of my own, he arrived home one evening with an application form for McDonald's, who were hiring for their two branches in Romford's shopping centre. I told him, with an unenthusiastic teenage grumble, that I would fill out the form and hand it in the next day, but he was having none of it. It was as though he could read my mind and see the plan I had already hatched to shred the form and claim I hadn't heard anything back from them. He made me fill out the application form in front of him, and he handed it in on his way to work the next day.

After a straightforward interview, I got the job at the McDonald's branch opposite Romford train station. I was a fully fledged crew member, complete with the brown uniform and baseball hat. They gave me full-time hours over the summer and then a weekend job when I joined the sixth form at Westminster City. The pay wasn't great – at about £3 per hour – but I got a free meal on my shift and had some money coming in, which gave me more freedom. I had the money to go out whenever I liked, and I could buy the clothes that I wanted – a godsend when it came to starting sixth form, which was uniform-free. Up until I could afford to buy my own clothes, I was relieved that I went to a school with a uniform. The cost wasn't easy for my parents, but it spared me the humiliation of not having the latest trainers, flashy clothes or the best dress sense. It was a social leveller.

Sixth form was a completely different experience from my first five years at Westminster City. It wasn't just the novelty of free periods without lessons or wearing our own clothes; it was that all of us had chosen to be there. The disruptive kids were gone, which meant that the bullying was over. I felt as if I had more space to be myself. I was loving learning and loving life, even if I was still hiding who I really was.

To my surprise, as much as anyone else's, I found myself going on dates with a couple of girls in the sixth form at Grey Coat. These never evolved into more serious relationships – my self-denial only took me so far – but my new-found dating life did seem to dispel any lingering questions over my sexuality from my classmates.

On Mr Nash's advice, I'd taken up three A Levels in English Literature, History, and Politics, but after a few weeks of hearing good reviews of the Religious Studies course, I opted to take it up as a fourth subject, having achieved a top grade at GCSE. But undertaking four A levels lasted all of a term, until

I decided that it was an unnecessary commitment and I was better off concentrating on three.

So, I dropped English Literature. Although it had always been my strongest subject, I wasn't enjoying it as much as I used to. When a class theatre trip was planned, which came at a cost of money I didn't have, it seemed like the right moment to call it quits. Unfortunately, this would mean telling Ms Soto, my English teacher for more than three years, that her star pupil was dropping out. Ms Soto wasn't just my English teacher, she was one of the very best teachers I'd ever had. She took my home-grown love of reading and turned it into a deeper love of English literature. Her classroom had been a sanctuary from the bullying over the years. We'd bonded over shared interests in drama, politics and even Star Trek. I knew I would be letting her down and she took it even worse than I had expected. She wasn't just disappointed; she was upset. She wasn't the only one. It took more than a term before the English department would speak to me again, but my mind was made up.

Our school always appointed a group of sixth formers as prefects, led by a head prefect and a team of deputy head prefects. There had been a widespread expectation that I would be appointed as head prefect, but to everyone's surprise, two of my good friends, Ben and Rachel, were appointed as joint head prefects, and I was made one of their deputies. I took the rejection badly, with a churlish sense of entitlement that probably justified my not getting the job. But what added injury to the perceived insult was an openly gay teacher telling me that he had heard one of the teachers justifying their decision in the staffroom on the grounds that

I was gay and wouldn't make a good role model for younger pupils.

It was a devastating blow. My worst fears about what being gay would mean for my future were confirmed. I was humiliated and hurt, but I was also completely enraged. I hadn't even admitted my sexuality to myself yet, and this was blatant discrimination. I had inherited Mum's defiant nature, so I wasn't going to stand for such an injustice. I wanted to know the truth of what they had said and decided to confront the teacher concerned in their office.

They reacted with shock to my account of what was alleged to have been said and strongly denied it. I would never know who was telling the truth, but as I left the office I was at least glad to have got it off my chest.

But the experience deepened my self-denial. I smothered the truth, but I was suffocating under the weight of my secret shame. I began to act up, searching for a release from the oppression of my own denial. I became more and more rebellious – partying, staying out late, slacking off. During year twelve, I found myself in more trouble than I had throughout my entire time at the school.

I'd made new friendships in the sixth form and enjoyed an underage pint – or several – on Friday nights at the Phoenix Pub on Palace Street. We soon progressed from pubs to clubs and from blagging our way into cheesy club nights playing 70s and 80s music to finding ourselves on the guest list for UK garage nights promoted by one of my friend's older brothers.

I also started to take days off to put in extra shifts at McDonald's to earn more money so I could go out more at weekends. I stopped handing in essays on time and came up with a myriad of excuses as to why they were late. Because my grades were always high, I got away with it longer than I should have. It was only when Mr James complained in the staffroom that my work was slipping and I was missing deadlines that my other teachers also spotted a pattern. I was summoned in to see Mrs Meadows and my form teacher, Mr Lloyd, to explain myself. This time, I didn't make excuses. I admitted my work ethic was sliding and I wasn't motivated, although I didn't acknowledge why. I was placed on an internal suspension for two weeks. I had to report to school for registration in the morning, and then I was sent around the corner to the St James's Library on Victoria Street to produce all the essays I'd missed, handing in at least one each day.

Fortunately, the tedious monotony – and the mountain of work I had to catch up on – acted as a deterrent for any repeat behaviour. I also knew I couldn't afford to mess up at this late stage. Any formal disciplinary action or drop in my predicted grades might cost me university offers, so as the end of year twelve approached, my mind snapped back to focus on my next steps. There was no 'Bank of Mum and Dad' to fall back on, or any cosy internships available to me through family connections. I had to make my own success, and that meant knuckling down and working hard.

With the encouragement of my teachers, Mrs Meadows and Mr Lloyd, I applied to join a summer school at Cambridge University, which was run by an amazing charity called the Sutton Trust. Founded in 1997 by the educational philanthropist Sir Peter Lampl, the Sutton Trust aims to support more students from working-class and under-represented backgrounds to access elite universities. I hoped that this might be my route in. Private schools had so much experience in supporting students to apply to Oxbridge, with mock interviews, coaching, even dedicated Oxbridge tutors. I thought some experience with the Sutton Trust might level the playing field.

I had a fantastic week at the summer school. Here I was at Cambridge – the world's third-oldest surviving university. It was beyond my wildest expectations. The stunning architecture. Beautiful gardens in full bloom. Dons and students cycling down King's Parade on their bicycles. Even the library of the History faculty was stunning, with stacks of books on shelves arranged across two floors, and rows of desk space. It was bigger than any library I had ever seen, and this was just the History library!

Throughout the summer school, I stayed in first-year accommodation at Clare College. The course was structured like a typical week for History undergraduates: lectures in the morning from 9 am, activities in the afternoon, some reading and writing time, and an essay due by the end of the week, which was marked by a Cambridge don and reviewed in a one-to-one meeting. We were given experiences that were alien to the majority of us from working-class backgrounds, of sitting and dining in the grand surroundings of the college hall for a three-course meal, punting down the River Cam, and taking in the grand surroundings of the university and its constituent colleges. I was in awe of the place, but I wasn't put off by feeling, at times, like a fish out of water in these unfamiliar surroundings. Maybe it was because the programme was full of working-class students or because of the inner voice that appeared asking, 'Why shouldn't this be open to people like me?' But the experience made me even more determined to win a place there.

At the end of the week, I sat down with Dr Polly O'Hanlon, a History fellow at Clare who also served as the admissions tutor. Her office was filled with books and papers on every wall, desk and table – exactly how I imagined a Cambridge don's office to be. The feedback on my essay on the rise of the Nazis in the 1930s was glowing. 'This is an undergraduate-quality essay and I think you should apply to Cambridge and to Clare,' she said, smiling. She was being sincere. Although I was used to positive feedback about my work at school, such a compliment from a Cambridge historian felt like real validation.

The Sutton Trust had done their job. I had arrived for the summer school in Cambridge already with the ambition to apply, but I left with the confidence to do it, knowing that I was good enough and that there were people like me who shared the same ambition.

Mrs Meadows had also encouraged me to apply to a summer school at RADA, the Royal Academy of Dramatic Art, which has produced some of the biggest names in stage, film and television. I won a place and was due to start almost immediately after the Sutton Trust summer school concluded. Unfortunately, I had arrived back from Cambridge with no money and I couldn't afford the fares from Upminster to Bloomsbury, let alone buy lunch every day. So instead of taking up the chance of a lifetime to spend a week at one of the world's most prestigious drama schools, I called in sick and spent the week earning extra money at McDonald's instead.

I think I always knew where I wanted to go after Westminster City, but looking back, I can't help but feel sad that I had missed such an amazing opportunity for the sake of a tube fare and lunch money. Sometimes, even when the opportunity is there, working-class kids are priced out.

With my heart set on Cambridge, I had to turn my mind to the application. The party lifestyle was put on hold as I spent my evenings surrounded by university prospectuses in the evening. I abandoned my previous plans to study Politics and decided to go for a range of History courses instead.

Mrs Meadows was delighted with the feedback I had received from Dr O'Hanlon and insisted I apply to Clare. My only hesitation was that I'd discovered the Clare College bar would be closed for refurbishment during my time at university. That was a deal-breaker.

A chance encounter at the school entrance with the chair of governors provided me with the alternative I was looking for. I had first met Lisa Jardine during the campaign to save Mr James. I knew that she was a professor at Queen Mary, University of London, but I had no idea just how pre-eminent a historian she was. To me, she was a warm, kind and generous leader of our school. She was fiercely committed to improving our educational standards and had stepped up as chair of governors to help turn the ship around after the Ofsted special measures were introduced. She had followed my progress with interest since then and was enthusiastic about my experience with the Sutton Trust.

'You must apply to Selwyn,' she said. 'My good friend John Morrill is there. He's a historian and vice master of the college. It is brilliant for History and right next door to the History faculty. You'll be happy there. Send me your application before you send it in,' she insisted.

I took Lisa Jardine up on her offer. I trusted her judgement. Cambridge required a separate statement and application form alongside the standard UCAS university application. Over a series of days and weeks, I drafted and redrafted my personal statements, sending each version across to Lisa and my old mentor Mr Nash, both of whom sent detailed feedback until we were all happy it was perfect.

A few weeks after my application had been sent, I received a letter from Selwyn inviting me for an interview. Suddenly, this all seemed very real. I knew my future was riding on how well I did, and the anxious countdown towards the big day began. The school arranged a mock interview with a careers advisor from the local authority, but they had no experience with Oxbridge interviews. Lisa Jardine came to the rescue again, spending time on the phone talking me through what they might ask and how I should conduct myself. Mr James also helped me prepare an essay for submission ahead of the interview, which he marked in his best handwriting. My part in the campaign to save him had paid dividends. He had taught me History from year nine through my GCSEs and would see me through my A levels. He turned my talent for History into a love for the subject. I may not have had the Oxbridge tuition provided by private schools, but between Lisa Jardine, Mr Nash and Mr James, I felt as if I had the best possible team fighting my corner.

In the days leading up to the interview, I felt sick with nerves. I was so terrified by the prospect of missing my train that I travelled up the night before and stayed opposite the college.

I had been filled with too many horror stories about Oxbridge interviews, like the tale, probably apocryphal, of a student who was told 'Surprise me' by their interviewer and chose to set fire to a newspaper in response.

Thankfully, if there was ever a time when Cambridge interview questions were designed to catch aspiring students out, it had long passed by the time I sat outside the study of the Selwyn admissions tutor. I was asked very general questions about why I wanted to study History at Selwyn, my academic achievements and my extra-curricular activities. No trick questions, and my hunch was that it had gone pretty well. Although as I left the interview, I worried afterwards that I had described myself as 'a politics junkie'. Was 'junkie' an acceptable phrase to be using in the mild-mannered company of a Cambridge don?

Then came the second round, which was a 'blind interview'. Candidates were given a piece of text with no attribution or context to analyse for discussion with the interviewer, who knew nothing about the applicant beyond their name. In this case, the interviewer was Professor John Morrill, Lisa Jardine's friend. If he had any idea who I was, he didn't let on. He was impressed that I was able to recognise the text as a speech given during Mrs Thatcher's premiership and could date it accurately because of a reference to the Department for Education and Science, which had since been renamed. Being a politics junkie was paying off.

In my final interview of the day, just as the daylight was giving way to dusk, I was quizzed on my essay by the director of studies in History at the college. It was the most challenging interview of the lot, without a doubt. I was grilled on my argument and stumped by his reference to 'gauleiters', regional officials in Nazi Germany, despite four years study-ing the Nazis. I thought I'd blown it.

The wait over Christmas was agonising. I was logging into my UCAS application several times a day just in case there were any updates, knowing full well I wouldn't hear anything until January.

Then, in the first week of the new year, a letter landed on the mat of Dad's flat in Upminster bearing the stamp of Selwyn College on the envelope. My hands were shaking as I picked it up. The envelope felt as though it had more than one sheet of paper in it, and I allowed myself to believe this was good news. I tore it open like a toddler with a Christmas present, and sure enough, there was a covering letter that began with congratulations on the offer of a place. I didn't read the rest of the letter – I was too busy jumping up and down, screaming with excitement. Sadly, no one was home to share my delight. Dad was at work. But I phoned him, Mum, Nanny Hill, Ray Rackham, Mr Nash, and Lisa Jardine to tell them the great news.

Mum and Dad were absolutely thrilled, although I was at pains to point out that an offer didn't guarantee a place unless I achieved straight As in my A levels. The mere offer of a university place, let alone one at Cambridge, was unprece-dented in our family and they were immensely proud. Mum wasted no time in broadcasting the news to the family as if I had already graduated, and Dad, though no less delighted, also underlined the importance of me knuckling down during my final months of study.

So I needed three A grades. I knew I could do it, but I had to put in the work.

In order to accept my place at Cambridge, I needed to return a number of forms including one from a parent agreeing to be a financial guarantor, committing to pay any tuition fees and bills that I couldn't. This was a formality, but one that really worried Dad. 'I'm not sure I can sign this,' he began. 'Are you sure you can afford it?' he asked, 'because I can't afford to pay if not. I just don't have the money.' I had a moment of panic. I had finally won a place at Cambridge but I risked falling at the first hurdle.

But I was soon able to explain to Dad that my tuition fees would be means-tested so I wouldn't have to pay, that I would receive a maintenance loan that would help me get by, and for extra cash, I would work alongside my studies as I had done with my A levels. By hook or by crook, I would do it.

My desperate plea was successful – Dad agreed to sign the form, apprehensively. I wondered how many other students who received Cambridge offers were having conversations like this. Not too many, I guessed.

As my A levels approached, so did the 2001 general election. I received a call from the local Labour Party. My local MP, John Cryer, was defending his marginal Hornchurch constituency from the Conservatives and they needed help. The Labour Party had sent a young organiser, Nadia Djilali, to get our dysfunctional and ageing local Labour Party into shape. I agreed to volunteer, and when I turned up, I brought the average age down by a few decades. I was one of the few local members who didn't regard Nadia as a 'Millbank Plant' sent by New Labour high command in Millbank Tower to give us our orders. I had only been a member for a couple of years, but even I could see the importance of having a well-organised campaign. I added knocking on doors and delivering leaflets to my list of weekly activities and did as much as I could around revision for my exams.

Polling day coincided with my first exam, the first of two History papers. I completed the first two questions with no problems, but when it came to choosing a third, my mind went blank. I panicked, sitting in the middle of the exam hall in a silent meltdown. 'You've blown it,' I was telling myself. 'You've blown your place at Cambridge.' This had never happened before. I had never panicked in an exam. After several agonising minutes, I pulled myself together, answered the question as best I could, left the hall and shared all my anxiety with friends at McDonald's, who suspected I was exaggerating.

I tried to put the horrible experience out of my mind as I got the tube back to Hornchurch and headed straight for John Cryer's campaign centre to help with the evening's 'get out the vote' campaign, calling constituents until 9.45 pm to make sure they had voted.

Nadia had invited me to the general election count. I arrived looking like a sore thumb. Everyone there was older than me and smartly dressed, whereas I had turned up in a green Ben Sherman jumper with a checked shirt underneath and a pair of jeans. I felt underdressed and a little embarrassed, but I was excited to be at my first election count in the vast hall of the local sports centre, filled with trestle tables staffed by counting officials. This was democracy in action, and I greeted it with all the exhilaration of being at a Cup Final match. The reality was sadly much duller as the long hours of waiting clicked by.

My job was to tally Labour and Conservative votes so the data could be fed back to Labour's election headquarters in Millbank Tower, giving them a sense of what was happening.

The news was mixed. Our hard work for John Cryer had paid off, and he kept his seat, albeit with a reduced majority. But the other Labour MPs, Keith Darvill in Upminster, and Eileen Gordon in Romford had lost their seats. So it was a bitter-sweet moment for Labour in our part of the world.

Over the weekend that followed, I fell into a deep depression. I thought I had already blown my A level in History and that my dream of a Cambridge education was gone. I was in floods of tears and felt even worse knowing that my emotional state was making it even less likely that I would do well in the exams still to come. Finally, Dad gave me the pep talk I needed to pull myself together. There was nothing I could do about my first exam, but there were still five to go. He was right, and I put all my focus and energy into my remaining exams.

Fortunately, the rest of the papers went well. But when they were out of the way, the waiting game began. I had started a job at the electrical retailers Comet, and I put in full-time hours there during the summer, which was a welcome distraction from my worrying. Plus, I was going to need the money for a holiday I had booked in Crete with school friends.

I was also going to need the money for university. My student finance application had been returned and declared that Dad's means-tested contribution to my tuition fees was £700 a year. Dad and I were shocked. He was a single parent on a car salesman's salary, which wasn't much. The Student Loans Company might have decided that Dad could afford £700, but reality said otherwise. Some hasty calculations with my student loan and interest-free overdraft persuaded me that I could still afford to go to university, but it was going to be tough, as I would need to pay the tuition fees myself. This felt terribly unfair, and my previous sympathy for the New Labour government's argument for means-testing fees disappeared. I thought the test meant that other families would pay, not families like mine.

When results day finally arrived, I was nursing a hangover from a party and sleepover we had at a friend's house the night before. With some sore heads, we made our way into school together on the tube. I was both desperate for my results and terrified of what they might bring.

I walked into the school library where Mrs Meadows and Mr Lloyd were sitting looking solemn. 'Well,' Mrs Meadows began hesitantly, 'you got an A in RS', she said, placing the results slip from the exam board down on the table. No surprises there. As the second slip was placed down, I braced myself for terrible news, but Mrs Meadows yelled, 'YOU GOT THREE As!' I leapt out of my chair, jumping up and down with relief, hugging them both, saying thank you over and over again.

I'd done it. Despite all the trials and tribulations of Westminster City and the turbulence at home, I had made it. I was sure that Cambridge would change my life. After years of seeing my parents struggle, I was convinced that this was the turning point in my life. This was going to be my great escape.

CHAPTER THIRTEEN

Going Up and Coming Out

Leading a student protest in Cambridge, 2004.

ONE OF THE oddities about Cambridge is that, wherever you're travelling from, when you're going to university for the start of term, you're always 'going up', and when you're leaving at the end of term, you're always 'going down'. I was going to have to get used to the strange nomenclature of my weird and wonderful new surroundings.

I had been preparing for my new life for weeks. A-level results day was in mid-August, but the Cambridge term doesn't start until the beginning of October each year. After a week of partying and lounging around on the beach in Crete, alongside countless other British school leavers, I had put in as many hours at Comet as I could and I started buying the essentials that I would need for my student halls.

All of it was now packed into Dad's overloaded car as we travelled up the M11 with Mum, who had made the trip to London from Preston to see me off. I know it was a big moment for them as well as me. Not only was I the first in the family to go to university, but it was also one of those rare days in my life when the three of us spent time together.

As we walked through the grand archway, the college looked beautiful in the warmth of the sunshine. The red brick of the building was complemented by the autumnal reds, oranges and yellows of the leaves on the trees outside. I had seen Selwyn already, but the sight of my new home was no less breathtaking to me than to my parents, seeing it for the first time. 'Nanny and Grandad would be so proud of you,' Mum said, beaming.

I swallowed the lump in my throat. My only sadness was that Nanny Libby and Grandad Streeting weren't there to see me too. I knew all my grandparents were proud of me – Nanny and Grandad Hill, and especially Grandad Pops. He was almost moved to tears when I told him. I could hear it in his voice when I'd phoned to tell him my results. 'I always knew you'd make it, Wes,' he said, his voice shaking. He would often say to me when I was growing up, 'If I had the money, I'd send you to Eton,' so it is probably fortunate, given his line of work, that he didn't try to go out and get it! As it turned out, St Peter's and Westminster City had seen me all right in the end.

Selwyn College is one of thirty-one constituent colleges of the University of Cambridge and first began to admit students in 1882. So it was relatively modern in the university's 800 years of history, but the pretty red brick and Ketton stone buildings of Selwyn's Old Court were just as regal and impressive as all the others to me.

It was obvious that Old Court was the centre of college life. There were students everywhere, bustling about. It was easy to spot the fellow first years, not just because they were flanked by proud parents. They all had the same slightly daunted expression on their faces as I did. Mum, Dad and I stepped through the grand archway into the court, where we were greeted by the magnificent college chapel, which stood proudly at the other end of the large, immaculately kept square lawn in the centre. To the right stood a building with a grand stone staircase that housed the college's hall, the senior common room for the fellows and bar for the students, and around the rest of the quad, a series of staircases leading to students' and fellows' accommodation. I had been to Selwyn twice before – to look around and then for my interview – but this was Mum and Dad's first time at Selwyn and their first visit to Cambridge. Mum was speechless and could hardly believe that this place would be my home for the next three years.

The first-year accommodation was in Cripps Court, where I had stayed the night before my interview. It was a fairly dull five-storey complex of 1960s student dorms organised around staircases across the road from Old Court. I had a standard room on the first floor with a single bed, a shelf, a built-in wardrobe and chest of drawers, with a desk and chair at the window.

We unloaded all my worldly belongings into the centre of the room. As I opened my welcome envelope, pamphlets and freebies came tumbling out, including a sexual-health pack containing an enormous pile of condoms. As if the sight of condoms and lubricant weren't embarrassing enough in front of my parents, there was a brightly coloured lesbian, gay and bisexual guide to the university too. I felt my face flush bright red. Did someone know? Had somebody said something? My stomach lurched before reason kicked back in. No one could have known my secret. This was something every first year received at the beginning of term.

Unpacking would have to wait because I could also see that there were a few essential items I still needed to get. There would be a matriculation ceremony on Monday morning, and the dress code was a lounge suit for men. I also needed an undergraduate gown for the occasion and for formal halls thereafter.

Matriculation. Gowns. Formal halls. This was all alien to me and required translation. Even the lounge suit raised questions. I had never owned a suit before. I had never needed one. Even at my grandparents' funerals, I had worn school trousers and a school shirt. I had no idea what a lounge suit was.

But I wasn't going to be intimidated; I was just in awe and soaking up every bit of my new surroundings. From that first day I've always felt there is something magical about Cambridge. I felt as if I was the luckiest person in the world to be included in all that history, tradition, and reputation for excellence.

I know it wasn't exactly the same story for Mum, however. She was so proud of me for going to Cambridge, but I know that whenever she came to visit over the years, she was always worried about being judged by others simply because she felt she always had been – for not doing well in school, for who her parents were, for being a young mother. Her visits over the years were the rare occasions when I saw her defiant nature slip.

Even though I was eighteen and about to start my new life at university, my parents hadn't yet escaped the ordeal of buying a new school uniform. We wandered into town to one of the robemakers in the city centre and then to Next, where my parents bought me a black suit, lilac shirt and purple tie, before going on their way. I knew they were still on a tight budget, so I really appreciated it and joked that at least this would be the last time they ever had to buy me a uniform. Mum seemed intent on an emotional goodbye as if we were never going to see each other again, and even Dad seemed to have something in his eye as he gave me a big hug and told me how proud he was. I didn't dwell too much on it at the time, but I know this was just as big an achievement for them as it was for me. All the hard work and sacrifices they had made over the years had paid off.

Now I could finally unpack, but it wasn't long before a knock came at the door. Others in my corridor were gathering in one of the larger rooms occupied by a girl called Sophie. She had already cracked open the gin at four in the afternoon. I could tell that we were going to get on like a house on fire.

Our eclectic mix of students all packed into the college bar that evening, feeling the same sense of excitement and apprehension about making friends with total strangers and trying to identify kindred spirits in the heaving throng of freshers.

It didn't take long for me to get into the swing of student life – rolling out of bed and into lectures, having dinner with my new friends, and frequenting Cindies, the main club in town. I was having a ball. Every day I spent at Cambridge, I felt so lucky to be there and I wanted to make the most of it.

Given my background – even my accent – whenever I tell people I went to Cambridge, the usual response is to ask whether I felt out of place or looked down upon. Occasionally, I marked myself out from the other students by wearing tracksuit bottoms as casual wear rather than for sports. But on the whole, I found Selwyn to be welcoming, friendly and inclusive.

I loved being part of a diverse student community, although I was shocked by the lack of ethnic diversity at Cambridge in the early 2000s. After attending primary and secondary schools in inner London, I missed it, but this was the first time in my life that I had ever encountered people who were privately educated. I had arrived with my own perceptions and stereo-types, perhaps even a hint of prejudice, about what they would be like: entitled, snobbish, conceited. I couldn't have been more wrong. The people I met, some of whom remain dear friends after all these years, were kind, down-to-earth, and full of the insecurities we all have about who we are, where we're going, how we'll fit in, whether we're 'doing life' right.

But I was aware that while every student earned their place at the university, some of us had overcome additional barri-ers to get there. It's like two athletes running the same course, but one of them facing hurdles to clear on the way. They may have run the same distance, but the one who cleared the hurdles is stronger for it.

There were a couple of occasions where my working-class background held me back. The Cambridge Union, not to be confused with the students' union, had a reputation as a prestigious debating society. It has played host to presidents and prime ministers, leading intellectuals and celebrities. Former presidents of the union include former Cabinet ministers like Kenneth Clarke, Michael Howard and Norman Lamont, the author Robert Harris, and the broadcaster Clare Balding. But at more than £100 for membership, it was far beyond my budget. The first time I set foot in the union to take part in a debate was after I graduated, when I was invited as a guest speaker in a debate on fair access to university. The irony was not lost on me.

The second time my class held me back was entirely self-inflicted. During my first week at Selwyn, I made my way down to the Kelsey Kerridge Sports Centre on the other side of town, where the students' union held their big freshers' fair – a showcase of every student-led sports club and society. Having been in every school play since the age of five, I immediately signed up to the mailing list for the Amateur Dramatics Club and the Footlights. The ADC is the oldest university dramatic society in England, and Footlights is the most famous for its comedy. Between them, they have produced some of the biggest names in acting and comedy, including Sir Ian McKellen, Emma Thompson, Rowan Atkinson and Stephen Fry.

I am almost ashamed to admit that I found their reputation intimidating and the fear of not measuring up overwhelming. Every term I would receive emails inviting auditions for new members, and every term, I bottled it. It is the only time I can recall being defeated on account of my class. Twenty years later I still I deeply regret missing out on something I'd loved doing so much.

The only other difference for me was when I returned home at the end of every term. For most of my friends, the university vacations were a break from the Cambridge pressure cooker, a chance to spend time with family, friends from home, or an opportunity for a well-deserved holiday. But for me, Cambridge always felt like the escape, and the journey home down the M11 was like landing back in the real world with a bump.

I worked as many hours at Comet as I could during vacations. Before I left for university, I had enquired about the possibility of transferring to their Cambridge branch, but the university strongly discouraged students from taking up part-time employment during term because of the intensity of the demands alongside education. This is a good idea in theory, but it assumes that students will be able to find work during the longer holidays, or not need to work at all. Luckily, my store manager at Comet in Romford, Emma Long, agreed to keep my job open full-time during the university vacation. It was a godsend. By the time my tuition fees, rent and food bill was deducted from my student loan, I was left with barely a hundred pounds for the whole term. Without those hours at Comet and the income it provided, I simply wouldn't have been able to afford my education.

While I had been at university, life had been moving on for Dad. He'd struck up a relationship with a woman called Joe-anne, who worked in accounts at the Nissan dealership where Dad worked. The first time I met Joe-anne, I could see why they were such a good match. She was warm, with a bright smile, and funny, with our sense of humour. She also had a young daughter named Georgia, who was about seven years old.

Dad and Joe-anne's relationship was so serious that, not long after I started university, they bought a house together in Chadwell Heath, about four miles from where we lived in Upminster Bridge. Chadwell Heath was less upmarket than Hornchurch and Upminster, but Dad had worked hard to get himself back on the housing ladder, and I was relieved to see him happy again with Joe-anne and it took no effort to build a rapport with Georgia, who was the same age as my brother Liam.

Our new home was a small two-and-a-half-bedroom house on a new-build development with a mix of shared ownership and housing association houses and flats. Since I was only a temporary resident, my bedroom was like a shoe box and a far cry from my en-suite room at Selwyn.

I avoided student politics when I started out at Cambridge as I wanted to enjoy student life and my studies, but was gradually pulled in. The Labour government's decision to replace the £1,000 up-front tuition fees with variable fees of £3,000 paid after graduation caused widespread student opposition. Having been saddled with a £700 bill for tuition fees that Dad couldn't afford, I was already unhappy with the system and worried about the risk of a slippery slope of rising student debt and the deterrent effect it might have on the poorest of us. So I joined a thousand others at the 'Big Noise' demonstration outside the Senate House, and then afterwards a meeting of the Cambridge University Students'

Union Council, where I found myself putting my hand up to volunteer for a vacancy on the CUSU Executive. I had been bitten by the political bug and was now secretary of the university's students' union.

It wasn't the only turning point in my student life. While I was on the CUSU Executive, I developed a crush on the Entertainments Officer. His name was Ed. Ed was tall, slim, with short, tousled brown hair and twinkling bright-blue eyes. He was handsome, even if his photo in the student newspaper revealed some dodgy blond highlights. Before long, we would find ourselves going for a pint together after meetings.

I was desperately confused and conflicted about how I was feeling until one night, it all came to a head. I'd bumped into Ed at Cindies. We were dancing together, getting drunk on shots and having a good time, until he suddenly announced he was going home. Despite my protestations, he left. Whether it was the alcohol, the undeniable attraction, or that I simply lost the will to keep on trying to be someone I wasn't, I sent him a text message: 'You're fit and I fancy you.' And who said romance is dead?! The moment I hit send, I felt my heart race. I had never told anyone how I felt about them before. Not a single soul. Now I had just told a boy at university that I liked him. Ed was openly gay, but it still felt like an enormous risk.

He replied mercifully quickly, suggesting we meet the next day, but I didn't trust myself to wait any longer. What if I woke up and decided to hide again? So I seized the moment and asked if I could see him immediately.

We met on Trinity Lane outside Clare College, in the shadow of King's College Chapel and the rear entrance to the

Old Schools. I could see Ed waiting and smiling as I approached. It was a freezing cold winter night, and I'm not sure if I was shivering with nerves or the biting cold as I walked towards him, reaching out to touch his soft, thick coat. We kissed, and it felt like the most natural thing in the world. Ed asked me how long I had felt like this. 'A while,' I replied shyly. He asked if I had ever told anyone. 'No,' came my embarrassed reply. So we said our goodbyes and agreed to meet the next day to give me time to see how I was feeling.

As I stumbled through the square court of Clare, happiness and relief were my chief emotions. But that was along with every other emotion that had kept me locked in the closet for so long. Guilt. Shame. And most of all, fear. The fear that I would lose friends and family. The fear that I was a bad Christian. The fear that I would be jeopardising my future career.

As I crossed Clare Bridge, tears flowed faster than the current of the river below. I knew I couldn't hide anymore. I was exhausted. There was no going back to being someone I wasn't.

The next morning, my head was pounding – from the booze as well as the tears. It took a few seconds to orientate myself and then it hit me. One of the most powerful feelings I had ever felt in my life: liberation.

I was smiling. I couldn't stop smiling. As I made my way over to the mirror on the wall of my pokey pyramid room at the top of the house, I started laughing. It was the uncontrollable laughter of relief. As I looked at my reflection, I finally recognised the person staring back at me.

Being gay isn't a choice, but I had spent so many years choosing not to be. I hadn't realised how truly exhausting it had been. I felt as if the weight of the world had lifted from my shoulders.

Having the courage to come out to myself had been the hardest part of the journey. Coming out to others proved relatively easy, not least thanks to Ed and my friends at Selwyn. But one by one, as I told people and word got around, I couldn't have wished for a better reaction.

That I was elected unopposed as the Selwyn JCR president weeks later underlined the point. To the extent anyone cared about my sexuality, it wasn't an issue. I was a fully fledged student politico by this point. The campaign against university top-up fees was building, and I wanted to play a more active part in it. So we continued to organise student stunts and protests and built towards the National Union of Students (NUS) national demonstration in London.

Aside from the demos, the politicking and drunken nights out with my mates, I spent most of the rest of my second year in a relationship with Ed. Although it lasted just seven months, twenty-five or so 'Cambridge weeks', the warmth and intensity made it one of the most meaningful relationships I have had. But when the year ended, so did Ed's time at Cambridge. As a finalist, he was moving to London to start a new career and, wisely, upon reflection, decided that keeping a relationship in Cambridge wouldn't allow him to make the fresh start he needed and would distract from my final year. As the last weeks of the year approached, the usual joy of the Cambridge summer, with May balls, end-of-year garden parties, and drinks out on the college grass, was tinged with sadness that a relationship with someone I loved was coming to an end.

Saying goodbye was hard but bottling up those feelings on the journey back home with Dad was even harder. I had been crying as I packed up my room that morning when Dad came to collect me. It wasn't just the end of term; it was the end of my first proper relationship. Perhaps I wouldn't have wanted to share a break-up with a girlfriend either, but I didn't have the freedom to choose whether to share that I had broken up with a boyfriend. While I had the courage to be myself at university, I hadn't yet found the courage to tell my family. As a result, going down from Cambridge meant going back into the closet.

The summer of my second year was turning out to be a disaster. When I phoned Comet before the end of term, I discovered my usual manager was on maternity leave and her replacement didn't want me back. So I started frantically applying for summer jobs, but it was too late. Nothing was available. I had no money and no prospects for earning any.

Thankfully, when Emma returned from maternity leave, she very much did want me back, but by then it was too little, too late. I picked up as many shifts as I could but arrived back at Selwyn for my final year as an under-funded politico. I also risked becoming an underqualified graduate. In my second year exams, I had achieved what was described to me as a 'bargain-basement 2:1'. I had spent too much time on demos or in the bar and not enough time in the libraries or the lecture theatre. I knew I had to take my final year more seriously.

I enjoyed the final year of my degree more than I had enjoyed the first two years of the course, mainly because I engaged with it more. But as much as I had told myself I was going to knuckle down and study hard, I just couldn't resist the pull of student politics. As my term as JCR president came to an end in December, I had my sights on the full-time sabbatical posts at CUSU. There was a widespread expectation that I would be a candidate for CUSU president, but competition would be fierce.

The election campaign was gruelling, even though the official period for it was only a week. One of my friends, Saba Arab, agreed to help run the campaign, but for the first few days we were on our own, printing manifestos and flyers and getting them up in as many places around the university as possible. By the end of the week, we'd recruited an army of volunteers who plastered posters everywhere, including the toilets, where we figured everyone headed at some point.

Fortunately, it worked. I was elected president of Cambridge University Students' Union by just twenty-two votes.

The distraction of student politics meant that I had fallen seriously behind with my studies again. The only way I was going to do better than a 2:2 was to spend the entire Easter holiday revising. After a word with my tutor at Selwyn, I made arrangements to stay in college over the Easter vacation, which meant forgoing precious income at Comet. But I used the holiday well, and by the time my finals came, I felt ready.

My exams finished relatively early. As I sat in the lecture theatre completing the last of my final exams, I let out a sigh of relief as the bell rang. No more exams. Ever. It was an amazing feeling and I felt pretty confident that I had done enough to secure the grade I wanted.

Sure enough, when the results were posted on the university's Senate House in the centre of Cambridge, I had done it. But in my final meeting with my Director of Studies, Dr Sewell was disappointed. 'When we saw you at your interview we had you down as one of the students who would deliver a first. I think you might have done it had you not spent so much time on student politics. I hope you feel it was worth it.' I think he even accused me of 'making a mockery of the system'.

At the time, I thought it was worth it. I had arrived in Cambridge determined to make the most of the student experience, and I had certainly done that, though on reflection, I could have done all those things and still applied myself more to my degree. Sorry, Dr Sewell!

Before I could graduate, there was the small matter of my college bill. The outstanding balance ran into thousands of pounds. Under the university's rules, unless I paid it, I would be unable to graduate, but without any holiday income, I was staring at the bottom of my student overdraft. The college refused to write off the debt, and my parents didn't have the money to lend. I was desperate. Fortunately, I was able to access a graduate loan from my bank because I had a job to go to, even though the salary was only around £11,000. It wasn't ideal, starting out with loans, but I had no other choice. And at least I had a good degree.

The sun shone gloriously on graduation day. Mum, Dad and Joe-anne were all there, Mum with my two-week-old baby brother, Brynley. In the new outfit she'd bought so as not to stand out against the other parents, all that stood out was how proud she was of her son. No one was made of money, so after a glass of fizz provided by the college, we wandered into town for a celebratory McDonald's. It wasn't the fancy feast that most Cambridge graduates tucked into, but it suited us to a T.

My Cambridge adventure wasn't over just yet. I had another year to look forward to as president of the students' union, but as I said goodbye to my friends, who were loading their cars and making their way off into the world, I realised that I had never experienced anything like my time at university and never would again.

CHAPTER FOURTEEN

Trying to Make a Difference

Leading an NUS demonstration, Trafalgar Square, 2006.

I WAS READY to get stuck into my new role and to make a change to the lives of students like me. Little did I know that my work with the students' union would help land me a dream job with one of the biggest student movements in the world: the National Union of Students (NUS). But it would be a steep learning curve, and require a lot of hard work and a year of struggling on a tiny CUSU salary to get to that point.

Education had changed my life, and I wanted to use my platform in the Cambridge students' union now to help others, especially to widen access to more working-class and under-represented students.

I also oversaw protests against the closure of the prestigious architecture school. Fighting hard to take on the uni bigwigs, our campaign was a huge success.

I was learning what big wins in politics felt like. Working with like-minded people to make an impact, getting stuck in and making a difference. I knew I was exactly where I wanted to be, doing exactly what I wanted to be doing.

And I must have been doing something right because it wasn't long before I realised I was on the radar of leading members of the NUS. It felt good to be noticed by an organisation whose goal is to ensure a quality education is available for everyone, regardless of their background or circumstances. NUS has often been seen as a training ground for aspiring Labour politicians and, looking at the cast list of former presidents, it's not hard to see why – with former Cabinet ministers Charles Clarke and Jack Straw among them.

But this was 2004, and New Labour was deeply unpopular with students, as it was with me, even as a lifelong Labour supporter. The Iraq War and the row about university top-up fees had broken the camel's back, and I resigned from the Labour Party in 2003. I found myself in direct opposition to the Labour government, and it seemed hypocritical to be a member any more.

The NUS held a conference every year during the Easter holidays when I worked so I had never attended one before. As president-elect of the students' union, I felt obliged to go as a delegate from CUSU, and I was astonished at what I saw.

The conference was a circus of student politics, with the grand ballroom of the Blackpool Winter Gardens providing the big top for all sorts of clowns. Revolutionary socialist groups were like that memorable scene from Monty Python's *Life of Brian*, where the Judean People's Front denounced the People's Front of Judea. In the middle of it all, some poor NUS executive committee member was in the chair acting as ringmaster, desperately trying to keep control of the rowdy conference floor, while delegate after delegate pompously raised points of order. It was the ultimate student hackfest.

Despite my hesitations to join, I found myself drawn further into it by a politics student named Henri Murison who was heavily involved in the Cambridge Labour Club. He appeared in the bar one evening and seemed determined to make it his mission to get me involved in Labour Students.

I began to see that I was not alone in the Labour Party in my views on Iraq and tuition fees, so I was persuaded by friends to get involved again. 'You've got to be in it to win it,' they'd say, and it proved to be good advice. Realistically, I was never going to be a Tory, and I wasn't a Liberal Democrat either.

So, my exit from the Labour Party was only brief. At Henri's suggestion, I tagged along to one of the Labour Students' caucuses. I was a sucker for a passionate campaign, and before I knew it, I was wearing a campaigning T-shirt for Rami Okasha, the Labour Students' candidate for NUS national president, and chanting, 'Go Rami, Go Rami, Go!' against the roar of activists for other candidates, in the bearpit of the NUS presidential hustings.

Unfortunately, the odds had been stacked against Rami by Tony Blair. The Labour government had scheduled a vote on tuition fees during the NUS conference, the day after his election. The timing couldn't have been worse, for Labour

Students or for NUS. Rami lost by just three votes and the whole conference, or at least the half of the conference who could be bothered, were loaded onto coaches in the middle of the night and driven down to Westminster for the final battle in the fight against higher tuition fees.

The vote in Parliament was a foregone conclusion. Although the Bill to introduce higher fees had scraped through its earlier stages in January by just five votes, many of the Labour rebels in the House of Commons had been bought off with concessions.

I had never sat in the visitors' gallery of the House of Commons before. But any excitement I might otherwise have felt at having first-hand view of democracy in action was outweighed by my anger at what was unfolding on the green benches below. But, like Alice following the White Rabbit into Wonderland, I had followed Henri Murison down the rabbit hole into Labour Students. My elected role as CUSU president would be coming to an end in July 2005, so as the next NUS conference approached that Easter, I was encouraged to stand for the National Executive Committee for the position of vice president for education. I was going to have to think hard about which side I was on here.

The Labour Students organisation remained deeply unpopular with those who feared that they were too close to the New Labour government, and with student union officers who hated that NUS was dominated by so many political factions and believed that politics should be kept out of it.

But, despite their shortcomings, I knew I was Labour and, thanks to Henri, I had got to know lots of the leading lights of Labour Students. Contrary to being terrible careerists, they struck me as people who really believed in working for change and proud to wear their politics on their sleeves. Plus, working for the NUS seemed like the perfect fit for me – not only was it a brilliant opportunity, but it would also be another chance to really make a difference.

There was another advantage to standing on a Labour Students' ticket. NUS elections were expensive. Labour Students paid for my leaflets, my T-shirts and 'Wes Streeting for VP Education' pencils. Not that this helped me much. I bombed in my first attempt at being elected as vice president for education.

The Labour Party had not been forgiven for its betrayal on student fees and Labour Students bore the brunt of it. Every Labour Students candidate for a full-time role was defeated, but I did get a big sympathy vote the next morning, topping the poll to be elected as a part-time member of the NUS National Executive Committee, the elected body of student representatives responsible for leading the union.

The part-time job with the committee was a gamble and arguably not one that I could afford. I was at the bottom of my overdraft every month at CUSU, I had a bank loan to repay on top of my student loan, and the NUS role came with an honorarium of just £270 a month after tax, plus some expenses. I could cut costs by living at home, relying on the goodwill of Dad and Joe-anne, but things would still be tight.

Dad was more than a bit puzzled when I told him that I would be moving back home at the end of my CUSU year to take up my NUS role. 'I don't understand how you've got a Cambridge University degree and ended up with a part-time job,' he said, not unreasonably.

I argued that this was a rare opportunity to gain experience that someone like me wouldn't normally have at such an early stage of my career. Where else would I have been lobbying Parliament, organising marches and demonstrations, or seen my words on the front page of the *Guardian* newspaper at the age of twenty-two?

Opportunities like this didn't come around often for people from backgrounds like mine. For me, it was a bit like the internships others take up to get into professions like banking, law, or journalism. They are far easier to access if you have the right connections and the backing of the Bank of Mum and Dad to compensate for the low or no pay. I'd managed to open my own doors to this job through CUSU, but I still lacked financial security. I was gambling on it paying off down the line.

So, rather than give it up, I got myself a second part-time job with Progress, a Labour-supporting think tank and magazine. It gave me an extra £500 a month after tax, which would help with the costs of roaming the country with NUS.

My second attempt to be elected as vice president for education was more successful than the first. A deal was struck: I, as part of Labour Students, would back Gemma Tumelty, the NUS national secretary, for the job of NUS president. In return, Gemma and her independent group of students' union officers would support my election. It worked – I won. Being elected as full-time vice president for education of NUS in April 2006 was a life-changing experience. It was a dream job, a perfect combination of both of my passions: education and politics. I was ecstatic. Although at £22,000, my salary was a lot lower than those of many of my friends from Cambridge, I found myself lobbying government ministers, sitting around the table with university vice-chancellors setting policy for the higher-education sector, and in the television and radio studios speaking up for students. It was only when Dad saw me on BBC News that he proudly said, 'I can finally see the point of what you're doing now,' with a big smile on his face.

My new role couldn't have come at a better time. Not only because I was broke, but because it was a welcome lift in spirits. Only two months before, my family had been shaken by the loss of our beloved Nanny Knott.

She had made it to the grand old age of ninety-six and died shortly before her ninety-seventh birthday. While it was hardly a shock, it came as a blow to her children, grandchildren, great-grandchildren, and great-great-grandchildren. She had been the glue that bound our family together and the focal point that kept every branch of our large extended family in touch.

Nanny Knott's funeral was held at a crematorium in Chelmsford. As with all funerals in our family, there were lots of tears, but lots of laughter, too. Mum always calls family funerals 'fun-for-alls' because they should be a celebration of life as much as mourning for our loss. My abiding memory of the service was that the huge congregation of well over a hundred people didn't appear to know the words of one of the hymns. 'You can tell that this isn't a God-fearing family,' I thought to myself, as I caught the eye of my cousin Ashley. We both started laughing. The sort of laughing that you know is entirely inappropriate at a funeral, much to the disapproval of the mourners around us. I knew that Nanny

Knott wouldn't have been offended. She wasn't religious anyway!

*

One of the things that saddened me most was that I couldn't really be myself at home. I felt comfortable being gay at work. The NUS, throughout its history, has been a pioneer for equality. It elected its first black president, Trevor Phillips, in 1978, long before most other organisations had ever had black leadership. It had campaigned for LGBT equality before it became the mainstream view. At home, though, I was still very much in the closet, and I thought I did a pretty good job at hiding my sexuality from my family. That was until one evening in the autumn of 2006.

I remember it vividly. I was lying on my bed, watching a DVD, when there was a knock on my bedroom door. It was Joe-anne. 'Can I talk to you?' she asked softly. There was something odd about her tone. Although I hadn't been around that much during my time in Cambridge, since moving back home after my year at CUSU, we had become close. Joe-anne was like a second mother to me. Easy to talk to. Fun to be around. Normally, there wasn't any hesitation or apprehension in her voice, but I could hear it now.

I sat up and nodded. 'Sure,' I replied, turning to face her as she stood in the doorway.

'While you were away, your dad was in here with your washing and knocked some papers off your desk,' she said quietly, walking into the bedroom and slowly closing the door so that we couldn't be overheard by Joe-anne's eleven-year-old daughter, Georgia, in her bedroom next door. 'One of them was a civil partnership invitation addressed to you and someone else.'

I didn't need to see my reflection in the bedroom mirror to know that I had turned a very telling shade of crimson. My heart was in my throat. I had been found out. That someone else was my boyfriend at the time, and the two of us had been invited to the wedding reception of Stephen Twigg, the former Labour MP, and his partner, Mark. The invitation made it glaringly obvious that we were a couple. And if she had had any doubt, I'm sure my reaction confirmed her suspicions.

I didn't know what to say. I felt such an overwhelming embarrassment.

I couldn't even make eye contact with my stepmum. All I could muster was a cautious 'Right . . .'

Joe-anne continued gently, 'Your Dad has put two and two together and I think he's made four . . .'

I repeated my dumbfounded, one-word reply: 'Right . . .'

An agonising silence filled the room, but only for a few seconds. Then Joe-anne said it: 'He's your boyfriend, isn't he?' There wasn't a hint of accusation in her voice, only care and sympathy.

I looked at her for the first time, sheepishly. I could feel my eyes beginning to water.

'Yes,' I confirmed, my voice almost breaking.

I had come out so many times since my first kiss with Ed on a side street in Cambridge. But one of the things I hadn't realised before I first came out is that it's not one singular event. It's a never-ending process.

'How's Dad?' I asked Joe-anne, fearing the answer.

'He's OK,' she said. 'He is confused. He is worried. He doesn't understand why you haven't told him, so I think you might need to give him some time. But we love you. We will always love you.'

That was all I needed to hear at that moment. Like so many other gay people who find themselves in the position of telling their parents or, as in my case, being found out by their parents, all we need to hear is that we are loved and accepted. Fear of rejection is the single biggest fear we have. Joe-anne left me to my thoughts. As soon as my bedroom door closed, I burst into tears and then quickly pulled myself together. My secret was out now. I could do nothing but wait anxiously for Dad to come home from work.

Coming out in Cambridge felt liberating. Being out in NUS felt wonderfully normal. Coming out at home felt terrifying.

I heard the front door go a short while later, followed by some hushed voices. I could hear Joe-anne's footsteps treading back up the stairs and into their bedroom. The house was silent, except for the sound of the television in the living room, where I knew Dad was waiting for me.

It was time to face the music.

When I entered the living room, Dad was sitting on the sofa staring at the television. He acknowledged me briefly and turned the television off. Silence filled the space vacated by the TV. I spoke first. I can't remember exactly what I said, but I do remember Dad's immediate reaction was sadness that I hadn't told him. He was full of questions. 'Why am I the last to know? Why did you think I wouldn't accept you? Are you happy?'

The answers were straightforward. I'd had long enough to imagine this moment. I hadn't told Dad because I was frightened of rejection. He wasn't the last to know; he was the first member of my family I had wanted to tell. I was worried he wouldn't accept me because, like most men his age, he'd made homophobic jokes in the past. I didn't think he was homophobic, but even the slightest bit of doubt made telling him a risk because of the fear of rejection.

The reference to homophobic jokes caught Dad off guard and he apologised almost immediately. He had no recollection of it and was taken aback that it had an impact on me.

The worries Dad had were ones shared by lots of parents, especially those who'd lived through the 1980s. Would my life be harder being gay? Would it affect my career? Would I catch HIV and AIDS?

He needed a few days to process it all. Of course he did. I sometimes feel that we can be a bit hard on our parents. Dad was born in 1965, at a time when homosexuality was illegal. Even after it was legalised, it remained taboo. As gay people, we all wish for those perfect coming-out stories where parents simply say, 'I love you and accept you and this doesn't change anything,' but life isn't like that. If I needed years to come to terms with being gay, I think Dad had earned a few days to work through how he felt.

I feel really lucky. I don't think Dad could have handled it better. It didn't take long for us to deal with any lingering awkwardness in our usual Streeting family way: with humour. I felt loved and accepted.

Telling Mum wasn't hard, either. Mum's family had always been accepting of diversity and difference. She was never going to judge me. I asked her not to tell my brothers and sister so that I could tell them myself, but that went straight out of the window as soon as she was off the phone. I was on MSN messenger at work, the noughties equivalent of WhatsApp on a desktop computer, telling my cousin Ashley, when he started giving me a blow-by-blow account in real time of Mum on the phone to my Aunt Amanda telling her the news. 'I've always wanted to be a trendy mum,' she said. Honestly, mothers. Who'd 'ave 'em?!

I'm so glad Dad found that invitation. It provided the catalyst that was needed for a conversation that was long overdue. I felt as if I was in a good place: free to be myself at home and loving my job at NUS.

As vice president for education, I was responsible for leading all of NUS's campaigns and advocacy work on education policy, from university admissions and course quality to student fees and finance. Alongside the newly elected NUS president, Gemma Tumelty, I developed a campaign to coincide with the introduction of the £3,000 tuition fees, called Admission:Impossible.

Complete with the *Mission: Impossible* branding, we organised a national demonstration that autumn in London. We worked and campaigned tirelessly, and within days of becoming prime minister in 2007, Gordon Brown announced an increase in student grants with an extra £400 million for student support. Gemma phoned me with the news and we were screaming with joy down the phone to each other. It felt as if we were finally making a real impact on students' lives.

I stood for election to be NUS national president on a platform to build a more 'representative and relevant NUS' and 'fighting for a fairer funding system' for students. I had the support of Gemma Tumelty, hundreds of student union officers, the Union of Jewish Students and, of course, Labour Students. Before I travelled up to Blackpool, I was due to return to Cambridge for a reunion dinner and to take part in the weird Cambridge tradition of receiving an honorary M.A. (Cantab.), which allows graduates to vote in elections for the chancellor of the university – not to be confused with a real masters degree!

Preparing for a big election and a graduation was stressful. As I packed my bags and made arrangements to travel to Cambridge, I received a call from Mum. She sounded panicked. Grandad Pops was in hospital. He had suffered a massive stroke and he was dying. 'You need to get here quickly to say goodbye,' she urged. I could hear in her voice that she had been crying. He was on the other side of London, at the Mayday Hospital in Croydon.

I managed to get as far as Liverpool Street when my mobile phone rang a second time. I was too late. He had slipped away and my chance to say goodbye had gone with him. I stood by the ticket barriers in shock, hot tears streaming down my face. I didn't know what to do. It was all too much. I felt under enormous pressure to get to Croydon, to get to Cambridge, and to get my speech ready for Blackpool, and all I could think about was Grandad Pops. I phoned Dad in a tearful panic – his rational thinking was exactly what I needed in that moment. 'Take a deep breath and do what you think is right,' Dad advised down the phone. 'You don't have to do anything you don't want to. People will understand,' he added.

I phoned Selwyn College to advise them that I wouldn't be able to make the graduation. I was gutted that I wouldn't see everyone, but it was the right thing to do, so I made my way down to Croydon. I arrived at the hospital to find Mum and my aunts, Eve and Amanda, waiting. They had been by his side during his final moments. We hugged and cried by his bedside, where his body lay, as if he were sleeping.

In some ways, his death came as a relief. He had struggled with breathing in his final weeks, and there was no telling how he might have suffered if he had survived for longer. He was no longer in pain.

His funeral took place a couple of weeks later, and, to everyone's amusement, it was a religious ceremony. The woman priest who led the ceremony struggled to hold back her own laughter as Vince, Grandad Pops' close friend and criminal associate, led a eulogy in which he gave a sanitised account of my grandfather's criminal misdemeanours. Still, if anyone needed us to pray for him as he met his maker, it was Grandad Pops.

He hadn't had an easy life, and he hadn't always led a good life, but he was a loving grandfather to me and I loved him in return. I would miss our debates and arguments. I wish I had spent more time asking him about his life and his crimes. I only visited him in prison once. I must have been about seven years old and I think he was in Wandsworth Prison at the time. I remember taking the train with my Mum and popping into a bakers on the way so that I could take some chocolate eclairs in for him. They were in a box tied with ribbon and they looked delicious. But when we arrived, the prison officers wouldn't let us take them in, which shouldn't have come as a surprise really. Still, I was devastated that I couldn't take him the treat I'd bought with my own pocket money.

I don't remember much of the visit besides the cake incident, only that I was surprised that Grandad Pops wasn't wearing a black-and-white striped uniform like prisoners did in cartoons. He was pleased to see us, and I was glad to see him, but I also remember how much I hated the experience. Our every move being watched by prison guards in a room full of other convicts and visitors, and the visit seemed to be over no sooner than it had started. I left there feeling sad about Grandad Pops' incarceration and decided that I didn't want to visit him there again.

I deeply regretted that I hadn't seen more of him as I got older. He was so proud that I'd made it to Cambridge, and I was sad that he didn't see me elected as NUS president just a few days after he died. He would have been even more thrilled to have seen me elected to Parliament, although I can almost hear him saying with his trademark wit, 'You work with even more crooks than I did!'

*

Being NUS president gave me an even bigger platform than my previous roles in student politics. I found myself on BBC Radio 4's *Today* programme, on the BBC and Sky News, writing opinion pieces in the *Guardian* and *The Times* and rubbing shoulders with the prime minister, Gordon Brown, who joked after the global financial crisis that, after my success in taking on HSBC, perhaps I should be brought in to deal with the rest of the banks. Earlier in my time with NUS, the bank announced that they planned to remove interest-free overdrafts as soon as students graduated, which could cost graduates, including me, hundreds of pounds a year. So, I set up a Facebook group called 'Stop the Great HSBC Rip Off!' which sought to mobilise students to protest and fight the bank's decision. Within days, thousands of students were signing up and sharing advice on how to switch bank accounts. It was incredible. But not long before the protest was due to happen, there was a phone call to NUS headquarters – HSBC were surrendering and wanted to talk! They wanted to make amends, so we asked for £300,000 to fund a ground-breaking piece of research into students' experiences at university. To their credit, they obliged, and fifteen years later, graduates still enjoy a grace period on their interest-free student overdrafts. I will say, it's one of my proudest achievements. It's what student politics should be about: organising collectively to make a real, practical difference. It's what all politics should be about.

My main impact as NUS president was almost accidental, and came five years after my term of office came to an end. As part of NUS' general election campaign, we launched a pledge for parliamentary candidates to sign that committed them to 'vote against any increase in tuition fees'. The pledge brought me into direct conflict with the Labour government, as many Labour candidates rebelled to sign my pledge against the urging of Peter Mandelson, Gordon Brown's de facto deputy prime minister, who was responsible for universities. A handful of Conservatives signed, and the Liberal Democrats signed up en masse. I had intended the pledge to cause a rebellion if Labour had been elected in 2010, hoping that the number of signatories would prevent any rise in fees. But the election resulted in a hung Parliament and the first coalition government since the Second World War. When the deputy prime minister, Nick Clegg, and other Lib Dem MPs broke their pledge to students, photographs they had taken with me and the NUS pledge in the House of Commons came back to haunt them in the 2015 general election with devastating electoral consequences. The Liberal Democrats lost forty-nine seats and were reduced to a rump of just eight MPs.

We may not have stopped higher tuition fees, but we nearly destroyed the Liberal Democrats. NUS had proven that breaking promises to students did not go unpunished. Students had power.

As well as making a difference to students in general, I also saw the transformational impact that NUS could have on individuals. There are many of us whose lives and careers have been transformed by our experience with NUS, but one stands out for me more than the rest.

I first met Hollie Williams at an NUS lobby of Parliament for students studying at further education colleges. She was a student at Worcester College of Technology. In the grand surroundings of the Central Lobby of the Houses of Parliament, with statues of former prime ministers and the patron saints of the nations of the United Kingdom looking down at the student campaigners assembled below, Hollie stood out in her bright red coat. She had long, thick auburn hair, green eyes almost hidden beneath her fringe and rosy pink cheeks. She wore that bright red coat almost like a shield. Before I had even spoken to her, it was obvious that she was painfully shy.

We exchanged a few words that day, and it wasn't until I was in Birmingham for an NUS conference that I finally got a glimpse through the window into the life she led. A mutual friend told me that Hollie's estranged father had been in a serious car accident up in Scotland and she didn't have enough money for a train ticket to get there. We had a whip round to raise the money for a train ticket and I offered to take Hollie up to Edinburgh. My boyfriend at the time was a student at Edinburgh University and she was welcome to stay in his spare room.

In between visits to her father, Hollie joined us on a Scottish Labour Students campaign bus around the central belt of Scotland, where we were campaigning in the Scottish parliamentary elections. She opened up about the life she was living. Her mother had died when she was young, and her father was nowhere to be seen. She had lived happily with her grandfather and her relationship with him made me think about my relationship with my own Grandad. Full of love and security. Unfortunately, he had fallen ill, and she became his carer in her early teens. When he died, she found herself living alone in his council flat in Hereford, just seventeen years old, living on benefits and trying to get herself an education.

I thought I'd had it tough at times, growing up, but Hollie's life had been way harder, and it was still full of hardships. Budgeting down to the last penny. Walking for more than an hour to and from college in all weathers because she couldn't afford public transport. But she was bright, and she had so much potential that everyone else could see except for her. I encouraged her to get more involved in NUS and Labour Students. Sometimes, perhaps, I pushed a little too hard. But she was successfully elected to the NUS executive and determined to go to university to study politics.

One of the powerful things about NUS is the networks it creates and the platform it gives its alumni. That was certainly true in Hollie's case. When she came to apply to university, she phoned me on the UCAS deadline day in floods of tears because she hadn't realised there was an application fee and she didn't have any money or family she could call upon. She felt she had fallen at the first hurdle. I paid her application fee and told her not to worry. When she won a place at Manchester Metropolitan University, she phoned me again in tears because she couldn't take up the place because she was required to pay a deposit for her first-year accommodation. This was a bit more expensive than a UCAS fee, but between me and my great friend Susan Nash, another Labour Student and NUS vice president, we put the money up for her and she paid us back during her first year. It brought to mind the way that our family looked out for each other in the East End. We never had much, but members of my family would hand over their last fiver if they felt that someone else needed it more. That's what families do for each other, or at least that's the way we were brought up back then.

Sometimes we do get to choose our family. Over the years, Hollie has become another little sister to me. The woman who left her council flat in Hereford to live in Manchester was unrecognisable as the girl in the red coat. I've watched her grow in confidence, happiness and security. She graduated successfully from university and started a career as a teacher before becoming a school business manager. I was proud to give her away on her wedding day, and now, happily married, she is living in Guernsey with her husband, where she works for a government agency. I wonder where she might have been had she not joined her college students' union?

Henry Kissinger famously said, 'The reason that university politics is so vicious is because the stakes are so small.' Student politics is often derided for being filled with young 'careerists' looking to climb the greasy pole into Westminster. Perhaps I am evidence for the prosecution, but I'm mounting the case for the defence: that student politics can be a force for good and an engine for social mobility. In my case, it had an even more powerful impact on my life and opportunities than a Cambridge University degree.

CHAPTER FIFTEEN

On the Move

With Labour Leader, Ed Miliband, and Cllr Jas Athwal, Ilford, 2014.

BY THE TIME my term as NUS president came to an end in June 2010, I'd had an experience like no other. It had taken me through the television and radio studios, through the corridors of power in Parliament and even through the famous black door of 10 Downing Street. I'd gained experience of leading an organisation of hundreds of staff and representing the interests of millions of people that few would have by the end of their careers, let alone a recent graduate and one who had grown up on a council estate at that.

I hoped that all this experience would stand me in good stead for a successful future, but that didn't change the reality of the present. I was twenty-seven, with a Cambridge degree and six years of unusual work experience under my belt. But I was completely broke. Even though I'd saved some money on rent by living at home, spending so much time travelling around the country, eating out on the road, and buying rounds on the NUS election trail meant that there was always more month than money left, whatever the time of year. On top of my student loan, I had clocked up £10,000 in a commercial loan and credit cards. I was worried about remaining trapped in debt and couldn't afford to take more financial risks. I needed to earn money to get myself out of debt and out of my parents' spare room.

I knew there would be some doors open to me as a former NUS president, like working for an MP, becoming a full-time trade union official or going to work for the Labour Party, which was now in opposition for the first time in thirteen years. I volunteered on David Miliband's campaign for the Labour Party leadership, helping to coordinate support from the youth and student sections of the party, but I wanted some wider experience outside politics.

I landed on my feet thanks to a contact in the local Labour Party, who introduced me to the government and public sector practice of PricewaterhouseCoopers (PwC) in the spring of 2010. During my time at Cambridge, I had attended a couple of careers talks and the world of management consultancy had never really appealed to me. But after an introductory coffee with one of the partners in PwC's education practice, it had a new appeal. This could be a great way of developing my interest in education and having a positive social impact, but in a private sector environment, building skills and experiences that I might take back into the public or voluntary sectors further down the track. It would also pay well and after six years of earning less than the average graduate starting salary, I was tired of being constantly worried about money and being in debt.

After a few rounds of conversations at different levels of the firm over a series of weeks and months and a literacy and numeracy test around May, I received a formal offer around June. I was going to join their consulting team, specialising in education, starting at the beginning of July 2010. I shared the news with my friends and colleagues at NUS, who were surprised. They imagined I would do something more political and didn't see me in a corporate environment. But I was walking straight from NUS into a job where my salary would double overnight. There would be more money coming in than going out. I could pay more than the minimum repayments on my loan and credit cards. I'd still be able to work around education, which remained my main passion.

I was ecstatic. It was more money than I had ever had and more money than either of my parents had ever earned, too. I felt as if I had financial security for the first time in my life.

My induction week was pretty surreal. I really felt as if I'd made it. Training days took place in swanky offices across the square mile of the City of London and Canary Wharf in London's Docklands. Those same Docklands Nanny Libby protested against back in the 1980s. It was ironic – I wondered what she would make of it all.

I was flitting between multimillion-pound buildings that were a stone's throw from the council estates I'd grown up on in Stepney. But this life, this career that was now mine, seemed a million miles away from where I had started. When

I was little, I could see the bright lights of the City from the top of our block of flats in Stepney, and I had never imagined myself there. Now, I could see Stepney from the skyscraper where we were training in Canary Wharf. I had gone up in the world, literally and metaphorically.

Like everyone else, I was nervous on my first day and keen to make a good first impression. I may have been suited and booted, but I still stood out like a sore thumb during the initial round of introductions between the new recruits. Everyone else had experience in accountancy or consulting. 'Former president of the National Union of Students' raised lots of eyebrows. Mine was not a conventional route into the firm, and this was never the career I had imagined for myself. But I was ready to leave my comfort zone and try something new.

As each day finished, I wasn't waiting around to make small talk, either. I was rushing straight for the tube and the train back to Chadwell Heath to knock on doors for the Labour Party to get our local council by-election candidate elected.

That candidate was me. So much for leaving politics behind for a new career in the City. My attempt to escape a political life for a while had failed before it had even started.

When the Labour Party put out a call for a candidate for a local council by-election a couple of weeks later, I thought it might be fate. I was immediately tempted. It would be a good way of keeping my toes in the political waters, although it would be a difficult election to win. Labour had only won it narrowly and unexpectedly in May – it had historically switched between the Liberal Democrats and the Conservatives. But, I had a lot of campaigning experience, and I knew I could get friends from Labour Students to join me.

The by-election took place in my first week at PwC, which made campaigning difficult. By day, I was undertaking my induction with other new recruits, and by night I was out canvassing voters.

On polling day, that Thursday, over a hundred volunteers were out during the day while I sat in the office, anxiously wondering how it was going. As soon as my work day ended at 4 pm, I ran straight to the tube station in Canary Wharf to head back to Chadwell Heath and the campaign centre.

The campaign was going well. The front page of the local paper, the *Ilford Recorder*, featured a large photograph of me with Harriet Harman, who was acting leader of the Labour Party following the resignation of Gordon Brown. She'd joined me on the campaign trail the week before and thrown her weight behind my campaign to ban the clamping of cars on South Road. All politics is local, after all!

In a close three-way fight against the Conservatives and Liberal Democrats, I won with 800 votes on a low turnout. Dad was with me at the count. It was a huge moment for us both – it was the first time he had ever voted for a Labour candidate! He was proud that his son had been elected as a local councillor, although he was keen to point out, to anyone that asked, 'I voted Streeting, not Labour.' Had Grandad Streeting still been alive, I suspect he would have expressed the same sentiment. I couldn't help but think of Nanny Libby and what she would have made of her grandson becoming a Labour councillor for Chadwell Ward in the London Borough of Redbridge. I felt proud to be carrying her political flame, and I have no doubt that she would have been proud of me.

Life was good. I had a new job, which more than paid the bills, and a new political outlet, which would feed my political habit.

Back at my day job, my unique NUS CV meant that I found myself in the unusual position of seeing my arrival as a 'former NUS president' at PwC circulated around the firm in their email bulletin to all staff with my photo. I even received an invitation to meet the chairman for coffee. I had started making acquaintances within the team and my career looked promising.

But one Friday afternoon, a few weeks into my new job, the phone rang. It was the compliance unit. They wanted to discuss the form I had sent in, registering my new position at Redbridge Council, as the firm's rules on outside interests required. 'There's a problem,' said the cold voice at the end of the line. 'The London Borough of Redbridge is an audit client. There's a conflict of interest here. You can't serve in this capacity for an audit client. It's against Audit Commission rules.' I froze while the stern instruction continued. 'You'll have to resign from Redbridge Council immediately.'

I put the phone down. My heart was pounding. What was I going to do? We'd already had a by-election in similar circumstances. I couldn't cause another, could I? But if I didn't stand down, would I be jobless and broke – again?

I explained the situation to the partners that had brought me into the firm as we sat in one of the side offices out of earshot from other staff in the open-plan set-up. They had never encountered a situation like this, and they were completely sympathetic, resolving to take up the issue and find a solution. The compliance unit was not so sympathetic. After a couple of weeks of wrangling, I was called in to meet with the partners again. There was little time wasted on small talk or polite formalities; I suppose they thought it was best to rip off the plaster. The news was bad: the Audit Commission rules were clear, and they required that the partners deliver an ultimatum: choose the firm or choose the council. They would give me some time to think it over, but – they added with an apology – they had to insist that I leave the office immediately and that I not return to the premises until I had made a decision.

As I walked out of the building that afternoon, I felt like a criminal. This all seemed so bizarre. Under local government rules, I would have to declare an interest and recuse myself from any decisions about our audit or auditor. There would be no conflict of interest. To their credit, the leadership of PwC raised my case with the Audit Commission to argue this point, but the Audit Commission was adamant that I had to choose.

Just when I thought I was set up for the future, just when I thought I was able to get my finances in order, I was back to that familiar feeling of having no money, again. If you've never experienced it, you are fortunate. It is a gripping fear, always worrying about the terrible consequences of direct debits bouncing, bills going unpaid, demand letters arriving and your credit rating sinking.

At least I was lucky enough to still have a home with Dad. As I sat there, contemplating my future, it took me next to no time to decide what the choice must be. Causing a by-election would be a breach of trust with the people who voted for me and an embarrassment the Labour Party would never forgive me for. So, I told my boss at PwC that I would have to resign. He understood, and the firm agreed to pay for an extra couple of months to help soften the financial blow, which was something, at least.

As soon as I got off the phone, I cancelled every non-essential direct debit, standing order and subscription I had. Until I had a new job, I would have to tighten my belt.

Thankfully, after a brief stint assisting with policy and writing material for Oona King who was running to be selected as the Labour candidate for the London Mayoralty, I managed to secure an interview for a job at a really special organisation.

The interview was at Bletchley Park, home of the codebreakers during the Second World War, and now a heritage museum and home to the Helena Kennedy Foundation.

The Helena Kennedy Foundation is a small charity named after the leading human rights lawyer supporting disadvantaged college leavers to access higher education. The trustees were recruiting for a new chief executive. It was a huge job – making sure the charity had a bright future, which meant tackling two years of deficits, as well as fundraising, and restructuring the mission of the charity, but it spoke directly to my own values and experiences and I was more than up for it. My only concern was that, at twenty-seven, I would be one of the youngest charity chief executives in the UK, so the recruiters might judge this too great a leap for me.

I talked it through with my friend and mentor, Matt Hyde, the Chief Executive of NUS. He put me in touch with Ann

Limb, the founder and chair of the charity. She said it would be competitive, but that I should go for it. She was waiting for me as I walked up the long path from the station to the mansion at Bletchley Park, where the charity was run from a small office.

The interview went well and within twenty-four hours I'd received the job offer from Ann over the phone. I was over the moon and hugely relieved. I had a permanent job again. My NUS experience was paying off.

I started a few weeks later. The students supported by the Helena Kennedy Foundation had some remarkable stories to tell. Mature students looking to achieve the potential that had been missed through their schooling. Ex-offenders seeking a fresh start. Victims of sexual abuse or domestic violence determined to break free of their ordeal. Lone parents wanting to provide a better future for their children. Refugees who had fled torture and persecution and were unable to access student finance while they were waiting for a decision on their asylum application.

Of course, I had first-hand experience of financial hardship and some of the students I met had experiences that reminded me of members of my own family, so I understood the kind of hurdles they were up against and was glad to help them with bursaries, mentoring and work placements wherever we could.

One of the things I've learned over the years is that professional networks are harder to build if you're from a working-class family. Even where we are able to build them, we are often reluctant to use them in a way that people from better-off backgrounds do. It's almost as if we view it as cheating.

But those born into more privileged backgrounds have a ready-made network of family and friends who provide advice, inspiration and connections almost by osmosis. I had now built, largely through NUS and Labour Students, a network of contacts that I could turn to time and again. It felt great to be in a position where I could give something back.

There was something powerful about the recognition the foundation provided to students who received a bursary award. Every student was invited to attend a special afternoon tea at the House of Lords to collect their certificates from Helena Kennedy. For some of them, it was the very first time that someone had told them they believed in them and their potential.

As a politician, I'm often told I've 'never had a proper job'. Putting to one side the fact that I worked at McDonald's and Comet and paid my own way through my A levels and university education, leading the foundation through two years of intense change felt a lot like running a small business, with lots of the same pressures. I had to worry about income generation, cash flow and whether we'd be able to run the payroll. Other people's livelihoods were dependent on my success or failure. When the charity had a rough patch, I took a pay cut, just as lots of business owners do.

With its finances back in good health, the charity would go from strength to strength supporting students, but I wasn't convinced that it could yet afford a full-time chief executive and I realised I just couldn't afford to carry on being paid for three days a week while doing a full-time job.

I started to cast around, and when Stonewall, the UK's leading gay equality charity, advertised for a new head of education to lead their programmes tackling prejudice-based bullying in schools. I was immediately interested. I could focus my energies on an issue close to my heart and with my own lived experience of homophobic abuse. Back in 2010, I'd had a tentative conversation with one of their directors, Ruth Hunt. Given the additional experience I'd now gained leading the Helena Kennedy Foundation, she encouraged me to apply,

I'd always admired the work Stonewall did to fight for the rights of the LGBT community, for people like me. It was formed in 1989 in response to a pernicious piece of Conservative Party legislation – Section 28 – which stated that local authorities should not 'promote the teaching in any maintained school of the acceptability of homosexuality as a pretended family relationship'.

Section 28 cast a long shadow over the education system and wasn't repealed until 2003. It had a chilling effect that stopped schools from acknowledging that gay people existed and from effectively tackling homophobic bullying. Kids like me suffered as a result. Words like 'that's so gay' or 'batty boy' were thrown around casually on a daily, sometimes hourly, basis without challenge at Westminster City. The failure to challenge homophobic bullying made it harder for me, and no doubt others, to feel safe in coming out.

Stonewall had been part of winning a whole series of land-mark breakthroughs for equality under the New Labour government: the end of Section 28, the end of the ban on gay people serving in the military, ending discrimination in the provision of goods and services, the introduction of same-sex civil partnerships and adoption rights. Those battles didn't just change laws, they changed hearts and minds, as the debate about these laws created more public discussion about acceptance and inclusion.

One of the things I was most struck by, as I visited secondary schools around the country during my time at Stonewall, was just how much the culture had changed since I was at school. Pupils would identify themselves openly as lesbian, gay, bisexual or trans in a way most of my generation never dared. With the support of their teachers, they were leading projects to tackle homophobic and other prejudice-based bullying. There were still big challenges. Stonewall research revealed that a majority of pupils who identified as LGBT experienced bullying, almost all heard homophobic language, and this impacted on their education and their own well-being. Things hadn't changed enough since similar taunts had kept me in the closet almost two decades earlier.

One of the best parts of my job was accompanying one of Stonewall's founders, Sir Ian McKellen, on school visits. Seeing this legend of screen and stage talking to pupils about his own experience as a gay actor and a pioneering champion for equality had a magic worthy of Gandalf himself. At the end of his assemblies, he would ask pupils if they knew why they had to work hard for exams. After leaving a dramatic pause, he would slip into his *Lord of the Rings* character and say, 'because if you don't . . . YOU SHALL NOT PASS!'

I can't even begin to imagine how I might have felt if I had seen someone as successful and well-loved as Ian coming into my school to tell me that it was OK to be gay. That you could lead a happy, fulfilled and successful life as an openly gay man.

I had to pinch myself as an adult that I was working with him. Sometimes, Ian and I would leave a school even more inspired than the pupils we left behind. At one school in Camden, a young Hijabi pupil told us why she had joined the school's anti-bullying club to tackle anti-LGBT prejudice. She said that, as a young Muslim woman, wearing a headscarf, she experienced prejudice and knew what it felt like and she didn't want her LGBT friends to go through it. She reconciled her religion's teachings on human sexuality with its teaching on how we should treat others. She told us that we don't all have to believe the same things to respect each other and that those of us who know what it means to experience prejudice have a special responsibility to stand with each other against all forms of hatred and bigotry. As I listened to her, I wished I could have recorded every word she said. Her words stayed with me. I use them regularly, and I have relayed them faithfully on this page. If this is what the future looks like, the kids are all right.

I arrived at Stonewall in 2012, just as the battle for same-sex marriage rights was building up. It was Stonewall at its best: waging a public-facing campaign urging politicians to 'Say I do to equal marriage' while at the same time working the phones and the tearooms of the Houses of Parliament to win over the waverers and see if compromise and consensus might be built to make sure that the ground-breaking Bill could navigate the House of Commons and the House of Lords.

The debate on equal marriage showed how much our country had changed on LGBT equality, but also how far our politics still had to go to catch up. The law was introduced by a Conservative-led government, in no small part thanks to their Liberal Democrat coalition partners, but a majority of Conservative MPs voted against it. It passed the elected MPs thanks to the votes of Labour MPs. Even more remarkably, it sailed through the historically more Conservative (and conservative) House of Lords. The unelected fuddy-duddies were more in tune with the voters than their elected counterparts.

The day it passed was a historic moment. Campaigners gathered opposite the House of Lords, serenaded by the London Gay Men's Chorus, waiting for the result. Success has many parents, and over the years, there has occasionally been an unedifying squabble over who made the difference. It was a huge number of activists, organisations and political leaders from across the political divide. It was politics at its best, making a real difference.

Alongside my more than full-time jobs, I was an elected councillor, which consumed at least two evenings a week, plus my Saturday morning advice surgery and going door to door to talk to local residents. Change was also afoot in Redbridge Town Hall. The twenty-six-strong Labour group of councillors elected in 2010 were divided, and dysfunctional. The divisions weren't political, but personality-based. It was turning into a complete shambles, and I knew something needed to be done.

I did not expect, however, that I would be a part of the solution. When a leadership challenge was mounted by another Labour councillor, Jas Athwal, I had initially declined to support him, even after we had gone for a walk in South Park and Jas had come to my aid after I was shat on by a passing bird, helping to get the damage out of my hair! But the Labour group had decided a change was needed and, to my surprise, Jas wanted me to be his deputy. We had to unite the group and aim to win in 2014.

After a vote of no-confidence was held in the previous leadership, we were elected uncontested. After just fifteen months as a councillor, I was deputy leader of the opposition.

My initial plan to build some life experience outside of Labour politics wasn't going well, but then life doesn't always go to plan. In politics, that's certainly true. Right place, right time can be just as important as the best-laid plans, and the best-laid plans can fall prey to events.

Life outside the office and the Town Hall was also good. Dad and Joe-anne had finally managed to get me to move out, although it took buying a house in the neighbouring borough to force the issue!

I rented a little one-bedroom flat around the corner from their house in Chadwell Heath. It came with some basic furnishing, which helped, as I didn't have any of my own. Dad and Joe-anne gave me their television as a moving present. I had finally flown the nest. For the first time in my life, I had my own place and freedom. The flat was on a new-build development, and the kitchen and living room were open plan, with barely enough room to swing a cat, but it suited me fine as a bachelor pad.

Life seemed to keep getting better and better. About six months after I moved, I met Joe Dancey. Well, it wasn't our first meeting. We'd occasionally said hello to each other over the years at Labour Party conferences, when I was representing NUS and Joe worked as a government special advisor to Valerie Amos, who served as Leader of the House of Lords. I had a bit of a crush. Joe was my type. Tall, dark hair, handsome and political. We had once shared a brief kiss on a friend's doorstep at the end of a long evening of drinking wine, but nothing had come of it.

It was London Pride 2011. I'd arrived late due to local councillor duties and caught my friends at the tail end of the parade, including Joe. We went off to a local Italian restaurant to get a late lunch and Joe and I sat opposite each other. We talked over wine and pizza, almost oblivious to the people around us, and continued in the best London Pride tradition: with cans of lager from the supermarket on the streets of Soho, which were filled with revellers.

It was all going so well until I announced that I had to leave. To go to a Take That concert. I know that reads like a tragic cliché, but a friend of mine had tickets and it had been arranged for months. I could see the disappointment cloud the twinkle in Joe's brown eyes. As we parted ways, I said we might come back into town from the Wembley Arena and meet them in Heaven, the famous gay club under the arches near Charing Cross station.

The beers continued to flow throughout the spectacular concert and the night felt young as we boarded the tube back into town. It was midnight by the time we arrived at Heaven, and the queue was hell. Of course it was. It was London Pride night. I thought we were looking at anywhere between half an hour to an hour to get in. I'd had enough and decided to bail, but then Joe appeared from the club. Someone had alerted him that I was planning to leave and he encouraged me to stay. It was all the encouragement I needed. Two hours later, I finally entered the club.

Absence had made our hearts grow fonder. In the packed, sweaty club, with the sticky floors pulling at our dancing feet, we kissed. Then we danced until the break of dawn. Leaving the club into the emerging light of the day, we shared another kiss at the top of Whitehall by Trafalgar Square as the sun came up, before going our separate ways.

I think I decided on our first date that Joe was a keeper. We went for lunch on London's Southbank and ordered a bottle of wine to lubricate the mildly awkward conversation. The sort of awkward conversation that reassures you that the other person likes you as much as you like them, but that doesn't quite set the nerves at rest. With our lunch finished, we went for a stroll along the river and got barely a few hundred yards before we stumbled upon an outdoor festival. Instead of another glass of wine, we opted for a bottle, sat on the grass, talking and laughing in the glorious sunshine of July.

We had so much in common. Joe had been a special advisor during Tony Blair's premiership, before going to work for Seb Coe at the heart of the London 2012 Olympic and Paralympic Games. We had a shared love for the Labour Party, a shared sense of humour, lots of mutual friends, and we enjoyed each other's company.

Joe also understood what I wanted to do and where I wanted to be. However much I loved my career outside politics, he knew I was a political animal and that politics was more than a part-time hobby. He knew what that meant and understood the choices ahead probably better than I did. Those choices were about to arrive sooner than I thought.

CHAPTER SIXTEEN

The End (and the Beginning)

The parliamentary candidate for Ilford North, 2015.

SO MUCH OF my life, and my family's, seems to have been unexpected. My nan surely didn't expect to marry a bank robber, end up cellmates with Christine Keeler, and give birth in prison. My nineteen-year-old mum's pregnancy was as unexpected as her decision to keep the baby. My traditional Tory dad and grandad surely wouldn't have expected their boy to be a Labour man. Not many people expect a kid born into poverty, who grew up in Tower Hamlets, to become a Cambridge graduate. A teenage Wes would never have expected to be finally at peace with who he was, and in a loving relationship with a fellow politics junkie. And I certainly didn't expect to put myself forward for Parliament at the age of thirty. I suppose by this point I should have learned to expect the unexpected, right?

I was enjoying my job and relishing the challenge of turning around Labour's fortunes on Redbridge Council, where we were aiming to win a majority for the first time in the borough's history.

My little flat in Chadwell Heath was in the safe Labour seat of Ilford South. Mike Gapes, my friend and the Labour MP since 1992, had no plans to retire, and I was in no hurry to become an MP, so it made sense to wait in the hope that I might be his successor.

But, as 2013 rolled on, I started to seriously consider putting myself forward to be the candidate in the neighbouring Ilford North, a suburban constituency on the London–Essex border. With a Conservative MP since 2005, defending a majority of 5,404, Ilford North was eighty-third on the 106-strong list of targets that Labour would need to win in order to put Ed Miliband in 10 Downing Street. I decided that, as deputy leader of the Labour group on Redbridge Council, with a good local profile, and as an experienced campaigner who could mobilise volunteers and money for the campaign, I stood the best chance of winning the seat for the Labour Party.

The people of Ilford North were also 'my sort of people'. Many of us had walked the same well-trodden path from the East End towards Essex, moving up and moving out of London in search of greener pastures. I understood and shared their values and their aspirations, and I believed that if anyone could win over previous Conservative voters in Ilford North, I could.

I decided to throw my hat into the ring. The selection contest would be tough. Unite the Union, at the time Labour's largest trade union affiliate, had a list of candidates they were determined to get selected. One of them was the chair of their London political committee, Mike Hedges, who was also a cabbie. At one point in its history, Ilford North was known as 'green badge valley' – home to the largest number of taxi drivers. Although he was from Islington, Mike thought that this connection gave him a good claim on the constituency nomination. An affable, decent man, his backing from Unite came with serious resources: well-designed glossy leaflets, slick videos, and high-profile endorsements, including visits to the constituency from former Mayor of London Ken Livingstone and the Unite General Secretary Len McCluskey.

Alongside Mike Hedges, who was proving to be a well-organised opponent already, other candidates were entering a crowded field. I needed to get my campaign in gear.

One of the biggest barriers in politics is money, and I didn't have any to spare. Although I was earning more money than I had ever had at Stonewall, I had no savings, a mountain of credit card debt, and large outgoings. I'd need three leaflets to be designed and printed to send to members, some note cards to leave messages when they were out, and enough postage to get at least one leaflet delivered by Royal Mail.

This is why we so often get MPs who are independently very wealthy or from a professional political background. Getting selected costs time and money that people in regular jobs or on modest or even middle incomes don't have. The selection process would take around two months to complete. I had a more-than-full-time job at Stonewall. When the application process opened for Ilford North on Friday, 29 August, I had been taken by surprise and hastily arranged to work from home so that I could get my application and first leaflet produced. I submitted my application two days later and on Monday morning went into work to negotiate some leave throughout September and October so that I could contact as many Labour members as possible. Under Ben Summerskill's leadership, Stonewall had fiercely guarded its party political neutrality, so alarm bells were ringing for them and I was grateful for the flexibility that Ruth and Ben afforded me. I knew that by putting myself forward for Parliament, I was making a choice that would have consequences for my future employment, but I equally knew this was a direction I had to take.

Running for selection was a big risk. In choosing to stand, I had sent a very clear signal about where I saw myself in a couple of years' time. I had chosen the Labour Party over my employer, just as I had with PwC. It was a gamble. I had to make sure it would pay off. Luckily, this is where the network I'd built up in NUS and Labour Students would come into its own. The call went out for money and volunteers to help. It felt like sending the Bat Signal into the Gotham City sky.

The call for help was answered. Donations of £10, £20, even £100 came in. That was the campaign materials paid for. Friends I hadn't seen for years gave up their time to call local members in phone banks organised by my friends. We had lift-off!

The thing that no one tells you about standing for selection to be a parliamentary candidate is just how hard a slog it really is. Unlike a general election campaign, where you're representing your party and a set of policies, in a selection campaign, you really must sell yourself. Every rejection feels deeply personal because in many respects it is. I spent hour after hour trying to get through to members. Responses varied from 'I'm too busy' to 'Please come to my house so that I can interrogate you for a couple of hours.' One member kept me talking for an hour on her doorstep in the pouring rain without an umbrella. I was soaked through to my skin, and my suit was so sodden that it was unsalvageable, even by the dry cleaner!

Everyone's hard work was paying off – I had secured the support of the majority of Labour Party branches and two trade unions and my campaign was building momentum. But this also meant that the pressure was mounting on me. In the final weeks of the campaign, I was told by friends in the party that my sexuality was being cited as a reason not to support me. No one had the guts to say it to my face and no one would have the guts to cite their own prejudice as a reason not to support me. It would always be cited as a more general concern about whether such a religious constituency would choose an openly gay MP to represent them in Parliament.

It hurt. Deeply. In that moment, I was taken right back to being seventeen years old, at school, hearing that a person I had trusted and respected believed I wouldn't be a good choice for head prefect just because I was gay. For all the progress that our country had made during my lifetime, most of which had been delivered by the Labour Party in government, bigotry was still a factor in a party that prided itself as the party of equality. I became anxious that this argument might take hold. If it did, people were very unlikely to say so. They were more likely to just quietly switch their support away on the day.

With Joe looking over my shoulder to make sure that I was doing my phone calls and ferrying me around the constituency in a hire car to go door-to-door talking to members, I became more anxious as the decision day loomed ever closer.

Two nights before the hustings and final vote, I cracked. I still hadn't written my speech. I suffered major writer's block and a crash in my confidence. I'd arranged for a few local members to turn up the following day so that I could practise my speech. What would they think when I turned up empty-handed? I needed a new suit to replace the one that had been trashed in the torrent of rain. I only had one other suit and it was suffering from constant wear on the campaign trail. It all became too much. Joe and I took a long walk at midnight in the streets around my flat to help clear my head and think about what I wanted to say.

The next morning we met at the Redbridge Institute for Adult Education for a dress rehearsal in the hall where the hustings would take place the following day. My friend Matthew arrived with a new navy suit from M&S, having been dispatched by Joe with my measurements that morning. I still had no speech, which generated glances of concern among those who assembled in the room. We opted to practise questions instead. The time was well spent. It got me in the right frame of mind, and, to Joe's amazement and mild frustration, we headed back to my office in the Town Hall, where I proceeded to bash out a draft speech from start to finish in one go.

D-day arrived. The candidates were assembled in a holding room, and one by one, we headed out to deliver our speeches and take questions. We couldn't see or hear each other's performances or the audience's reactions.

When my turn came, I walked in to applause and took to the podium. 'If I were sat where you are today, I'd be asking two questions,' I began. 'Who is best placed to beat Lee Scott? And why do they want to be the MP, not for any old constituency, but *here* for Ilford North?' Over the course of the campaign, I hoped that I'd convinced them that I was the answer.

The final question was a hostile one. The tension rose in the room as an older woman rose to put what she hoped would be a killer inquisition: 'You talk about your experience, but to me, you are just a boy. How can you claim to have the experience to be our MP?' I knew her to be a supporter of another candidate. But her query was almost word for word a question that Joe had thrown at me the previous day. My age had been the biggest hurdle I'd had to overcome with wavering members, so I knew exactly how to respond.

I was the youngest candidate. But I also had experience that few people my age had: senior leadership experience in the voluntary sector, media experience, campaigning experience, local government experience. Experience that few MPs have of growing up in poverty, of paying my way through university in retail jobs. I shared all this with the room before concluding with the story of a woman I had met who was a victim of domestic violence living in overcrowded accommodation with her children and being let down by the NHS. 'I don't know what it's like to live that woman's life. I haven't walked in her shoes. What matters is that I had the empathy to listen and the experience to be her advocate: with the council's housing department, with the police and the NHS. That's the experience I have, and that's why I'm ready to be your Member of Parliament.'

The audience erupted in applause. I returned to the holding room feeling confident. One of the endorsers for another candidate turned to her friend within earshot of my friend John and said, 'That's just swung my vote.'

The result was emphatic. As the votes were counted, it became clear that I was going to win on first preferences with more than fifty per cent of the vote. When the result was announced, it was eighty per cent. I'd won. The other candidates were gracious in defeat, and we made our way into the hall for the declaration to a big cheer and a team photograph behind the new parliamentary candidate for Ilford North.

The campaign had been gruelling, but the hard work was just beginning, and my world was about to be turned upside down.

When I returned to work, I sat down with Ben Summerskill and Ruth Hunt to discuss my future at Stonewall. 'How will you juggle your role here with your role on the council and the general election?' they asked. 'I can't,' I admitted. They were taken aback by my candour, but I'd come to the conclusion that it was impossible to be a senior manager in a national charity *and* the deputy leader of the Labour group with key elections to fight *and* a parliamentary candidate in a target seat. Something had to give. I'd known, ever since I first got involved in a mock election at Westminster City, that I wanted to be an elected politician one day. If that dream was to become a reality, I'd have to give up my job.

It was the right decision, but I was terrified. Just as I had justified getting into debt and earning less money at NUS, on the basis it was a once-in-a-lifetime opportunity, now I was leaving a good career and a steady income in the hope of some big breaks: into power locally in Redbridge and into Parliament at the general election.

*

The new year arrived, and with it, a harsh encounter with my new reality. After six weeks of talking to potential recruiters and applying for jobs, I discovered that being a parliamentary candidate makes you highly unemployable. Potential employers know full well that they won't be your number-one priority. My hopes of finding a three or four-day-a-week job were dashed. I decided to go freelance.

This was not an easy decision to make. Anyone with a background like mine will understand just how terrifying the concept of taking a job with no regular salary, or even guaranteed income, truly is.

Thankfully, I landed clients. Ironically, much of the work involved helping charities to open the door to the Conservative-Liberal Democrat coalition in government. For Magic Breakfast, a wonderful charity that tackles childhood hunger through primary-school breakfast clubs, I helped to formulate their campaign strategy and got their inspirational founder, Carmel McConnell, into Number 10 to make the case for government funding to David Cameron's senior advisors, which ultimately delivered millions of pounds into the programme. I also managed to persuade Downing Street to provide videos from David Cameron and Nick Clegg in support of a campaign by the British Youth Council to encourage young people to vote in the general election. For the Labour Party, I was tasked by then Shadow Education Secretary Tristram Hunt to write the party's policy on tackling anti-LGBT+ bullying in schools.

But money was still tight, so when a flat came up to rent in a new development in Barkingside, Joe and I decided to take the plunge and rent the flat together. My friend Richard moved across from South London to help with the campaign and the rent. The only albatross that remained around my neck was £10,000 worth of credit card debt that I had racked up during my time at NUS, which was costing hundreds of pounds each month just in interest payments. Joe very generously agreed to loan me the money to pay them off and to start paying him back after the general election. It was a huge weight off my shoulders.

All of this gave me the time I needed to focus on fighting elections. In May 2014, Jas Athwal and I made history by leading the Labour Party to a majority on Redbridge Council for the first time in the borough's history. I joined Jas's cabinet as Deputy Leader of the Council and Cabinet Member for Health and Wellbeing.

Matthew Goddin, the borough organiser, who masterminded our winning campaign, agreed to become my organiser in Ilford North. Although the local election results had been good for Labour across the borough, we were still hundreds of votes behind the Conservatives in Ilford North. We had to throw the kitchen sink at the campaign.

We campaigned throughout the week and at weekends. The NUS and Labour Students mafia paid dividends in volunteers turning up to help. We had campaign visits from Labour Leader Ed Miliband and other members of the shadow cabinet, and as we approached polling day in May 2015, we were knocking on doors more than any other candidate in Britain.

The election was going to be close, and I knew it was time to pull out all the stops. It was time to deploy my secret weapon: Mum. Mum drove down from the North West and was overwhelmed by the campaign she saw in full swing. She was bursting with pride, and she showed it: on school gates, at tube stations, on the doorsteps. 'He's my son,' she would shout at the top of her voice. Years living up North had not suppressed her cockney accent. 'He's such a good boy, and he'll work so hard for you.' She clearly made an impression. For years later, people would tell me, 'I met your mum during the election! She's lovely, isn't she? She's so proud of you.'

The biggest surprise of all came on polling day. Dad, a life-long Conservative voter, came out to knock on doors for the Labour Party with my stepmum, Joe-anne. To voters, his open-ing gambit was, 'I'm normally a Conservative voter, but I'm proud to campaign for my son.' He made damn sure no one would make the mistake of thinking he was a Labour Party member! It meant so much to me that he came out to help.

We knocked on doors until 9.50 pm that day. We knew it would be close and that every vote would count. We returned to one of the campaign centres to watch the exit poll come in, surrounded by volunteers. As Big Ben struck 10 pm, I really believed I would win. But then the BBC exit poll appeared – the Conservatives were projected to be the largest party again, with 316 seats.

We hoped that Labour's stronger performance in London would carry us, but as I watched the results come in, surrounded by close friends and family in our flat, it became all too obvious I was going to have to concede defeat.

'I've lost,' I announced to the assembled gathering. The room fell silent. I explained why the results across London pointed to a defeat in Ilford North and the conversation turned to what a shame it was and how we couldn't have worked harder.

The only person who still believed I had won was Mum. It didn't matter how much I tried to explain national swings and why Labour's narrow hold in Tooting and a big defeat in Battersea pointed to defeat in Ilford North; she wasn't having any of it. 'You've won. I know you have. I can feel it,' she persisted, as defiant as ever.

As I cracked open another can of Kronenbourg, I set about writing some thoughts for a concession speech at the count. The atmosphere in the flat was sombre. To try and lift the mood, Joe decided he and I would fly away on holiday as soon as we could and started investigating flights to San Francisco.

'I've got no money and no job,' I told Joe. 'What am I going to do?'

At about 3.30 in the morning, I gathered together my family in the flat – Mum, Dad, Joe-anne, Joe and his mum, Mary – and told them that we would go to the count at the Town Hall, keep our chins up, thank those who had turned up to help and show dignity in defeat.

I was shaking hands with the volunteers when, seemingly out of nowhere, Keith Prince, the former Conservative Leader of Redbridge Council, appeared and grasped my hand in his.

'Well done, Wes, you've clinched it, mate.' I gawped at him in disbelief. 'Sorry, what was that?' I asked, stunned. 'You've clinched it,' Keith repeated.

I didn't have time to tell anyone what I'd heard before the defeated Conservative MP, Lee Scott, appeared to do the same. 'Congratulations, Wes,' he said, shaking my hand.

The entire time I was wallowing in assumed defeat, the reality at the count was that the results had been too close to call. No one thought to tell me, I suppose.

Until this point, I had held it all together – the excitement, the nerves, the panic, the adrenaline. But, feeling a lump swell in my throat, I rushed to the nearest door into the lobby of the Town Hall and burst into tears. Within seconds I was surrounded by jubilant Labour volunteers as my parents looked on, stunned and jubilant with tears in their eyes. I could hardly believe what was happening.

I was told the results were about to be announced and that I was needed on stage.

I turned to Joe. 'I don't have a victory speech!' I said in a complete panic.

As we assembled on stage, I messaged some friends. 'Ilford North result imminent. You need to watch this.'

The declaration was underway. 'Lee Scott, the Conservative Party candidate, 20,974. Wes Streeting, the Labour Party candidate, twenty-one thousand . . .' I couldn't hear the rest through all the cheering in the hall. As I turned to shake the hands of the other candidates, Lee Scott, who had just lost his seat and his job, leaned in and gave me a big hug. It was an extraordinarily generous gesture and the mark of the decency of the man.

The results were still coming in across the country. I didn't know what sort of Parliament I would be walking into, but the constituency that some people said would never elect an openly gay MP had bucked the trend in doing so.

*

When you're elected as an MP, you're handed a brown envelope at the count addressed to the 'Newly Elected Member of Parliament'. I felt like Charlie Bucket receiving his golden ticket to Willy Wonka's Chocolate Factory. Inside the envelope were instructions about where and when to appear at the Houses of Parliament and a telephone number to ring.

I was one of the first MPs to arrive on Friday, 8 May. The sun was shining, and the daylight slightly grated against my weary, tired eyes. I'd had barely any sleep.

I had walked the corridors of the Palace of Westminster before as a visitor and campaigner, but now I had goosebumps as I was shown around the House of Commons as a Member. My majority was just 589. Who knew whether my time in Parliament would last more than a single term, but I resolved there and then that if I ever walked into Parliament without that same feeling of awe at the privilege and responsibility I had been given, I would know it was time to leave.

My parents were keen to come and see my new place of work. I took them around the grounds, taking in centuries of history. It was a far cry from the walks I had taken years ago – leapfrogging over the bollards on Cable Street with Mum, or strolling down the Roman Road with Grandad when Dad would struggle to get a look in. I'm not sure they could quite believe that their son now worked in a literal palace. Nor could I, if truth be told.

Mum, who had spent election day proudly telling voters in Ilford North that 'he's my son' as she handed out leaflets, was now giving a repeat performance to every House of Commons official she met, as I showed her around Parliament for the first time, along with Joe and my Aunt Amanda. Suffice to say I moved her on as quickly as possible before she gave away too many childhood stories, relieved that she hadn't brought along my baby photos. Dad and Joe-anne were equally proud when they visited a few days afterwards. Thanks to my new parliamentary assistant, Jay Asher, we found our way to the roof terrace and took a photo as a family with the iconic clock tower that houses Big Ben in the background.

With the family tours over, it was time to get down to work. I was still waiting to be allocated an office, so I was 'hot-desking' in a meeting room with a group of other newly elected Labour MPs. We were all in the same boat: trying to figure out what we were supposed to be doing and where we were supposed to be. It was only when I saw them all sorting through their post and expressed surprise that I hadn't received any that I was told that I should go to the MPs' post office. Sure enough, when I arrived, they were relieved to see me. 'We were wondering when you'd come in. We've got three big green sacks of post waiting for you!' No one had told me! I would need to recruit some staff, find a new constituency office in Ilford, and start writing my maiden speech. A Labour leadership election was to be held, and candidates were already ringing to canvass support to ask for my nomination. It was a big decision.

There was so much to think about as I stood at the cash machine on the ground floor of the Palace of Westminster, but my thoughts about the future were rudely interrupted by the bleeping coming from the machine. My attempt to withdraw £40 had failed due to insufficient funds. My negative balance flashed up on the screen. I was almost at the bottom of my overdraft and available funds were just £20. With that, I withdrew my last £20 from the cashpoint and thanked my lucky stars that I had won.

The Voice From the Radio

THE VOICE FROM the radio comes like a bolt from the blue. I haven't heard it for nearly thirty years, but I recognise it immediately, and my heart almost bursts with happiness. 'I would like him to know how proud I am of what he has achieved against not easy odds,' it says, slightly more crackly than I remembered it. The voice belongs to Mrs Dodd, my old head teacher from St Peter's. I have a lump in my throat and my eyes are moist as I listen to her talking about me.

The BBC tracked her down for an episode of Radio 4's *Profile*, in which they featured my story. The timing is extraordinary, coming just as I draw this book to a close. Even now, all these years later, she appears to guide me onwards. I've looked for her many times over the years. I've always wanted to thank her for everything she did for me, but I've never been able to find her. Now I know why. She remarried and is now Ann Howarth.

Listening to Ann Howarth describe me as 'a delightful boy, quite shy, self-contained,' I am transported back thirty years to the little boy I once was. Shy and self-contained. She was right. How had I forgotten, even as I've delved deep into the vaults of my own memories to write this book? Perhaps it's because it has been so long since someone described me in such a way!

In the years that have passed since then, I have found my voice and my confidence. That boy from Stepney is still there. I carry his experiences with me every day. They drive and motivate me: my values, my politics, and the things I still want to achieve.

My life is so different now. I'm proud of my working-class roots, but I lead a middle-class life. I have a mortgage. I have savings. I have financial security for the first time in my life.

Dad and Joe-anne are still happily married and living in Essex and hope to pay off their mortgage before they retire. Mum still struggles to make ends meet, working as a cleaner in the North of England, but at least I am now in a position to help her. She is happy. Nanny and Grandad Hill are still going, despite Nanny Hill's ongoing battle with cancer, enjoying the beautiful views and the wildlife from the garden of their little bungalow in North Wales. The rest of our East End family can be found scattered across Essex and further afield. Like so many other East Enders, they've moved onwards and mostly upwards. We tend to see each other only at weddings and funerals now.

I wish I could tell you that the opportunities I've experienced in my life are available to everyone. That all we need to do is pull ourselves up by our bootstraps and we can make it. That poverty is a choice, not a trap. That we live in a classless society. That things can only get better. But experience and evidence tell us otherwise, and I am afraid that the chances for children from backgrounds like mine are worsening.

On a recent visit to a primary school in my constituency, a girl – maybe ten or eleven years old – asked me why children couldn't learn remotely from home instead of attending school. Given the experience her generation had during the Covid-19 lockdowns, I was surprised by her question. Most children were happy to be back. As I left the class, her teacher explained that she had moved home four times since the start of that term. The girl was simply exhausted.

One afternoon in my MP advice surgery for local residents, a woman came to see me with three girls in tow. She described her ordeal of fleeing domestic violence, holding down three jobs to provide for her girls but still being evicted because she couldn't keep up with her rent. She had been relocated to temporary accommodation on the other side of London, where she had limited cooking facilities and no washing machine. Her eldest daughter was studying for her GCSEs, and her two youngest were at primary school. That woman was commuting more than an hour across London to get her children to two schools, before taking herself off to three jobs during the day, picking her kids up to take them back across London, making them a basic meal and then hand-washing and pressing her daughter's uniforms. Her eldest daughter described the challenges of sharing a room with her mum and her sisters. She was revising for her GCSEs under the duvet with a torch in the evening because she could see that her mum was exhausted and needed to rest. As they spoke, they held each other's hands as her mother told me that her daughter had spoken of taking her own life in desperation at the situation. I am not ashamed to admit that I cried with them in that case. Despite my best efforts, they were relocated to Wolverhampton. More than a hundred miles away from their family, friends, the kids' schools, and Mum's jobs.

Another case that broke my heart was that of a boy who came up to me at the end of a talk I had been giving at another local primary school. He asked to see me privately, which was very unusual. Children his age, no more than eleven years old, rarely asked to speak to an MP privately. His head teacher offered us her office and the three of us sat around the table with some tea and biscuits. 'You grew up in a council flat, didn't you?' he asked nervously. 'That's right, I did,' came my reply. I was surprised that he knew that much about my background. Then the penny dropped. 'I was wondering if you could get me a council flat for my family,' he said. He was living in a bedsit with his mum and two brothers. He described how sad his mum was. How unfair it was that they didn't have a home of their own. I had to sit there and explain to an eleven-year-old boy, who was just like me in so many respects, why I couldn't immediately provide something that I'd had when I was his age. Something I knew his family deserved. After he left, his head teacher explained that his school work was suffering and his behaviour was deteriorating. I wrote him a letter afterwards, promising to do my best for him, and I urged him to work hard at school like I did so that he could grow up to be whoever and whatever he chooses to be. In this case, there was a happier ending. We found his family a permanent home, his school work picked up, and his head teacher reported that he was doing well after progressing to his new secondary school.

The injustice of these cases is enraging. These children are beginning life with their hands tied behind their backs. Some people will blame the parents. Sometimes there's an element of truth to it, but tell that to the mother now raising her children in Wolverhampton, who fled her abusive partner and worked every hour she could, but couldn't make ends meet because the link between a hard day's work and a fair day's pay has been broken.

Growing up in that council estate in Stepney, I thought that I had it bad. In many respects, I did, but the tragedy is that things are worse now than they were in the 1980s. The council flat that I wanted to escape is something that children today aspire to. They don't have the security of a home over their head; they're being pushed from pillar to post in grotty temporary accommodation. They don't have the support of extended family to help with childcare or to make up the shortfall with the weekly shop because they're often uprooted away from their families, across towns and cities, sometimes across the country. No Nanny Libby or Grandad Streeting to help. They don't have the stability of a great state education to set them up for life because no sooner do they settle into a new school, making new friends, than it's time to move again. No chance for a Mrs Dodd or a Mr Nash to work their magic.

This is Britain in the 21st century. A great country that has so much going for it, but also a country of staggering inequality, intolerable poverty and wasted potential.

We're sold the myth of meritocracy, but there's a class ceiling in Britain. Children from working-class backgrounds arrive at school already behind their peers. They're twice as likely to end up leaving school without GCSEs in English and Maths than their better-off classmates. Efforts to close the gap at sixteen have not only stalled, but they are showing signs of widening. Privately educated pupils are seven times more likely to win a place at Oxford or Cambridge universities. Even high-performing state schools take in half the number of kids from poorer backgrounds than the average school. All of this has a bearing on who pulls the levers of power in Britain. In politics, business, law, media, creative industries and sport, Britain's most influential people are five times more likely to have been to private school. Even when working-class kids break through the class ceiling into elite professions, we tend to earn less than our counterparts from more affluent backgrounds.

But perhaps what should worry us even more than the presence of the class ceiling is the absence of a floor. The safety net in our country is threadbare. The number of children living in poverty stands at more than four million, and it is rising. It limits their choices and life chances. The public services that made such a difference in my life – council housing, education, social security – are being steadily eroded. Those who bear the brunt of it are children from backgrounds like mine. How can these children reach their potential and fly when the weight of their poverty hangs around their ankles, dragging them into the ground?

Hard work matters. Individual effort counts. My father and his father taught me that. Sometimes people on the left of politics don't appreciate this enough. The state can't solve every problem. Sometimes bad public services are part of the problem and the people they are supposed to help feel more like victims of the state rather than supported by it. I think back to some of Mum's experiences with the NHS and the Department for Social Security.

Better public services are part of the answer: a great state education system that helps children to realise their potential, decent and affordable housing to provide security, accessible health services that promote good health and well-being, social care that gives children born into the worst circumstances the very best start in life, a social security system that provides both a safety net and a springboard to help people back on their feet. They are essential, but they aren't, on their own, sufficient.

Family has a role to play in providing a stable upbringing for children and mutual support and care when times are hard. Their task is made much easier if they are rooted in a community which has the opportunities of decent pay and good conditions at work. Without the security of a decent, affordable home and an income that does more than just pay the bills, families struggle and break down, and the kids are often left paying the long-term price of hardship and unfulfilled potential, and so the cycle continues for another generation.

In case it isn't obvious by now, the story I've shared with you isn't a self-aggrandising homily to my own success. It's not really about me at all. It's a hymn to my family, to my parents and grandparents, to great teachers, and to the wonderful people in my life who gave a kid from a council estate in Stepney all the chances he needed to get on in life. You played your part too, dear reader, if not for me, then for other kids who rely on your taxes to give them a fighting chance in life.

I'm in no doubt about how I made my journey from council house to House of Commons. I am the product of a family that loves me; a welfare state that housed me, fed me, and clothed me; a health service that cared for me; a state education that nurtured me, inspired me, and backed me; a university that opened doors for me; a student movement that gave a platform to me; and a rewarding career that has sustained me.

Now I have the chance to give something back in return, to improve the future of kids like me.

Thank you.

Wes Streeting

January 2023

Acknowledgements

THIS BOOK WASN'T my idea. The primary thanks (and blame!) for this book must go to Tom Perrin for having both the idea and the persistence to get me to commit to it. I nearly said no.

My reluctance might have won the day were it not for the encouragement of two great friends and fellow parliamentary authors, Michael Cashman and Jess Phillips. Both of them inspire me, so it meant a lot to have their support and words of wisdom along the way.

Having decided to go for it, I needed an agent. Thank goodness Jess introduced me to Laura Macdougall at United Agents because she has been an absolute godsend, helping me to navigate the weird and wonderful world of publishing as a rookie author.

I knew I wanted to publish the book with Tom because he understood my story and the mission of the book, even before I did. That was in no small part thanks to the great care that Rachel Sylvester took in telling my story to readers of *The Times* in the interview that caught Tom's attention.

The team at Hodder & Stoughton have been terrific. Rowena Webb's enthusiasm for the book gave us lift-off and helped me to shake off any lingering doubts. Thanks are also due to Leni Lawrence, Vickie Boff, Zakirah Alam, Rachel Southey and Richard Peters.

For better or worse, I insisted on writing this myself, rather than relying on a ghostwriter, but I was conscious that a book like this needed a very different style from the opinion pieces and speeches I've become accustomed to in my day job. Caitlin Mellon has been a dream to work with, helping me to elevate my writing to bring the story to life. More than that, she's helped me to rediscover my love of writing for pleasure.

Between them, Caitlin, Tom and Sophie Bristow cut tens of thousands of words, mostly to the detriment of stories from CUSU and NUS, which undoubtedly made this a better book! But when I reflected back on my time at Cambridge, NUS, HKF, and Stonewall, my abiding memories of happiness involve the brilliant people I worked with. I'm lucky to have known them. Similarly, throughout all the trials and tribulations of British politics since 2015, I've been kept sane by my office buddy, Peter Kyle, the brilliant staff and interns who've ·worked for me, members of the Ilford North Labour Party, who've always had my back and the people of Ilford North who've elected me to Parliament three times.

I was adamant that I would write this book without it interfering with my work as MP for Ilford North and Shadow Health and Social Care Secretary. I was able to achieve this goal thanks in no small part to a brilliant team that I can always trust and rely upon, Matthew Goddin, Barney Dowling, Dr Tom Gardiner, Dr Sarah Harrison, Bal Ghataore, Sam Gould, Will Prescott, Hollie Wickens and Anna Wilson. Thanks are also due to Keir Starmer, Matthew Doyle and Sam

White for giving me their blessing to go ahead, or else I would have turned it down!

The sacrifice of what little free time I had to write this book came at the expense of my partner, Joe Dancey. Over more than a decade he's put up with selections, re-selections, local elections, three general elections, a referendum and the rollercoaster of British politics. He tolerated me sitting with a laptop by the pool on holidays, over Christmas, and working late into the night and in what little free time we have during weekends at home. Joe – thanks for your love and support and for giving me a dress rehearsal on the audiobook by listening to me read each chapter out aloud at least twice!

Thanks are also due to friends who were willing to read and comment on drafts: Andrew Adonis, Richard Angell, Jay Asher, Matthew Goddin, Roger Liddle, Adam McNicholas, Will Prescott and Amy Richards.

To all my long-suffering friends, who I don't see nearly enough, thank you for your unconditional love and support along the way. You know who you are.

I would not have written this book without the blessing of my family. Mum, Dad, Eve, Amanda, Sara, and my grandparents were instrumental, especially for the earlier chapters. This is their story as much as it is mine, and they have been willing to share memories with me, and therefore you, that are both joyful and painful.

The best moments in the writing process were hearing back from my parents about how much they'd enjoyed reading the drafts. Theirs are the reviews that matter most.